IMAGE IMPACT FOR MEN

IMAGE IMPACT FOR MEN

The Business and Professional Man's Personal Packaging Program

Edited by
JACQUELINE THOMPSON

A & W PUBLISHERS, INC.
New York

Published by
A & W Publishers, Inc.
95 Madison Avenue
New York, NY 10016

Manufactured in the United States of America
Designed by Jennie Nichols/LEVAVI & LEVAVI

10 9 8 7 6 5 4 3 2 1

Library of Congress Cataloging in Publication Data
Main entry under title:

   Image impact for men, the business and professional man's personal packaging
   program.
   Includes index.
   1. Success. 2. Businessmen. 3. Grooming for men. 4. Men's clothing. 5.
Self-perception.
I. Thompson, Jacqueline.
HF5386.I462 1983   650.1'088041 · 82-11403

ISBN 0-89479-120-6

CONTENTS

IMAGE IMPACT FOR MEN

PART I

IMAGE ASSESSMENT: WHERE ARE YOU COMING FROM? WHERE ARE YOU HEADED?

1

TAKING INVENTORY: The Anatomy of One Man's Image Overhaul

by William Hussey

Meet L. Mayson Roberts. He's a fictionalized depiction of a real, and quite well-known, business executive. He is chairman of the board and chief executive officer of a *Fortune* 500 industrial company I'll call Atlantic Industries. The company had revenues of over $2 billion in 1981 and after-tax profits of around $200 million. A substantial company, a substantial record—and a substantial man to head it up.

If you had met Mr. Roberts a short twelve years ago, there would be little you'd recognize in this imposing and charismatic figure. Instead, you'd have met Len Roberts, a competent, workaday engineer in the manufacturing department of a subsidiary of Atlantic Industries. He had gone to Purdue University and received a B.S. degree in mechanical engineering. Always good with his hands and of a practical turn of mind, Roberts nevertheless had ambition beyond mere technical facility. He had a keen analytical mind, got along relatively well with his peers despite his cool manner, and had a real but unfulfilled knack for high-risk, venturesome decisions.

Thus, Len Roberts had the basic equipment—intellectual and emotional—for a management career, but none of his superiors had noticed. Why? Why wasn't he singled out and given an opportunity to exploit this latent management ability? The reason: Roberts's talent was masked by his all-too-distinct image defects. He was overweight, out of shape, a poor public speaker, a careless dresser, and he was sometimes indifferent in manner. These negative attributes, superficial as they were, had little effect on his engineering work, but they would make a lot of difference if he was to achieve his goal and break out of his technical career path into general management.

.In fact, it took Len Roberts several years to identify his problem as one concerning outward appearances rather than substance. And another year to become motivated enough to do something about it. The conversation that triggered the change in this talented but seemingly run-of-the-mill engineer was casual enough. It was initiated by one of Roberts's best friends at work, his immediate superior. His friend and sometime mentor saw the diamond in the rough in Roberts. He knew firsthand Roberts's capacity for hard work, his intellectual accomplishments and potential, but he also realized there was not much he could do to help unless Len were willing to make some rather drastic changes and improvement in his outward manner. The friend realized that Roberts, with some expensive professional counseling, could achieve enormous success.

Cautiously, the friend broached the subject of Roberts's image and the fact that he had the wrong one for a man with his lofty aspirations. He suggested Roberts see a "personal image consultant"—a professional who could advise Roberts about a range of image matters, from his dress to how to implement his career goals. A professional image consultant, at the very least, could be more candid than his friend could in pointing out Roberts's shortcomings. His friend had seen other men, less gifted than Roberts, achieve their business and personal goals after they had retained one of these behind-the-scenes experts in image improvement.

Roberts ultimately saw not one professional consultant but four. And, in addition to his two-year-long image-improvement program, he enrolled in three night-school management courses. His hard work paid off. Company officials began to notice this bright young man in the manufacturing division. Soon he was being singled out for special assignments; and eventually the company underwrote the cost of Roberts's M.B.A. in marketing that he earned with honors in an accelerated program at the Harvard Business School.

But let's backtrack and examine the process that transformed this ordinary-looking engineer into a $300,000-a-year executive with a magnificent home in a desirable suburb of a large city and a spacious seaside house for his wife and three children.

In Roberts's first consultation with his image consultant—a public relations counselor who specialized in grooming executives for senior management positions—his more obvious defects came under scrutiny. The personal PR counselor analyzed Roberts in a broad, diagnostic context, seeking to isolate the more troublesome aspects of his image problems in order to formulate specific solutions. Given the magnitude of Roberts's ambition, the consultant was able to zero in on his appearance, manner, and style—even his name—and then recommend a complete image overhaul to cover all aspects of his problem.

For his weight and fitness, for instance, the PR counselor advised Roberts to join a health and racquet club and get some form of exercise daily. Next, a wardrobe expert advised Roberts on his dress, which was appropriate for an engineer but abominable for an aspiring general manager of a huge American corporation. Once Roberts looked the part, his personal PR man sent him to a speech consultant to rid him of several annoying verbal "tics" and to coach him on public speaking. He himself took charge of Roberts's "packaging"—his comportment, business manners, and management style, plus the setting of long- and short-term career goals.

The PR counselor had a definite program mapped out for his client. Since Roberts aspired to a top-level management position, the PR counselor realized that his client was not going to achieve that goal overnight; what he needed in the meantime were intermediate goals he could achieve in relatively short order. In Roberts's specific case, he had to progress further within his department before he could take a larger leap into general management. Through his experience with other clients, the PR counselor knew that observable, measurable progress would spur Roberts on, bolster his self-esteem, and encourage him to take the strategic next steps to get ahead. Thus began the twelve-year transformation of engineer Len Roberts into CEO L. Mayson Roberts.

Let's look at Roberts's image-change program in depth.

First, Roberts joined a local health and racquet club, where he turned himself over to a physical education specialist. The trainer saw that Roberts was at least thirty pounds overweight, was soft and flabby, had little stamina, and moved clumsily. Through years of neglect, his body was in sore need of a reconditioning program. Before beginning any serious effort to change Roberts, the trainer suggested that Roberts undergo a complete medical examination. Though Roberts was only thirty years old, losing weight and participating in strenuous exercise and athletic programs could conceivably place a tremendous strain on his heart and other vital organs. His muscle tone, too, had to be improved slowly. A doctor had to be consulted.

After a thorough physical—including an EKG and other sophisticated diagnostic procedures—Roberts was cleared for a full, unrestricted program of exercise and athletic activity. Since his weight was also a factor, the physician put him on a diet. Roberts had been a devotee of junk food; he was cautioned against foods that had a high caloric content and little nutritional value. Aside from that, his was the simplest of regimens; he was to eat in moderation—about half the amount he had been eating—and choose food and drink from the spectrum of the four basic food groups: fruits and vegetables; whole grain breads and cereals; lean meats, peas, beans, and nuts; and dairy products. Only moderate amounts of alcohol and no sugared soft drinks were allowed. Combined with the exercise program, this diet assured measured weight loss as well as a healthy firming and toning of muscle tissue.

After he had lost the desired amount of weight, bringing his shape into reasonable proportion, step two in the short-term transformation of Len Roberts went into effect. His PR consultant arranged for several sessions, including a shopping expedition, with a professional wardrobe specialist.

"The starting point," said the dress expert, "is to understand that clothing plays a role in your career advancement. You may not get promotions *because* of your wardrobe, but it's harder to advance *in spite of* your wardrobe. You can read a lot of books about image but that's only part of it. You have to be on guard against self-deception. Who are you? What message do you want your attire to give other people? Don't kid yourself anymore."

It was true. Roberts had been deceiving himself. Until he was brought up short by his first mentor on the job and later by his personal PR counselor, he believed he looked about right. Unfortunately, when he looked in the mirror, he saw something that others did not see. Because all the engineers in his department dressed in rather slipshod fashion, he thought he could too. Dress wasn't important. The wardrobe adviser convinced him that he had to stand out from the crowd, not continue to fall into the careless clothing and grooming habits of his peers.

The dress specialist began by evaluating Roberts's somatotype—the general classification of his body size and configuration. With minor variations, all human beings fall into one of three basic morphological types: the *endomorphic,* or generally short and heavy-set; the *meso-*

morphic, or tall and athletic looking; and the *ectomorphic,* or slender and angular. A person's build dictates the kind of dress, colors, and patterns that best suit his frame.

Roberts was an endomorph. He was below average in height, was thick around the middle and could be called "pear shaped." The adviser—who selected a wardrobe that attenuated Roberts's basic morphology and subtly created the illusion of a mesomorph—was aided in this project by a surprising ally, Roberts's wife. He knew that more than 65 percent of all the menswear purchased in this country are bought by women, or men accompanied by women. The wardrobe expert welcomed this extra pair of eyes and brought Mrs. Roberts along on their shopping trips. He had two objectives: he wanted her to understand *why* certain garments were appropriate attire for her husband; and he felt her participation would strengthen her husband's resolve in this area. In short, she would help make Roberts's wardrobe change an achievable goal.

Step three was taken almost simultaneously with the selection of an entirely new wardrobe. Speech and comportment go hand in glove with appearance, and thus a third consultant, a specialist in public speaking, was engaged. Roberts had never paid too much attention to how he sounded or what he looked like when called upon to speak. Most of his presentations up to now had been given to groups of other technical personnel and he approached these assignments in workmanlike—but uninspired—fashion. The speech expert was able to convince him that every opportunity to speak is an opportunity to shine, to stand out from others. And who could say when some top-level executive might not drop in on a meeting to observe that up-and-coming, articulate engineer who always gave the interesting presentations?

Motivating Roberts to help himself and continually adapt to the ever-dynamic management environment in his company was, perhaps, the most challenging part of the PR consultant's plan for Roberts. But there were other formidable obstacles, financial as well as psychological, to overcome. Many of them were brought up by Roberts himself. There was the cost of the various image services, none of them cheap, some of them very expensive. Indeed, the whole two-year program would end up costing Roberts close to $25,000. Conscious of his individuality, Roberts also expressed fear that he'd turn into a carbon copy of other executives—the "cookie cutter" syndrome. Moreover, the spare time he used to spend with his family now would dwindle to weekends at best. But through determination, the support of his family, and the respect and confidence he developed for his quartet of image consultants, Roberts persevered. And once he became 100 percent convinced of the efficacy of his consultant's career-advancement plan and adopted a gung-ho attitude toward it, Roberts made rapid progress. Soon he was ready for step four.

This brought his personal PR counselor to the fore. That advisor would now pull together and "package" all the disparate aspects of Roberts's improved image. Through extensive role-playing in front of a videotape camera, he helped Roberts develop a new *persona* for his job, another for dealing with people outside his organization, and yet another for his social life. Social ease and business finesse were in fact the twin objectives.

The counselor took Roberts through a three-phase process to be used as the framework for every interpersonal situation he faced. He had Roberts ask—and answer—three questions:

- What is the image I *do* project?
- What is the image I *want* to project?
- How can I *improve*?

Each question involved all the constituents of effective communication—speech, voice, dress, posture, gestures, and eye contact. After each videotape session, Roberts and the PR counselor analyzed Roberts's performance to judge how well he was integrating the improvements in his image wrought by the individual specialists. Their objective was a consistent, credible, unified persona.

As Roberts's confidence grew, he began to seek out opportunities to speak—at company meetings, at technical conferences, even at local community affairs. When he had a critical speaking engagement, he'd work on his presentation with his speech coach.

Because Roberts became so visible at work and could not only identify puzzling manufacturing problems but communicate effectively to get them solved, it wasn't too long before he was promoted to head his department. Then corporate-level executives began to invite him to represent the engineering staff in general management meetings. The company's senior executives appreciated his clear explanations of complex technical matters.

At this point in his career ascendancy, a small but significant decision was made. Contrary to the old saw about a rose smelling the same, a person's name, the PR consultant claimed, engenders an immediate response in other people. The name "Len Roberts" was a prosaic one, hardly designed to push him to the forefront with life's winners.

Christopher P. Anderson, in his book *The Name Game* (Simon &

Schuster, 1977), cites many examples of name changes which also changed the direction of the recipients' lives. "What's in a name?" asks Anderson. "Among other things, the difference between success and failure in the business world.... Names are charged with hidden meanings and unspoken overtones that profoundly help or hinder you in your relationships and your life."

Would Rawleigh Warner be any more effective than William Warner? Or Woodrow Wilson than Thomas Wilson? Or did John Getty become J. Paul Getty—and thus a success? Len Roberts didn't waste any time fretting about his name change. It was accomplished swiftly and with no apparent negative reaction at work. It was almost as though it was expected. In this manner was born L. Mayson Roberts.

The PR counselor's game plan for Roberts, as I said at the outset, was a continuing program of change—some of it rapid, some of it painfully slow. After those initial two years, Roberts began to get recognition beyond his department. Gradually, promotions began to come, first in small increments within the department, later at the divisional level. And finally, clutching his newly minted Harvard M.B.A. degree in hand, he made a quantum leap into leadership of the corporate marketing department. A couple of years in this high-visibility job and Roberts was tapped for a vice-presidency.

The time was now ripe for L. Mayson Roberts to become better known beyond his company's corridors. During this phase of Roberts's career development, his personal PR consultant hit his stride. He began planting stories about Roberts's accomplishments in the business press, and articles with his byline began appearing in trade magazines with national circulation. After intense coaching from his panel of experts, Roberts started to show up on radio and television talk shows as a spokesman for his company and industry. He was building a constituency, a forum for himself that would make his position within the company almost unassailable. He needed this impregnable fortress, knowing that the competition in the upper reaches of management is fierce. Fortunately, his game plan, created just a few short years earlier, had prepared him for such executive-suite infighting. And when he had doubts, his secret arsenal of personal image consultants was available with advice and an action plan.

The rest is corporate history. Shortly after his forty-second birthday, Roberts was elected president of the company, heir apparent to the chairman, who was three years away from retirement. Those three years were spent cementing all he had learned to build a secure edifice from which he could function as the company's CEO for many years to come. The transformation was complete.

Sound familiar? Of course. But how often do we look behind the facade of successful business and professional leaders to discover what contributed to their rise? How deeply do we examine their origins? Chances are that the Roberts scenario, with minor variations, is being repeated daily in business, the professions, and the arts by truly ambitious people.

How do we measure up? Do you, like Len Roberts, have any counterproductive outer attributes that are limiting your chances of attaining a high position in your chosen field?

The impact you make on others is in direct proportion to the way you look, move, and sound. Take a good look at yourself in the mirror. When you speak, notice how you sound. Be aware of how your presence affects others.

Here is a checklist designed to help you interpret the signals you've been getting—and possibly ignoring—from your friends and associates. Be brutally honest with yourself in deciding whether to check a statement because it applies to you.

_____ People assume I am a lot older or younger than I really am.

_____ My clothes make me stand out from the crowd, causing people to make comments such as, "I wish I had the nerve to wear an outfit like that," or "You always look so unusual, so *different* from everybody else."

_____ People often tease me about my clothes.

_____ People often tease me about the colors I wear.

_____ People often tease me about the way I coordinate my outfits.

_____ When I look around a room full of my peers, I frequently feel shabby or inadequate compared to them.

_____ If my co-workers run across me after-hours—on the street, in a restaurant, or at a party—they often don't recognize me.

_____ People sometimes make negative comments about some aspect of my grooming (e.g., greasy hair, scuffed shoes, dirty fingernails, smoker's breath).

_____ Salesclerks in a crowded store tend to wait on me last.

_____ Strangers often express surprise when I tell them what I do for a living.

_____ I am frequently offered jobs well below my levels of ability and training.

_____ Often, I'm not considered for jobs that are ideal for me because interviewers claim the jobs aren't good enough for me, that I wouldn't be challenged, and would therefore quit.

_____ I don't often look other people straight in the eye when I talk to them because it makes me uncomfortable.

_____ Supposedly in jest, people sometimes mimic my mannerisms.

_____ People wince or give me an odd look when I shake hands with them.

_____ Strangers immediately call me by my first name instead of addressing me more formally as Mr._____ .

_____ I am often surprised by the violent reactions my seemingly innocuous comments elicit. Other people say, "If you could only have *heard* the way you sounded when you said that," or, "If you could only have *seen* the way you looked."

_____ When I enter a room full of people I tend to hesitate, walk slowly, and keep my head bowed.

_____ In meetings, I try to sit where I think I'll be least noticed.

_____ I seldom gesture because it's too demonstrative and theatrical.

_____ Frequently, my facial expressions don't match my feelings. I know because people say that I'm confusing them and ask for clarification.

_____ Because of my natural facial appearance, I tend to look happy or sad or angry when I am actually feeling quite neutral.

_____ People tend to fidget and look away while I'm speaking.

_____ Often people don't take what I say seriously.

_____ Because people haven't been able to hear me distinctly, they ask, "Would you repeat that, please?"

_____ People interrupt me, implying that what I have to say is much less important than what they have to say.

_____ People frequently take offense at things I've said when I thought I was complimenting them.

_____ Even when I am communicating a relatively simple thought, people are always asking me to re-explain what I mean.

_____ In restaurants and other public places, my companions frequently look uncomfortable and ask me to lower my voice.

_____ I have trouble getting my ideas accepted at work.

_____ When I finally meet people with whom I've had numerous telephone conversations, they usually express surprise— " You're Jim Smith. You're not at all what I expected!"

_____ I suspect that the unflattering things people say in jest about my speech habits are actually true.

_____ In business or social situations requiring small talk, I often become tongue-tied, and awkward silences develop.

_____ Because I don't make a habit of identifying myself at the beginning of telephone conversations, people usually interrupt to ask, "Who is this please?"

_____ People frequently tell me I've picked the wrong time or place to bring up a certain subject.

_____ I have trouble remembering strangers' names, even after I've just been introduced.

_____ I tend to be late for appointments.

_____ Even when I'm the host, the waiter seldom brings the restaurant check to me.

_____ When I want to express appreciation, I usually just pick up the telephone rather than write a thank-you note.

_____ I have extended telephone conversations, even though a visitor may be sitting in my office waiting for me to finish so we can resume our meeting.

_____ My business correspondence looks sloppy (e.g., filled with penned corrections, misspellings, showing a disregard for the usual business-letter format).

_____ People seem to think I'm too self-critical and make such comments as, "You don't like yourself much, do you?"

_____ I often find other people putting me on the defensive.

_____ People comment that I ought to broaden my interests.

_____ I have a "yes, but" response every time anyone offers me any constructive advice.

_____ I allow self-doubt to render me incapable of making many decisions.

_____ I don't handle job frustration and stress well.

_____ I have trouble eliciting cooperation from difficult co-workers.

_____ I don't know how to turn a failure to my advantage.

_____ Colleagues often take credit for my ideas or successes.

_____ Although I'm performing at the peak of my ability, I am invariably passed over for promotions.

_____ I think going after personal publicity is the mark of a show-off.

_____ I seldom return calls from casual acquaintances because I don't have time to enlarge my circle of friends.

_____ I often feel that life controls me rather than vice versa.

_____ Although I have plenty of free time for leisure activity, my social calendar is usually empty.

_____ The women to whom I am attracted are seldom attracted to me.

_____ On dates, women comment, "You seem lost in your own thoughts."

_____ Women seldom want to go out with me a second time.

_____ At social gatherings, I either feel awkward because I am standing alone in a corner or I stick with the person I came with throughout the entire affair.

_____ I'm not a joiner. I'd rather spend my leisure time in solitary pursuits.

This checklist contains sixty negative statements covering all aspects of your visual and aural image. If you checked twenty statements or less, you are either another Dan Rather—you project a superior image— or self-delusionary. Between twenty-one and forty checkmarks indicate there's considerable room for improvement in your appearance, dress, speech, gestures, manners, and poise. A score of forty-one to sixty means you are desperately in need of the image advice contained in this book. A total image overhaul should be your first priority, starting right now.

2

SELF-IMAGE:
Evaluating Yourself
from the
Inside Out

by Mara Gleckel

The way you are treated in this world depends largely on the way you present yourself—the way you look, the way you speak, the way you behave. If you look undeserving, chances are you will be treated that way. If you act defensive, you invite attacks. On the other hand, if you act strong and confident, people will respond to you with respect, if not deference.

Unfortunately, many men present themselves poorly. Instead of acting confident, they appear overly agreeable. Instead of behaving assertively, they behave aggressively. Instead of acting as if they are in control of a situation, they let the situation appear to be controlling them.

If such men could only see themselves as others do, they would probably correct their negative behavior automatically—and, in the process, raise their own self-esteem. But since we cannot step outside ourselves and look at our own actions, the process of change is more complicated.

In this chapter, we'd like to help you determine whether your persona—the image you present to the world—accurately reflects your inner self. We want you to examine *why* you look, speak, and behave the way you do and analyze how those exterior attributes are helping or hindering you to achieve your goals in life.

WHERE AM I COMING FROM?

Before you decide what you would like to change about yourself, you should first consider your past. There is a cause-and-effect relationship between your past experiences—particularly what happened to you in your family—and your present behavior, and, by extension, your future course of action.

The way you respond to people as an adult is largely based on the way you learned to respond to members of your family as you were growing up. The childhood behavior that got you attention, approval, or punishment has a profound effect on the way you behave today.

For example, your relationship with your parents is probably the most significant interaction you experienced during your formative years. And for the rest of your life, you will tend to respond to other people in significant authority positions in the same way you related to your mother or father. And you will expect to get the same response from these authority figures that you got from your parents. For example, if your father was overly critical and made you feel inadequate, the slightest criticism from a male boss is likely to provoke in you those old feelings of childhood inadequacy. On the other hand, if your father was accepting of both your assets and liabilities and made you feel loved regardless of what you did, you will feel more secure and react with more confidence around men in authority positions.

If you don't like the way you respond to other people—if your response is distrust, fear of becoming close, a sense of feeling left out—you're not stuck in that response. Once you become aware of what's going on inside you emotionally, you are much freer to do something about it. You will be more likely to see people as people and not as surrogate mothers, fathers, or siblings. Here is an exercise that may help you locate the source of these old patterns of behavior.

Exercise #1 — "My father made me feel..."

Think about how you related to your father and how this affects you now. (Use the same exercise to analyze your childhood relationship with your mother.)

• Did your father love you unconditionally, or was his love predicated on whether you did as he asked?

• Did your father make you feel as if nothing you ever did was right? That whatever you did, he could do better?

• Did your father approve of you for being a "nice guy" and popular with all the kids in the neighborhood, or did he encourage you to play the role of "tough guy"?

• When you are with a group of men today, do you always expect to be the center of attention, or do you feel cowed?

Think of other questions that address the same point: how your childhood relationship with your father colors your present-day relationships with other men. When you've answered these questions as openly and honestly as you can, it will become clear to you how your past influences your present.

Take John, for example. He let his boss play the role of father to him. His boss would actually say to him, "You're the son I've always wanted." He would open John's mail, walk into John's office unannounced even when he was in the middle of a meeting with someone else, and, in general, constantly tried to make John feel childlike and incompetent. John was furious most of the time but still felt it necessary to act grateful and appeasing. He could not act adult or authoritative in the presence of his boss. When he became aware of what was going on he knew the only solution for him was to change jobs. Fortunately, he didn't sabotage his own career goals by doing so. He stayed a sufficient length of time, not only to complete a project he had been assigned but to learn the things that would help him move on to a better position. But if he had not become aware of what was happening and made his plans accordingly, he might have exploded in anger and ended up quitting before he got what he wanted out of the job.

Exercise #2 — "My co-workers represent..."

The role you played in your family—and may still be playing—also influences the way you behave today, for people generally react to their colleagues in the office in the same way they once reacted to other family members.

Take the case of Jim, a younger brother who got attention in the family only when he did something outrageous. Always the rebel at home, he continues to act that way at work. He always comes in late, wears flamboyant and inappropriate clothing, fights with his peers, defies his supervisors. It won't do him any good to go out and get a different job because the same thing will happen all over again. What he must do is realize that his behavior is inappropriate in the office. He must learn that there is a lot more room in the real world than there was in his own small family, and find more positive, less self-destructive ways to get attention.

• Think about the people in your office. Who are your supervisors, your peers, your subordinates? Then think about the people in your family. What was your position in the family? In each group—home and office—who is (or who was) the highest achiever, the lowest achiever, the most dependable person, the favorite, the smartest? Take a piece of paper and fold it in half. On one side list the people in your family and the roles they play or played. On the other side, list the people in your office and the roles they play. This is an easy way to see who's playing the same roles.

• What role do *you* play in the office? What role or roles did you play at home? Do you see yourself relating the same way to each set of people?

• Do you feel guilty in the presence of your boss? Do you always have to please? Do you get feelings of jealousy when others are praised? Did you respond the same way with your brothers and sisters? Were you the dependable one at home, the one who always mowed the lawn, took out the garbage, and did other chores? Are you the dependable one at work, and do you feel put upon by those who are less responsible? If you're not the dependable one, do you take advantage of the one who does the detail work? If you are a low achiever, do you try to get the high achiever to do your work for you?

• Think about how you get what you want on your job. Do you do it by having a temper tantrum? By being manipulative? By rebelling? How does that fit in with how you behaved at home?

If you often think things like, "They'll be sorry if I quit" or "They will sure miss me," it's similar to thinking about running away from home. If you come in late regularly and are reprimanded, do you say, "I'm sorry, it was an accident," or "To hell with you, I'm quitting"; or do you call in sick the next day? Your response is probably the same as it was when your parents corrected you.

If you were the center of attention in your family, you may want to be the center of attention in the office. If you were competitive with your father, you may be competitive with your immediate supervisor. If the only way to get approval in your family was achievement, you will try to achieve at work. But as an adult you may have to stop looking for constant approval and wait for recognition to come later.

Part of the reason many people are unhappy at work is that they may be responding at work the way they did in their early family life. But we are no longer children. We are adults with options. And we can choose to react in healthier, more adult ways.

Exercise #3 — "My name was..."

There are various "names" that you may have been called as a child—
"tough guy," "rebel," "good boy," "baby," "big brother," "book-
worm," "bad boy," "mommy's favorite," "teacher's pet,"
"easygoing"—that are still affecting the way you envision yourself
today. However, the old behavior that accompanied those names may
no longer be appropriate. And it may be time to change it.

• Discover the name or label from your childhood that fits you. The
name may never even have been verbalized, but you felt its pull. It
identified you. You may discover that more than one name applies. For
instance, you may have been "tough guy" and "rebel"; "good boy"
and "easygoing."

• Now consider the "name" you would like to sport as an adult.
Some possibilities are "superman," "superdad," "macho," "responsible," "successful," "powerful," "star," "glamour boy," "leader," "executive," "achiever," "helper," "generous," "kind." What is your adult
name? Again, there may be more than one name you want to apply to
yourself.

• Finally, ask yourself whether your old, childhood name or names
are affecting your ability to attain your new, adult name. For example, if
your childhood name was "good boy" and you now wish it to be
"strong," consider whether you are sabotaging your attempts at forcefulness by acting too pliable. If your name was "nice guy" and you
would like to change it to "macho," you may find that the image you
project is still more feminine than masculine. To change, you're going
to have to start competing head on with other men, at least for the
attention of women.

If your childhood name was "teacher's pet" and you now want to be
thought of as "leader,"you may find that the rewards you got—and still
may be getting—for being an authority figure's favorite may be prevent-
ing you from making the kind of assertive moves that accompany
leadership. As somebody's favorite, you can count on constant emotional support. As a leader, you must take risks and stand up for your
beliefs and ideas, even if that means going it alone for a while.

Write down the name that fit you as a child and the name you would
like to have describe you now. Under the childhood name, list the
benefits you remember and perhaps still are receiving, such as attention, love, friends, admiration. Then, under your adult name, list the
things you feel you would have to give up to attain that name fully.

For instance, if your name was "good natured" and you now want to
be "boss," you would have to give up having everybody love you,
being everyone's best friend, the one no one ever criticizes, the one

who always gets invited to parties. On the other hand, there are certain rewards that go along with being "boss," especially if you are a good one: status, money, self-respect, and possibly a way of behaving that is much more closely attuned to your true personality than the set of behaviors you adopted to get all those childhood goodies.

"Mommy's little boy" who wants to become an "independent man" will have to give up being taken care of and placated and risk making his own mistakes. Again, there are rewards he will eventually gain—a sense of true independence, of doing what he wants to do, of being in control of his life without having to worry about constantly pleasing other people. On the other hand, in a society where economic rewards sometimes mean "alone at the top" and "the buck stops here," he might decide it's more advantageous to stay where he is, under his mother's or some other woman's domination. Even though he doesn't achieve his high financial goals, he won't be lonely. As a high achiever, he might have to settle for less camaraderie, and to take responsibility for his failures as well as his successes.

In other words, every change requires a tradeoff. You will have to ask yourself if you are willing to make the sacrifices that accompany change in order to garner a totally new set of rewards. So be honest with yourself:

• Do you prefer the rewards that accompany the old name?

• Is the reason you're not attaining the new name because you're unwilling to give up the things—emotional, physical, financial or otherwise—that go with the old name?

The answers to these questions have nothing to do with morality. Whichever set of rewards you prefer, the important thing is that you decide which is right for *you*. And once you understand what you really want, you will feel more in control of your life and be less likely to just let things happen to you. And you will be much further along in arriving at an image that is both new and natural.

MAKING YOUR IMAGE FIT YOUR ASPIRATIONS

There are advantages and disadvantages to every kind of image. A man who looks extremely urbane and cultivated, for example, might find he is treated as a curiosity and not taken seriously by a lot of men. Furthermore, he might not be accepted by his colleagues on a friendly, informal level. A man who is a "glamour boy," on the other hand, may have plenty of female admirers, but he will probably have a more difficult time establishing rapport with his male business associates.

It might be too drastic a personality change for an urbane man to start acting and looking macho, or for a macho man to try looking highly cultivated. But both types of men could at least modify their image if they want to neutralize some of the negative reactions they get. For example, the urbane man might try to warm up his look— substitute a pipe for a cigarette holder, wear less formal and more casual clothing styles—so that people would find him less aloof and intimidating. And the "glamour boy" might try to look less fashionable and noticeable and more conservative and ordinary.

In short, it's important that you find your *own* style and adapt it to the requirements of your business and personal life. "Adapt" is the key word here.

Exercise #4 — "I want to look..."

• Take a good look at yourself in a typical outfit. Does the way you look now fit your career or lifestyle goals?

• If not, study the following list of qualities and check off those that best describe how you would like to look:

_____ proper	_____ businesslike
_____ authoritative	_____ casual
_____ creative	_____ masculine
_____ sexy	_____ fashionable
_____ boyish	_____ understated

• Is the way you look now close to the ideal look you have chosen? If not, what would you change? Is it merely a matter of changing your accessories? Or is your clothing all wrong, too? Don't discount the importance of body language in this equation. Are your posture and gestures inappropriate for the look you would like to project? And what about your facial expression?

YOUR BODY LANGUAGE

What does the way you move your body say to others? Let's find out.

Sit in front of a full-length mirror. First, place yourself in a position that you find most comfortable. Study how you look. Then put yourself in the position you find the least comfortable. Again study the way you look. You can stand or sit but be sure to bring in all parts of your body.

How do you look in each position? Comfortable? Uncomfortable? Nervous? Calm? Vulnerable? Tough? Friendly?

Do you feel your body is saying what you want it to say? Are you holding yourself in, arms folded, when you would like to be more open, friendly and outgoing? Are you sitting in tough, masculine positions, legs spread apart, looking threatening, when you would *like* to look approachable?

Once you are aware of how you look you can make little changes here and there to project an image you feel more comfortable with. You could concentrate on looking more welcoming if you're trying to make friends. Or if you're turning people off by looking too tough, you could try assuming less masculine postures. You don't want to erase your personality but it can sometimes be helpful to modify extreme postures if they stand in the way of achieving goals.

INNER CHANGE→OUTER CHANGE→CHANGED REACTIONS IN OTHERS

When you change your persona, be prepared for new responses from other people, some positive, some negative.

A new image will undoubtedly attract new types of people. On the other hand, old friends may not like the "new you" and either pressure you to revert to the "old you" or walk away.

If you are sure your new look is helping you achieve your goals, you must decide whether maintaining the old ties is so important to you that you are willing to forgo individual achievement. If you are one of many supervisors and you want to become a middle manager, stepping out of the group is important. Obviously, some of your co-workers aren't going to like it. Consider the fact that you may have outgrown many of your old buddies anyway, and it's time to give them up and move on. Reaching a higher plateau in your company or your profession always means leaving some people behind and selecting friends from your new peer group.

3

DO YOU HAVE IMAGE INTEGRITY?

by Barbara Blaes

Jim was angry. "I always look neat. I'm clean. I take daily showers. I keep my hair trimmed. What more do they want?"

The man pacing my office did, indeed, look neat. But he did *not* look like an executive. His company had sent him to me with instructions to make him look like what he was—executive material.

Jim arrived for our appointment wearing a three-quarter length plaid overcoat and Tyrolean hat. His suit was brown, wrinkle-free polyester, topped off with a light-blue plaid tie. On his feet, he wore brown loafers with tassels.

Then there was Walt, a lab technician who attended an image-improvement seminar I gave in Denver. Walt was going to night school to become a chemist and hoped to be promoted within the small lab where he worked. How did he dress? He always wore khaki, from his open-neck shirt and webbed belt to his pants with the sharp creases. He moved with quick precision and sported a crew cut.

"I got used to looking like this in the Marines," he explained. "It still makes sense to me. It's easy. Neat. Nothing ever clashes."

When I asked what chemists wore, he said, "Oh, they dress casually. After all, they look out the window at the Rocky Mountains, not Madison Avenue. They wear corduroys and flannel shirts. Their hair is always longer than mine. Some even have beards."

Walt was puzzled because his superiors did not take his aspirations seriously. They seemed to think he'd stay a technician for the rest of his life.

David, in contrast, wore traditional, three-piece suits and white shirts. He was twenty-five years old, had just graduated from Columbia with an M.B.A. and was launched on a career with an important insurance company. Two hours with me was a graduation gift from his mother who was, understandably, concerned about his penchant for wearing clogs with his suits and his defiance about his full red beard.

David came to me reluctantly. "The suit, the white shirt—that's as far as I'll go to sacrifice my individuality. I intend to get my promotions on my ability, not because I look like a carbon copy of everybody else."

These three men were making essentially the same mistake. They all lacked what I call "image integrity." The elements of their image—clothing, accessories, hair, speech, voice, body language, and manners—were inconsistent, out of synch with each other and with the professional environments in which they were trying to get ahead. The overall impression conveyed was that of men who didn't know who they were or where they were headed. And, as a consequence, neither did anyone else!

Any man wishing to adopt a more appropriate image must first answer three basic questions—and answer them as honestly and objectively as possible.

QUESTION #1: HAVE I DEVELOPED A CLEAR SENSE OF MY OWN PERSONAL STYLE BASED ON AN HONEST AND CURRENT SELF-ANALYSIS?

Everyone has an image, whether he designed it consciously or not. Let's examine what kind of image you've adopted, and why.

The way people look and speak is often heavily influenced by childhood role models and experiences. Your parents' standards and ideas about dress could be influencing you to this day.

One of my clients told me he had six sisters and one brother. In order to simplify laundry sorting, his mother always bought blue shirts for him and yellow shirts for his brother.

"To this day, I can't wear yellow shirts," he told me. "Yellow happens to look good on me, but I can't escape the feeling I'm wearing my brother's shirts."

Another client said his father always told him never to call attention to himself; he shouldn't set himself apart and act or look any "better off" than anyone else. He was taught to be and to look like "a regular guy." Today, he has a real problem in developing the necessary leadership skills for corporate advancement and in choosing clothes that promote a successful, on-the-way-up image.

Perhaps, you were always dressed in clothes that could "take it." Or maybe your family discouraged attention to appearance altogether because it was considered *un*masculine and sissified. If your family wasn't affluent, you may have been encouraged to "wear it out," even if the garment had been worn by your two brothers before you. One client showed me a topcoat he'd worn for ten years. It was dated in style, a bad color for a man with his complexion, and fit poorly because he'd lost weight recently. "I know I should get rid of it," he said, "but you'll have to force me to do it. I just can't because it's still a perfectly good coat. There's another five years' wear in it."

Consider, too, your family's attitudes toward weight. Some families value bulk and equate it not only with health but with personal qualities such as reliability, strength, and stability. They view thin people as untrustworthy, superficial, and lacking forcefulness. If this is the case, you may be unconsciously sabotaging your own efforts to lose weight.

Speech and voice inflection are two other image elements that may go back to childhood. Perhaps the primary means of communication in your family was shouting and "fighting it out," which might explain why today people say you speak too loudly or accuse you of being raucous and boisterous. On the other hand, your family may have specialized in silence and withdrawal, and you were religiously trained never to raise your voice. You may have been discouraged from arguing. "My mother drilled it into me that 'silence is golden,'" one client said. "Now I really have trouble holding up my end of a discussion, especially in a heated professional debate."

Finally, as you got older, you were encouraged to express your ideas on controversial subjects, or was that discouraged?

In addition to early family influences, we are often haunted long into adulthood by a friend's remarks and opinions. Someone in one of my seminars said a girl told him years ago he reminded her of Bob Hope. "I've tried to act like him ever since," the man said, acknowledging it was silly. "It sure was a strain to come up with all those one-liners. I probably wasn't ever very funny, but I kept it up, because everybody likes Bob Hope, and I wanted that to rub off on me."

Another client wasn't comfortable wearing bright ties, but he wore them regularly. Why? Because ten years before his college roommate had told him he looked drab and should wear more color.

These are some of the factors that may have contributed to the image you developed over the years, an image that may now need updating. One thing you must constantly evaluate is whether your image is contemporary and representative of you and your life as they are today. You may still be dressing, speaking, and behaving as you did years ago, although your circumstances have changed dramatically since then. If this is the case, don't you think it's time for a change?

Present as well as past influences can also affect your image adversely. I often hear: "My wife thinks I look fine," or "My girl friend likes me to use this cologne," or "My daughter says, 'The stores are full of pastels for men. Get with it, Dad.'" The moral: Don't let women's opinions automatically determine your image. It's okay to want to please the women in your life, but not to the point where their ideas of what you should look like keep you from finding your own best image.

Before fashioning a new image, you need to rid yourself of these hobbling influences and reassess yourself honestly. Take a good, long look at yourself. Carefully analyze both your strong and weak points. Take special care in analyzing your faults. From my experiences with clients, I can tell you that many people go to exaggerated, misguided lengths to hide minor flaws, often to the detriment of their overall appearance. One man I know let the hair on the left side of his head grow ten inches long, then combed it across his bare head. Those few, long hairs stopped just above his right ear. Baldness is completely acceptable on male executives, much more so than poor attempts at camouflage.

When I mentioned this example in a lecture, another man said, "I do that with my hair, even though most of it's gone now, but I never thought about it. I just kept combing it the same as I had since I was a kid. It never occurred to me to change."

I have heard men attempting to camouflage faults explain: "I wear a beard to cover my weak chin"; "My ears stick way out. That's why I wear bushy sideburns"; "I'm so big, if I stand up straight, I'll scare people."

By overcompensating for what they consider their faults, these men created even more complex problems for themselves. The man with the beard wanted to rise in the banking profession. He was sure his imagined weak chin would hold him back. Instead, his beard was not appropriate in his environment. The man with the full, bushy sideburns wasn't aware that they gave him an image of someone lower on the socioeconomic scale than he belonged. The man who worried about scaring people because of his size looked tired, lazy, and sloppy instead.

In formulating your image—the person you want to become—make sure that it grows out of who you truly are. Your image won't work if you don't feel comfortable with it. Don't try to look and act like a woodsy outdoorsman if Keats, sherry, and a fireplace are your preference. Don't try to be an urban sophisticate if you're a country boy at heart.

QUESTION #2: ARE ALL THE COMPONENTS OF MY IMAGE IN HARMONY WITH EACH OTHER?

A successful man is most often a well-integrated person whose appearance and behavior create a consistent, believable public image. He is a total entity, not an assemblage of disparate parts. His appearance, speech, and manner complement each other and reflect the best of himself.

Unfortunately, too many men's images send out conflicting messages, confusing people instead of attracting and influencing them. I have seen many men whose image was almost perfect—yet was ruined by one discordant detail. Here are some of the more obvious "image wreckers":

• Anklet socks exposing bare shins, worn by an otherwise impeccably groomed executive during an important business meeting.

• Penny loafers worn with a business suit.

• A weak Wally Cox voice issuing from a man who looks like Arnold Schwarzenegger; or, conversely, a cultivated baritone speaking voice (à la George Sanders) emanating from a man who looks like a country singer (à la Willie Nelson).

• Extreme or exotic facial hair patterns worn on anyone who isn't a member of the Hell's Angels motorcycle gang—or a character actor who specializes in playing psychos.

• A slouching posture and shuffling walk on an otherwise efficient professional manager.

• Sneakers that a man wears for all occasions—including a black-tie charity ball. (Howard Hughes did this.)

For some men the problem lies not in one detail but in a whole area of their looks. The placement officer at a prominent university told me that she had sent a graduate on a job interview and had received this comment from the man who interviewed him: "I liked the young man you sent me. He spoke well and had a good record, but he just didn't look sharp enough. His top shirt button was open under his tie, his shirt was a little rumpled, his hair a little tousled, his shoes not shined. He looked as though he'd just gotten out of bed."

An exaggeration? Perhaps. But, needless to say, the young man didn't get the job. In his case, the colors he wore were all right, the clothes appropriate. He just wasn't well groomed. Conversely, a man may be meticulously groomed but wear poorly fitting clothes of cheap fabrics and hybrid colors.

Image inconsistencies confuse people. Consider John, who told his boss that he wouldn't mind going to Detroit to give a sales presentation and postpone his vacation. He sighed deeply as he spoke and his body slumped. Do you suppose his boss accepted what he *said* as an indication of his true feelings, or judged them by how John *behaved*?

Then there's Hank, who dresses very well in upper-middle-class garb and yet uses obscene language to fit in as "one of the boys." And Richard, who told his female colleague that he'd listen to her idea with an open mind, though her recommendation conflicted with his, while locking his arms across his chest and narrowing his eyes. He said one thing, but his body language indicated the opposite.

QUESTION #3: IS MY IMAGE IN HARMONY WITH MY ENVIRONMENT?

Once you have defined the image you would like to present to the world, and noted those details of appearance or behavior that conflict with or undermine that image, your next step is to decide what image is appropriate to the roles you play in life. When you are in a professional setting, do you have a professional image? In a social setting, a social image?

Think of your image as a form of communication. With it, you want to send out messages that will evoke a positive response in others. At work you will wish to communicate qualities such as commitment, loyalty, stability, and intelligence. In order to do this, you must never wear cheap, extremely casual, or loud clothes. You should look as though you could meet with executives and not be out of step, not cause anyone embarrassment because of the way you look, act, or speak.

One executive told me that one of his employees dresses so casually he looks as though he's off to a baseball game, not to serious work.

"How can I really believe in him," he asked, "unless he begins to look as though he means business?" Another said, "I have a man in my office who indulges himself with big, gaudy rings and atrocious clothes. He's good, and I'd like to promote him, but I know that if I send him out to represent me, he will inspire an immediate turn-off."

Men often don't realize that the look of leadership, authority, and power can be learned and used as a career skill. It is one career variable completely under your control, yet so many men discount it. They dress in ways that communicate the wrong values, attitudes, and roles. Here are some of the more obvious stereotypes, followed by the message their image is sending.

College Boy
This man is still on campus. He wears corduroy jackets and dungarees and walks with a swinging gait on thick rubber-soled shoes. He may be twenty-three or fifty. He often sees easy answers to complex problems and presents them with a wide-eyed glow. *Message:* "I may be bright, but I have some growing up to do before I can handle responsibility."

The Male Model
This man is trendy. He brings his interest in looks, fashion, and fads into the office. He can lift one eyebrow at a time—and does. He likes cufflinks. He wears the latest fashion, whether it's cowboy boots, astronaut watches, or pink plaid jackets. *Message:* "I change my mind a lot. You can't depend on my stability."

Old-Fashioned
This man spends a lot of time wondering why he's never promoted. He deals poorly with female colleagues, averting his eyes, grinning and patronizing them. Often he's overweight. He looks drab and tired. His clothes and eyeglass frames are outdated. *Message:* "I'm not open to change and don't get any new ideas."

Disheveled
Men who don't seem to care about their appearance are in this category. They are frequently in poor physical condition, move awkwardly, and slump. Even though they are talented, they present themselves negatively. Their clothes are nondescript and wrinkled. Their ties are pulled down, and their shoes aren't shined. They're not quite dirty, but not quite clean. Too much time elapses between shampoos. *Message:* "I don't care about my appearance or myself, why should I care about my work?"

Few men are pure examples of the preceding types, but if you recognize part of yourself in any of them, take heed. The image you project may be holding you back.

A distinct image or business style accompanies every profession. A lawyer, for example, is expected to dress and comport himself one way, while a man in advertising or the arts is expected to look and act in a different way.

IMAGE-CHANGE SUCCESS STORIES

Jim is an example of a man who overcame his appearance problems and developed an effective, professional image. You met Jim at the beginning of the chapter; he's the one who was told that he'd better look like an executive or he'd never become one.

Shortly after we worked together, Jim left the company and eventually became a highly successful independent consultant. One day he was called back to his original company to bid on a consulting project. He arrived wearing a conservative, expensive, charcoal suit, white shirt, and burgundy tie with a small print. He wore wingtip shoes and high black socks, and carried a brown leather briefcase. He left his Tyrolean hat at home. He was proud of the way he looked and what he had accomplished. He walked with a new assurance.

"I couldn't believe the difference in the way I was treated this time by everyone in the office," he later told me. "I had no idea how negatively I must have been perceived before."

Walt, the lab technician, and David, the insurance-office man, also adopted new images. Walt finally realized that people evaluated those in solid khaki outfits as military people, deliverymen, gas station attendants, or janitors. He saw that if he wanted to be a chemist after he qualified through his course work, he'd better start to look like those he worked with. "Look as though you belong," I advised him, "not like an outsider." He let his hair grow out a little and began wearing corduroys and flannel shirts. Occasionally, he wears a sport coat and trousers. During our last conversation he joked that he might even grow a beard and smoke a pipe.

David soon understood that he didn't have to make a political statement through his appearance, that he could hold onto his individuality without the help of clogs and a beard. He finds it more effective now to use his appearance to serve as a quiet, dignified support for his personal and professional strengths. "If people aren't distracted by the way I look, they're more apt to trust me and to listen to me," he said.

In our busy world, people are usually far too distracted to wait to be proven wrong about their first visual and aural impressions of strangers. Naturally, we all want to be judged solely on our merit and ability, our personality, and that inner core that is our best self. But the reality is that initially we are judged by the image we present. Often, we don't get a second chance. This is true at a job interview, a sales encounter, a professional conference—any situation in which we are meeting new people. The first impression is vital. Make it count!

PART II

YOUR APPEARANCE: WHAT OTHER PEOPLE SEE AND HOW TO IMPROVE IT

4

CLOTHES CONSCIOUSNESS: Building Credibility Through Your Wardrobe

by William Thourlby

Studies show that when you walk through a door, even though no one in the room has ever seen you before, you create what the social psychologists call a "threshold effect." In one tenth of a second these strangers are forced to form instant judgments about you, based on the only criteria available for that decision—your clothing, which covers up to ninety percent of your body. In that decisive moment they will make ten decisions about your

1. economic level
2. educational level
3. trustworthiness
4. social position
5. level of sophistication
6. social heritage (that is, your parents' and ancestors' social position)
7. educational heritage (your parents' and ancestors' educational level)
8. economic heritage (your parents' and ancestors' level of affluence)

9. success (in previous and current endeavors)
10. moral character

To be successful in almost any endeavor, you must be sure that all these judgments made about you are favorable, because *you never get a second chance to make a good first impression*. Understanding this and controlling how you want people to perceive you is *power*. You achieve this powerful edge over your competition by packaging (or dressing, if you will) yourself to turn off the least number of people, thus exposing yourself to the greatest number of possibilities for success.

While it is certainly true that your speech, body language, education, and background are all important components of the success formula, they require time and closer inspection to evaluate. Clothing, on the other hand, is the first and most obvious criterion from which a stranger can form an instant judgment.

Oliver Wendell Holmes said, "The greatest thing in this world is not so much where we are, but in what direction we are moving." Your wardrobe will help other people decide where you are moving—up, down, or nowhere in particular.

On the following pages, I will give you a step-by-step program that will enable you to build a wardrobe keyed to that unwritten—but nevertheless very real—American business success code. If you aspire to move up in business, I advise you to invest in appropriate, well-tailored business attire. Remember, your goal is to impress your corporate superiors, peers, and clients—not the avant-garde wing of the fashion establishment. The man most likely to move ahead is the man who invests his money to suit where he makes his money. He builds his credibility—to a greater or lesser extent—by way of his wardrobe.

BUILDING A BUSINESS WARDROBE

Your product or industry, your client mix, the climate where you live, the economy, and some good common sense are the factors that control your wardrobe decisions. But the overarching principle is still the axiom: "Nothing wears as well as tradition." Erring in the direction of tradition will serve you well no matter what you do for a living or where you live. Moderation expressed by the clothes that you wear reflects status and a solid upper-middle-class background.

Now let's examine in more depth each of the factors that contribute to your wardrobe decision-making.

Your Product or Industry

The product that your company sells or the industry in which you are employed is an important factor to consider when building an appropriate business image. Are you involved in the sale of a tangible or intangible product? Is it a big-ticket item or relatively inexpensive? Is it a product for the general consumer or for industrial users? These are the types of questions you should ask yourself in order to decide how to "package," or dress, yourself.

In general, the more directly a product influences the customer's finances, family, or future, the more serious an image you should present. For example, if you are employed in the insurance, securities, or health-care industries, you should dress in clothes that convey an impression of seriousness: suits; dark ties; white, blue or ecru (that is, pale yellow) shirts. However, if you are involved in the marketing of luxury, recreational, or novelty items, you can package yourself more casually. Sport coats, slacks, and less formal ties are appropriate.

Start thinking of yourself as a product and start packaging yourself to accomplish the task at hand.

Client Mix

The second important influence on the way you dress, or package yourself, is your client mix. What type of customer do you call on or does your company have? What is the educational background, social status, and economic level of these clients? The answers to such questions will help you determine what type of appearance you should present to them—what "look" will make the best impression on them.

For example, if your customers are predominantly wealthy homeowners, you should package yourself so that your appearance says that you come from a similar background. If your appearance suggests that you come from a lower socioeconomic background, you will have little chance of being accepted and trusted by them. Likewise, if you call on or do business with highly educated prospects, such as engineers or college professors, your appearance should suggest similar educational attainment.

Again, whatever your client mix may be, take the time to analyze those customers to make sure you package yourself in a way that will attract rather than repel them.

Climate or Geographic Location

The old adage, "When in Rome, do as the Romans do," does not apply to traveling salesmen or executives. You should be consistent in your appearance whether you are in Florida one day and California the next.

Traditional, well-tailored clothing is acceptable anywhere.

On the other hand, although you should not change your image by dressing exactly like the natives, you should remember that some areas of the country are more formal than others. For example, the East Coast is characterized by more formality in business dress than certain parts of the South or West Coast. Therefore, your appearance should vary in formality to reflect the local custom.

Before you set out on a business trip, analyze the climate and geographic region with regard to its formality in business dress and package yourself accordingly. If you study these factors and apply what you learn to your image, you will begin to notice that this approach will get you more hearings—and more extended ones—with your prospects. While the right image won't help you close the deal if you're not a good closer, it will make you appear more credible to your customers, clients, or prospects. As you package yourself correctly for your clients, you will notice you are being more warmly greeted and accepted by them. They will begin to consider you a friend rather than just another traveling pitchman or smooth-talking executive. You will find yourself invited to their homes to meet their family, to their clubs to meet their friends. But you will never be invited to any of these places if you continue to wear the kind of clothes that set you apart and make you appear different.

Economy

Ask the average man why he doesn't buy at least one quality suit a year (that's the bare minimum), and invariably he says, "I can't afford it." You ask, "Why?" He says, "I just bought a $15,000 car, a $585 driving lawn mower, and a $7,500 swimming pool." He forgets that all of these so-called status symbols can't be taken with him to the office or to a client's office. What he does take to the office every day is his clothing. In fact, his wardrobe in business is his primary status symbol, the one area over which he can exert complete control. I think it is time most ambitious men realign their priorities and decide whether they are investing money in the things that will help them make even more money, or investing in the things that only take money out of their bank accounts with no promise of putting any back in.

Start thinking in terms of "investment clothing." When you buy clothes for business, you are investing in your future; you are helping yourself succeed. Therefore, you should always buy the very best you can possibly afford. When you purchase an article of business attire, always think in terms of durability and versatility: How long will it last and how often can I wear it?

There are several ways to stretch your wardrobe dollars and still buy expensive, quality clothing. For example, make your first three suits solids—no stripes or plaids. In addition, make sure those solid-colored suits are within the same color family so that any accessories (shirts, ties, belts and shoes) you buy can be worn with all three suits. Then, just by changing the accessory item, you can change your outfit dramatically. Because your accessories are interchangeable, you can get the maximum wear from your suits without anyone suspecting that you only own three suits. If your suits are dark-colored, all the better. Dark suits are more versatile since they can be worn in more different ways.

Common Sense

If your business wardrobe is not near the top of your financial priorities, it will show. Your clothes will tell on you. For instance, some men outfit themselves in accordance with their active social life and fool themselves into thinking they can, with the addition of a few clothing items that are more conservative, manage to don the same wardrobe for business. Don't think such men's bosses can't see where they place their priorities, especially when it comes time to slip a few pink slips into the salary envelopes of selected employees because of a business slowdown or recession. Never give your employer even the slightest excuse to think you aren't fully committed to your job.

STEP ONE—BUYING A SUIT

Don't be confused by all the rhetoric on the subject of suits—how to choose one, get a proper fit, judge the smallest detail to make sure you are buying quality. When it comes to choosing a suit, there are only two major choices with a few minor variations to consider. Men are lucky—unlike the situation women must contend with when it comes to fashion—because the basic suit never really changes.

The major choice concerns a suit's cut. Do you look best in the traditional American natural-shoulder suit or the European cut? The traditional American suit is distinguished by natural sloping shoulders, modestly tapered jacket, and notched lapels. (See Figure 4-1.) The European-designed suit is much more dramatic in fit with high armholes, padded shoulders, a severely suppressed waist, and peaked lapels. (See Figure 4-3.)

Now let's get down to facts. Aside from the "glamour" professions like entertainment, advertising, and publishing, top executives in most American corporations wear traditional clothing that does not call attention to itself. (See Figure 4-2.) "Quiet reliability" is one way to

FIGURE 4–1. The classic, two-button American-cut suit is distinguished by its natural sloping shoulders, modestly tapered jacket, and notched lapels. (Credit: Hart, Schaffner & Marx)

FIGURE 4–2. The double-breasted suit looks best on the man with a slim or medium build. Because of its dash and flair, it is most appropriate for men employed in the "glamour" industries. (Credit: Hart, Schaffner & Marx)

FIGURE 4–3.   The European-cut suit is dramatic in its styling and fit. It has high armholes, padded shoulders, a severely suppressed waist, and peaked lapels. (Credit: Men's Fashion Assn.)

describe the look. In fact, if you work outside the glamour industries, take a second look at any item of clothing that you are complimented on. You want other people to be concerned about what's on your mind, not what's on your body.

The suit is the basic component of a business wardrobe. It is the canvas on which you paint your personality, background, and future. Choose it wisely!

Color or tone is crucial

Imagine a color or tone chart that grades from one to ten. Number ten is the dominant figure color, the color that will convey the most power and/or authority. Guess the color? It's black, of course. Farther down the scale are midnight blue and charcoal gray, and finally reaching number one, the all-white Good Humor Man look. To be taken seriously as a businessman in America, you must wear suits that rate five or greater on the color chart—tan, medium grey and darker. Stay away from black, however. It is too severe for most men and may make you look like an undertaker. Pastels, at the other end of the scale, are for leisure time only.

Small details in tailoring distinguish the classic suit

They are the hallmark of investment clothing. They transcend time. Therefore, in choosing a suit, look for these traditional details:

The Soft Shoulders   Look for a shoulder with no padding. The natural-shoulder suit (i.e., American cut) conveys that "I've got nothing to hide" reliability. It's the look most business executives want to project. Padded shoulders, on the other hand, might have negative connotations. On an unconscious level, they convey the notion that you have something to hide or that you're insecure.

The 3½-Inch Lapel   Find a clean, classic notch styling as close to a standard 3½-inch width as possible. This suit will stay in style for years. Although the width may vary slightly, going wider to 4 inches or narrower to 2 inches, the 3½-inch width will remain a standard. It will look neither outdated nor trendy. The very fact that you are not caught up in the whim of high fashion gives you a look of stability, like a man who is here to stay.

The Plain Notch Lapel   This lapel is the style to buy. It has no tabs and is not a peaked lapel. Also avoid fishmouth or European notches. All of these styles move in and out of fashion and can make your otherwise perfectly wearable suit obsolete. The classic notch lapel is a staple. It has no contrasting or matching top stitching, no top stitching around the edges of the lapel, just the clean lapel look. Top stitching on lapels is too casual for traditional business attire.

Two- or Three-Button Styling Your jacket may have two or three buttons, but make sure those buttons are made of bone or horn—no shiny plastic, please. Two-button styling with some slight tapering is usually the more flattering to the average male figure. Two buttons allow your jacket to be tapered more easily. However, any obvious or extravagant tapering of the jacket—as in most European-cut styles—should be avoided for the same reasons you steered clear of padded shoulders. Your physique should be showcased by the suit. The suit should not be used to rebuild or reshape your body.

Vents Side or center vents are both acceptable, but top executives seem to prefer the center vent. It's the more conservative of the two styles.

Inside Pockets Your suit pockets should be built into your jacket, rather than applied to the outside of the jacket like patch pockets. A flap should cover the pocket opening with the exception of the breast pocket. Patch pockets are acceptable on summer suits only.

Straight-Leg Pants For suit pants, the width at the knee and the bottom of the pants should be about the same. If you have large feet and need an extra one and one-half inches to balance a large shoe, fine, but no more. Flaired and tapered pants come and go but they are not part of the classic business look. Suit pants should always be worn with a belt and contain no fancy, unnecessary pockets.

THE SHIRT

The shirt is as powerful a status indicator as anything you wear. You can ruin your entire image by having the wrong collar style or wrong color shirt. Frayed collars or heavy stitching are other image destroyers. In short, choose your shirts with the utmost care.

Collars The collar of a shirt is the focal point of your wardrobe package—and often where men go wrong. When men try to save money on shirts, the collar is a dead giveaway. The collars on cheaper shirts tend to pucker, especially if they aren't laundered properly. A puckered shirt collar is counterproductive for the man who is trying to project a look of power and authority. My advice is to spend more for a quality shirt and always send your shirts to the laundry.

There are only four basic collar styles appropriate for business:

1. The classic straight collar is recommended for all suits and sport coats. It is a traditional favorite. (See Figure 4–4.)
2. The tab collar, with or without the collar pin, is another favorite for suits whether or not you wear a vest. (See Figure 4–5.)
3. The Windsor collar has a wider spread and is frequently worn on custom or semi-custom-made shirts with a disappearing collar band to accentuate or lengthen the neck. This collar can be worn with vested or nonvested suits. (See Figure 4–6.)
4. The classic button-down collar is recommended for more casual business wear, with nonvested suits, and with sport coats. (See Figure 4–7.)

Try to remember that collar lengths should seldom vary from 3¼ inches to 3½ inches; otherwise, the collar becomes associated with a fad. Also avoid collars with heavy stitching, contrasting thread, noticeable button combinations or large collar-roll effect. (By large collar-roll effect, I refer to a collar that forms a semicircle from the base of the collar out to the button-down points. It is also known as a "Hollywood button-down.")

Shirt Materials   Your choice of shirting materials is relatively simple once you realize you must stick to the classics. The best shirt material is still cotton broadcloth. If you send your shirts to the laundry, which I recommend, you may buy the 100-percent cotton. If you prefer wash-and-wear, you should buy the cotton polyester blend for its durable press qualities. Be sure you always select blends with a larger percentage of cotton than polyester, however (e.g., 55 percent cotton, 45 percent polyester, at least). This is necessary to keep the collar from fraying prematurely or having the collar material ball up around the neck.

Here are the acceptable shirting materials for business wear:

Broadcloth: This should be your first choice. It has a fine, close weave that works both for business and casual attire.

Oxford cloth: This looser, basket-weave material is somewhat more casual than the broadcloth, thereby lending itself to wear with non-vested suits and sport coats.

End-on-End: This material is similar to oxford cloth except that there are colored threads interwoven with white threads. This shirt is particularly effective in pastels since the white threads soften the color of the shirt.

Batiste: This is a very lightweight, luxurious material, used mostly for warm-weather wear. However, because of its lightness, it does not stand up well to laundering and lacks durability. This material should be worn only with a suit.

Jacquard and Pique: These materials are reserved for very dressy business or semi-formal occasions.

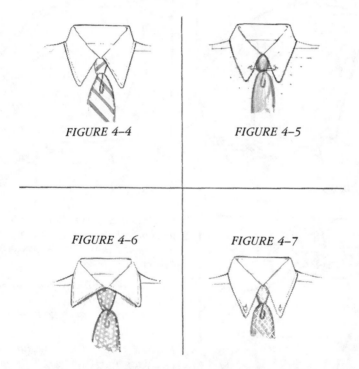

FIGURE 4–4   *FIGURE 4–5*

FIGURE 4–6   *FIGURE 4–7*

These are the four basic collar styles appropriate for business. FIGURE 4–4 shows the classic straight collar, simple and always correct. FIGURE 4–5 depicts the pinned collar. It is a tab collar that can be worn with or without the pin. FIGURE 4–6 is the Windsor collar, a stiff, cutaway collar popularized by the Duke of Windsor. He used a larger knot of his own invention (i.e., Windsor knot) to fill the wide gap between the collar points. FIGURE 4–7 is the button-down, recommended for more casual wear. (Art credit: Linda Tain)

Pockets and Fronts   Choose shirts with either the fly or French front. Always avoid any exaggerated stitching or elaborate button configurations. If you are not sure if what you have in your hand is a classic shirt, don't buy it. If you are having your shirts made, never have pockets put on them. If they are ready-made, one pocket is acceptable. I hope it goes without saying that you should never wear plastic pen or pencil holders in that shirt pocket.

FIGURE 4–8.

FIGURE 4–9.

FIGURE 4–10.

FIGURE 4–8.   The full-cut shirt is the only choice for the large-boned man or the man who is overweight. (Art credit: Linda Tain)

FIGURE 4–9.   The regular-cut shirt has some tapering to the waist. It is worn by men of average weight and build.

FIGURE 4–10.   The body shirt is severely tapered, thus "hugs" the body. It looks best on the slim- to medium-figured man. (Art credit: Linda Tain)

Taper and Cut   There are three different cuts available in dress shirts. They vary from manufacturer to manufacturer in name, degree of taper, and stylistic features; but they are generally known as full cut, regular taper, and body shirt. (See Figures 4–8; 4–9; 4–10.) Your weight and body configuration will dictate which cut suits you. Just make sure the shirt does not bag on you, conveying an impression of disorderliness.

Cuffs   There are really only two cuff styles: the barrel cuff, otherwise known as the classic single-button cuff; and the French cuff, which requires cuff links. The French cuff is more glamorous, but both are acceptable in business.

Monograms   Whether you choose to have your initials embroidered on your shirt is a very personal decision. I would look first to see what my contemporaries are doing before I decide. If you opt for a monogram, it should be placed over the heart, nowhere else. In fact, put it any place else and it will be regarded as avant garde and showy. Choose a dark color and the smallest legible monogram lettering.

Collar Stays   When buying shirts, check to see that they have removable collar stays. The stays should be removed before the shirt is laundered so that pressing the collar does not leave an imprint or crease around the stay, or, worse yet, melt the stay itself. Do not hesitate to trim the stays if they are too long.

BLAZERS AND SPORT COATS

If you could only have one sport coat to use for more informal business occasions as well as strictly for pleasure, I'm sure you would choose the classic navy blue blazer. If you decide that your budget can only accommodate one blazer, then buy a wool/polyester blend for year-round use. Purchase the single-breasted blazer with traditional natural shoulders. Always insist on brass buttons.

For a more complete informal wardrobe, your next choice should be a tweed (preferably the neutral dark Harris tweed) or dark herringbone. Both can be worn with solid gray slacks or several other color choices, giving you maximum versatility. These sport coats can also be used for extremely casual wear over jeans.

SWEATERS AND VESTS

Sweaters come in two basic types: lightweight and dressy; or bulky, for outdoor use.

In choosing your sweaters, keep them basic and simple. This is not the clothing item to use to display your wild color sense or design ideas. In lightweight sweaters, I recommend the V-neck style in such basic colors as navy blue, baby blue, tan, and gray. The heavier-weight bulky sweaters can be anything from ski sweaters to the large cardigan, V-neck, or turtleneck styles. If you have a short neck, remember to choose the mock rather than the full turtleneck.

Vests, for all practical purposes, are strictly a sports item if they are made of any material other than your suit material. Here is where you can let loose a little with a plaid, suede, or even smart sweater (sleeveless) style.

SLACKS

For openers, stick to dress slacks. Why? Because dress slacks work both for dress and casual occasions. They can be worn with blazers and sport coats. Then, with a change of heart, you can also wear them with an open sports shirt or sweater.

I recommend belt loops because they take away the problem when you gain and lose a little weight. When the waist of your slacks begins to feel a little loose, you can always cinch it in again with a belt. Besides, a belt helps you look the part of a gentleman. If you choose a pair of slacks with no loops, ask the tailor to put them on from the extra material at the pants cuffs.

In choosing the colors for slacks, stick to basic solid grays, and light, medium, and charcoal tans and blues. These colors mix and match with every jacket, sweater or sports shirt. Just avoid all the tricky gadgets that designers, in a fit of ingenuity, sometimes add to slacks. Remember: tricky clothes are for tricky folks.

COATS AND OUTER WEAR

Every trade or profession, including yours, has its own dress code, even if it is unwritten. And your success, in part, is bound to depend on how you measure up to those standards. Therefore, look at your raincoat or trench coat as a very important investment.

There are basically only two types of raincoats you should consider: The classic raglan shoulder, fly-front, executive raincoat is the most common. (See Figure 4–11.) This coat is the first and best choice for the senior executive of any large company. The second choice is the trench coat. (See Figure 4–12.) It was originally worn by British officers in the

FIGURE 4–11. The traditional raglan shoulder, fly-front raincoat—khaki colored only—is ideal for business wear. (Art credit: Linda Tain)

FIGURE 4–12.   The tan trench coat, originally worn by British officers during World War I, adds panache to a businessman's appearance. (Art credit: Linda Tain)

trenches and battlefields of World War I and its styling has changed very little since. When used in combat, every part of the trench coat had a use. The gun flaps shielded the shoulder from the rifle kick; the shoulder yoke gave extra protection against the rain; the inverted pleat or riding wedge at the back enabled the wearer to ride comfortably on horseback. Even today, trench coats whose only practical use is to shield the wearer from the rain contain these same styling details. But do not fall prey to any jazzy extras, brass buttons, hand-grenade holders, and on and on. Enough is enough. The trench coat is also a good choice for business wear and will add a certain dash to your appearance.

For either coat, there are two essentials to bear in mind:

• Buy only the classic khaki tan—no soft pastels, basic blacks, or flashy iridescents.

• The raincoat or trench coat should come to at least two inches below the knee. If you are tall and self-conscious about your height, the coat should hang to the middle of your knee, and the sleeves should be one inch to one and one-half inches longer than your suit coat sleeve.

TOPCOATS OR OVERCOATS?

Today we live in a world of almost totally controlled temperatures. Overcoats are no longer such a necessity. Topcoats, because they are lighter in weight and bulk but still afford warmth, have almost replaced the big, heavy overcoats of yesterday.

There are four classic topcoat or overcoat styles that you should consider when purchasing a winter coat for business.

Chesterfield   This is the most formal of the four styles and should be a serious contender for your clothing dollar as an all-round coat for business and more formal occasions after six P.M. The basic Chesterfield comes with a fly front. It is a fitted coat and gives good line and balance to your silhouette. The classic Chesterfield colors are navy blue, brown or medium to dark-gray herringbone. (See Figure 4–13.)

Polo or Camel's-Hair Coat   This coat comes in either the single- or double-breasted model. You will recognize this coat by the half belt in back on the double-breasted model. *Don't* buy the camel's-hair wrap-around version with the full self-belt. It is too casual for most business situations. (See Figure 4–14.)

British Army Coat, or British Warm   This classic originated, like the trench coat, in World War I. The coat is double breasted, has epaulets,

FIGURE 4–13.   The Chesterfield topcoat, with its velvet collar, can be worn for business or more formal occasions. This fitted coat comes in solid navy or brown fabrics or in gray herringbone as shown. (Art credit: Linda Tain)

FIGURE 4–14.   The polo or camel's-hair coat comes in either the single- or double-breasted model. The double-breasted model, shown above, always has the half belt running across the back. (Art credit: Linda Tain)

FIGURE 4–15.   The British warm or British army coat originated, like the trench coat, in World War I. It is double breasted with epaulets and is usually made from the tightly woven English melton cloth. (Art credit: Linda Tain)

FIGURE 4–16.   *The raglan sleeve topcoat takes its name from its shoulder seam, which is slanted diagonally to the neckline. It is available in a wide variety of fabrics and colors. (Art credit: Linda Tain)*

and is usually made from the original wool melton cloth woven in England. It is a tough, well-woven fabric that travels well and feels very warm when you are wearing it. (See Figure 4–15.)

Raglan Sleeve Coat This coat takes its name from its distinctive sleeve. A raglan sleeve has a seam that is slanted diagonally and extends all the way to the neckline; thus, each sleeve extends all the way to the neckline as well. The raglan sleeve coat is available in a wide variety of fabrics and colors. It is popular because it is so easy to slip on and off over suits. (See Figure 4–16.)

WHEN THE OCCASION IS FORMAL: FORMAL WEAR

Every man looks good in a tuxedo. If your business or social life requires you to wear a tuxedo three or more times a year, you should think seriously about buying one of your own rather than renting. When buying that tuxedo, think in terms of the long pull. Don't make emotional buying decisions: "I have blue eyes so I'll look good in an iridescent blue." Stay with the standard black or midnight blue. (See Figure 4–17.)

Remember, you will wear your tuxedo indoors, entertaining, dancing, and sitting, so get a lightweight wool worsted or a polyester/wool blend for year-round use. In the summer you can wear the same tux pants with a white evening jacket.

Single-breasted jackets are the best style. Double breasted are clumsier and must always be kept buttoned to look good. Furthermore, they go in and out of style from year to year. Choose the natural-shoulder jacket since its good taste transcends the fads. Stick with a center vent as side vents, like the double-breasted style, come and go.

There are basically three collar choices for your tuxedo jacket: the shawl collar, peaked lapel, or standard notch lapel. Lapels are covered in either of two fabrics—satin or grosgrain. Both are fine but satin is best.

Tuxedo pants are straight legged and in the same fabric and color as your jacket. The side seams on the pants are covered by a braided or satin stripe. The bottoms of the pants are *never* cuffed.

Formal Shirt The shirt you wear with your tuxedo is white and box pleated. If you are shorter and want a smaller pleat, fine, but avoid the jazzy extras. Stick with a simple white shirt.

Cuff Links and Studs These items can be pearl or plain gold, but the simple black enamel style set in gold is best.

FIGURE 4–17.   The traditional tuxedo is black and single-breasted. The lapels are covered in satin. The tuxedo pants have a satin stripe running down the side and the pants are straight legged with no cuff. (Credit: Bill Blass/After Six)

Bow Tie   Wear a silk bow tie with your pleated shirt. A clip-on is all right if it looks good. The tie must be the same color as the tux and made from the same fabric as your lapels, either satin or grosgrain.

Shoes   No one is going to see your great tux if you wear a pair of everyday shoes. Instead, all eyes will be riveted to your inappropriate shoes. The proper shoe to wear with a tuxedo is made of black patent leather. You can get these with laces, or as plain pumps with a bow on the instep. In the long run, lace-up shoes are more practical. Finish off your footgear with a pair of solid black, silk, over-the-calf stockings.

TYPICAL YEAR-ROUND WARDROBE OF THE BUSINESS EXECUTIVE

First, build a year-round wardrobe. Once it is completed, you then add those necessary summer and winter items to supplement your basic wardrobe.

Five Suits (two of them under two years old)   Your suits should be vested and lightweight for year-round use. Choose suits whose colors fall in the 5-to-10 range on the light-to-dark color scale (grade 1 is white; grade 10 is black). A good complementary selection of suit colors and patterns would be:
  Solid navy blue
  Navy blue pinstripe
  Charcoal gray
  Muted glen plaid
  Charcoal gray pinstripe

Shirts (in the collar style most becoming to you)
  12 white broadcloth—barrel cuffs
  2 pastel blue
  2 striped (blue and gray; or burgundy)
  2 ecru

Slacks (two pairs)
  Solid gray (medium to dark shade)
  Gray patterned or tan (year-round blend)

Sport Coat
  Navy blue blazer (year-round weight with gold or brass buttons)

Ties
3 solids (navy blue, deep burgundy, black—faille)
3 foulards (dark shades, small designs in blue, burgundy, or gray)
3 regimentals (dark, classic burgundy, blue or white)
2 ties for evening (pearl gray solid; dark pin dotted)

Belt
black leather with brass buckle

Socks
1 dozen black, over-the-calf style (wool or wool/polyester)

Shoes (black leather, three pairs)
lace-up wingtip
lace-up cap toe
tassel loafer
shoe trees and shoe bags for travel

Handkerchiefs
1 dozen white linen with hand-rolled edges

Watches (two)
simple gold watch with a classic face; dark leather band
gold watch with more elegant band for evening and formal wear

Raincoat (one)
classic raglan shoulder, French front raincoat; *or* trench coat (khaki color)

Topcoats (two)
British warm or Chesterfield
Formal coat (dark) for evening occasions

Additional Clothing Items for Summer Wear

Three Suits
Blue seersucker
Light tan (wool/polyester)
Blue-stripe seersucker

Sport Coat
summer blazer or summer madras

WARDROBE RECOMMENDATIONS FOR THE SUCCESSFUL ATTORNEY

An attorney is under more pressure to make a good first impression than almost any other professional. Why? Because most of a lawyer's real work for his clients is unseen; that is, by the client. An attorney may put in thirty or forty hours preparing for a client conference and then spend only fifteen or twenty minutes actually with the client. Therefore, the decor of a lawyer's office, the demeanor of his staff, and his own appearance must all communicate excellent education, social and cultural heritage, success, and the many other attributes which clients feel are important in the attorney they choose to represent them.

By "appearance," I do not refer exclusively to dress. Your appearance includes how you style your hair, care for your hands and nails, attend to your teeth, and polish your shoes. Most importantly, appearance includes your physical fitness, the shape in which you keep your body. In the trade, all these things add up to your personal "packaging." Sure, we all know about Clarence Darrow's tobacco-stained sweaters and Melvin Belli's velvet vest and matching briefcase. But are you a lawyer of Clarence Darrow or Melvin Belli's stature? If you are, maybe you can get away with such eccentricities too. Otherwise, better adopt a more traditional image.

For the trial attorney determined to win his case, there is a solid, competent look he should strive for in order to establish credibility with juries. In short, the smart lawyer packages himself to distract—or even worse, turn off—the smallest number of jurors or judges.

A fail-safe legal wardrobe would contain the following:

Five Suits
   (two under two years old; year-round weights and vested)
   3 solid gray (color shades fall between 7 and 10 on the light-to-dark color scale)
   1 solid blue
   1 blue pinstripe (that looks solid at 15 feet)

Shirts
   12 broadcloth (all white)

Ties (10)
   Foulards or regimentals (all ties at a distance either should look solid, or the design should be indiscernible)

Shoes
  Black lace-up (wingtip or cap toe)

Socks
  1 dozen (black or several pairs navy; over-the-calf style)

WARDROBE RECOMMENDATIONS FOR THE SUCCESSFUL ARCHITECT OR ENGINEER

There are professions that don't require a man to dress in a formal business suit every day. In fact, such an outfit might even be inappropriate depending on the specific circumstances. My goal—and I hope yours—is that no matter what your occupation or profession, you always look as if you are dressed for the occasion or situation. Common sense and good taste are the watchwords.

If I had to single out one group of men who are universally known as poor dressers, it would have to be engineers. There are good reasons why engineers ignore their dress. When they are in college, and even later, they are told that their superior education automatically elevates them several status notches in other people's eyes. In addition, they work on and near dirty equipment, run around messy job sites, and get oil, water, and all manner of chemicals and grease on their clothing. Consequently, few engineers buy quality clothing, just what is on sale. This makes the average engineer look underdressed when called into a conference with a corporate president, and overdressed in factories and on job sites.

But these reasons are really excuses for not learning how to dress right, and at the same time resolve the very real problem of how to dress well when working around greasy equipment and in construction areas.

The factors we discussed earlier apply here: Analyze your industry, company, client mix, and geographic requirements. Remember, each company within an industry has its own distinctive style and unwritten dress code, ranging from extremely conservative to outlandishly contemporary. After noting what your peers and superiors are wearing, adopt that "style" yourself, but always lean toward the more conservative end of the corporate wardrobe spectrum.

The key to the successful engineer's wardrobe is medium-to-dark gray, brown, or blue suits with white button-down shirts, and regimental striped ties. Grays, browns, and blues are likeable yet serious colors. The natural shoulder in your suit indicates that you are traditional and conservative, hence dependable and responsible. The button-down shirt reinforces the impression that you are straightforward, trustworthy, and well educated.

An engineer should wear a vest only in a serious management situation. In general, vests create too formal an effect, thus tending to look out of place on engineers. They are certainly not for everyday wear.

A word of caution is necessary here. If you are an engineer or architect, you will probably have more sport coats and blazers in your wardrobe than other professionals. So don't be caught in the mix-and-match trap. In short, *never wear a suit coat as a sport coat; never wear suit slacks with a blazer or sport coat.* If your suit coat's cut and buttons are informal enough to pass as a sport coat, it is not a true business suit and you shouldn't even own it. Suits are traditionally worn for situations of a serious nature. Sport coats are for less serious occasions. Blazer suits, on the other hand, shouldn't be worn at all. A hybrid of the serious suit and informal sport coat, a blazer suit is neither fish nor fowl. Consequently, it is seldom appropriate for either the formal or informal situation, and generally looks incongruous no matter when you wear it. In fact, the blazer suit has almost as many negative connotations as the lower-middle-class leisure suit. The blazer suit is nothing more than a blatant attempt to sacrifice good taste and tradition for economy.

An ambitious architect or engineer's wardrobe would contain:

Five Suits
   year-round, solid, some vested and all in the same color family. How dark they are depends on your client mix and responsibilities.

Shirts (12)
   6 white button-down oxford cloth
   3 blue button-down oxford cloth
   3 white broadcloth (for more formal business affairs)

Ties (6)
   2 regimentals
   2 foulards
   2 solids

Belts
   black or dark brown with a brass buckle

Socks
   1 dozen black or brown over-the-calf

Shoes
   3 pairs (dark brown or black; all lace-up wing, cap or plain toe)

Slacks
   2 dress slacks (solid in dark gray, dark tan or brown)
   2 casual (chino or khaki)

Sport Coats
   1 blazer
   1 sport coat (Harris tweed solid)

For Wear in the Field

Overshoes
   1 pair from L. L. Bean; tan

Eisenhower Jacket
   blue or dark gray

Outerwear
   3/4–length field jacket

Take the same care and pride in your field look as you do in your office look. People are making judgments about you in both places. Keep your overshoes, Eisenhower and 3/4–length jackets in your car so they are always available for emergency trips to construction sites.

5

ACCESSORY AWARENESS:
Those Small Details That Create a Large Impression

by Don Bachman

There are only two types of men who don't have to worry about their appearance: rock stars and eccentric millionaires. If you don't happen to fit into one of these categories, keep reading.

Clothes—those wardrobe items that cover most of your body most of the time—are primary communicators. In the previous chapter, you learned how to select the major items comprising a business wardrobe—suits, sport coats, slacks, topcoats, sweaters, and vests. In this chapter, you'll learn about accessories, those secondary visual communicators that can make or break your appearance. After all, an outfit is only as good as the quality—and appropriateness—of its accessories. To influence others and stand above the crowd, you need more than just the right suit with the right tailoring. You also need to showcase that suit with the right tie, pocket square, jewelry, belt, and shoes. And to sharpen your image further, you must also own the right wallet, gloves, attaché case, luggage, and umbrella.

In considering accessories, let's start at the top of your head and work our way down to your toes.

HATS

During the 1960s and 1970s, when longer hair on men was fashionable, men's hats took a nose dive in the popularity polls. Today, men are wearing their hair shorter and male headgear is enjoying a resurgence. I don't think we will see the hat return as the status symbol it was at the turn of the century, but its popularity is definitely growing. Why? Primarily because men are rediscovering that hats not only protect you from the elements but add a distinguished, "finished" look to a business outfit as well.

The most popular dress hat is the fur-textured felt with a silk or grosgrain ribbon band. It's referred to as a fedora, or "snap-brim model" because it's worn with the back of the brim snapped up and the front of the brim turned down. The preferred hat colors are the darker shades of gray, brown, or blue, with the ribbon bands an even deeper tone than the hat itself.

Many hats that were once considered strictly for sport or casual wear are now acceptable with some business attire. These hats include the snap-brim Irish tweed, the rough-finish Tyrolean, and the crushable cloth-checked or plaid hat worn with the brim turned down.

For warmer climates, hats are also appropriate. Here, cool, lightweight models are worn exclusively. In Florida, for example, you will see businessmen wearing the flat-topped, stiff-brimmed straw hat called a "boater." You might also see men wearing a planter's hat, with its modified porkpie crown and large three- to four-inch brim with rolled edges; the panama, with its straight crown creased down the center, black grosgrain band and 2¼-inch brim; or a modified version of the fedora, made of straw, coconut palm or other lightweight materials.

TIES

The tie is important because it is an extension of your face, where other people tend to focus their attention when they look at you. We've all heard the old saw about the eyes being the window to your soul. Think of your tie as the window to your background and personality. You might as well view your tie that way because, on a subconscious level, that's the type of impact your ties make on other people every day of the week.

If you want your ties to make a positive statement about you, you must consider everything about a tie—its length, width, texture, color, and pattern—before you add it to your wardrobe.

Materials   Ties are made from a wide variety of fabrics, but silk, silk-polyester blends, cotton, and wool are still the best bets. They are not only traditional tie fabrics, but they knot well, hang correctly, and continue to look good after many wearings. If a tie is made of any other fabric, don't buy it!

Patterns   Ties come in solids, regimental stripes, club ties, polka dots, and small geometric patterns—foulards. (See the examples in Figures 5–1, 5–2, 5–3, and 5–4.)

Solid-colored ties in burgundy, dark blue, and brown are classics that belong in every man's wardrobe. But avoid solids with shadow stripes or raised designs. A rich-toned, solid-colored tie in pure silk setting off

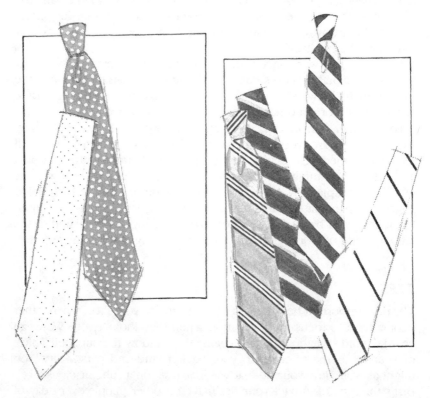

FIGURE 5–1.   The pin dot (left) and the polka-dot tie are always appropriate. The smaller the dot, the more formal the tie. (Art credit: Linda Tain)

FIGURE 5–2.   Regimental-striped ties, with their diagonal stripes of varying widths, are ideal for a more casual look. (Art credit: Linda Tain)

a well-cut suit presents a most commanding business look.

Regimental-striped ties have wide diagonal stripes. A variation is the repp, which has the diagonal stripes on a fabric with a cross-rib weave. Neither of these ties should have more than three colors. The background color should coordinate with your suit. With striped ties, the more subtle the coloring, the more formal the look. The bright, perky tones lend to an informal look.

Club ties are silks and silk blends displaying a repeated small design, such as a bird, sailboat, club insignia, or corporate logo, usually set against a navy blue, burgundy or brown ground.

FIGURE 5–3.   The club tie, made of silk or a silk blend, showcases repeated small designs such as horses, lions, sailboats, club insignias, or corporate logos. (Art credit: Linda Tain)

FIGURE 5–4.   The foulard tie has small, repeated geometric patterns throughout. (Art credit: Linda Tain)

Polka-dot and small-geometric-patterned ties afford a very neat and "together" look. The smaller the dot or design, the more formal the tie. In fact, ties with pin dots share the same degree of authority as solid ties because such ties look like solids from a few feet back.

Length The length of the average tie is about fifty-five inches. Making allowances for the tie knot and the length of your torso, the tips of all your ties should ideally touch the top of your belt buckle. (See Figure 5–5.)

FIGURE 5–5. The tip of a man's tie should just touch the top of his belt buckle. (Art credit: Linda Tain)

Color Coordination If you're just starting to build a wardrobe and working on a tight budget, you can limit yourself to two ties per suit. But that's the minimum. You might color-coordinate your ties to your suits as follows:

Suits	Shirts	Ties (predominant color)
medium to dark blue	white; cream; light blue, red or navy stripes	red; burgundy; dark blue
dark gray	white; ivory; light gray, black or red stripes	burgundy; black; light gray; red
medium gray	white; ivory; light blue; red, blue, or black stripes	red; burgundy; rust; black; olive; blue
dark brown	white; ivory; cream; beige; dark brown stripes	brown; gold; medium green; rust; beige; yellow
tan to light brown	white; light blue; yellow; cream; brown, green, or blue stripes	red; copper; yellow; dark green; olive; brown; light blue; dark blue; burgundy

Bow Ties Except for formal affairs, the bow tie is rarely seen any more. In general, a bow tie does not connote an up-and-coming executive. In fact, the only men I know who wear bow ties comfortably are men who have "made it" in the art world and in the business world as entrepreneurs. They have already achieved their career goals so they can afford to be slightly eccentric.

Other ties the ambitious business manager should avoid are novelty ties, bizarre patterns, large polka dots, large, modernistic geometrics, and, for that matter, any large shapes. For example, stay away from ties with large splashes of wild colors. Those pastel Pucci geometrics fall into this category unless you feel invincible, live in the Sun Belt, and have made it to the top of a glamour industry like television or film production.

Care of Ties Since you've spent a lot of time and money in selecting your ties, it's only natural to give as much attention to their care. These seven rules will help you extend the life of your ties:

1. Hang silk, silk-polyester, and cotton ties on a hanger or tie bar.
2. Roll up wool knit ties and store them in a drawer. Knit ties stretch out when they're hung.
3. Always untie the knot when removing your tie. Don't slip the knot and pull the tie over your head, storing it that way until the next time you wear it.
4. Never wear the same tie on two consecutive days. Silk fibers need a day or two to rest and return to their original shape.
5. Stains and spots on ties should be blotted with cold water, but never rubbed. Excessive rubbing will break down the silk fibers.
6. A persistent spot or stain may sometimes be removed by holding it over a steaming kettle for a few moments. This will loosen the stain and you will be able to brush it away when it dries.
7. Badly soiled ties should be professionally cleaned by a reliable dry cleaner.

NECK SCARVES

There doesn't seem to be any middle ground with scarves. A man either enjoys wearing them with his topcoat or will have nothing to do with them. If you happen to enjoy that extra bit of protection on blustery days, you may take your pick from the available silk, cashmere, and wool scarves on the market. A silk scarf in a solid or print adds panache to any topcoat. But the classiest scarf of all is a cashmere backed with a silk foulard lining. Plain cashmere or wool scarves are generally available in burgundy, blue, or subdued checks and plaids. White silk scarves are great—if you happen to be flying in an open-cockpit biplane. They look slightly ridiculous with most office attire.

POCKET SQUARES AND HANDKERCHIEFS

The pocket square is usually made of silk and comes in solids or multicolored tie prints. The handkerchief, in contrast, is made of quality cotton or linen and is normally restricted to white.

Either the pocket square or the handkerchief can be tucked into the breast pocket of a suit or blazer to add another dash of color to your outfit and brighten your appearance. The pocket square should not be so flamboyant that it stands out by itself and magnetizes all viewers, however. Rather, the colors should harmonize with your tie but never

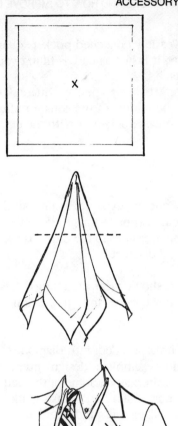

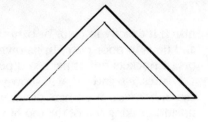

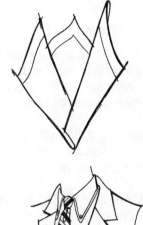

FIGURE 5-6
STEP 1: With your handkerchief or pocket square still folded, pick it up at the center.
STEP 2: Allow the points to hang in an irregular fashion. With the points down, stuff the handkerchief/pocket square into your breast pocket.
STEP 3: Puff out the material peaking over the top of the pocket.
(Art credit: Linda Tain)

FIGURE 5-7
STEP 1: Leave the handkerchief/ pocket square folded in its usual square. Next, fold it in half diagonally to form a triangle.
STEP 2: Fold the two corners of the triangle up so that the center point falls below the two outside points.
STEP 3: Place the handkerchief/ pocket square in the pocket with the center point closest to the body. Arrange the points in an irregular fashion as they peak out from the top of the breast pocket.
(Art credit: Linda Tain)

match it exactly in color or pattern. Wearing a matched pocket square and tie is in poor taste. In its own way, it is just as bad as filling your breast pockets full of pens and pencils.

Figures 5–6 and 5–7 will show you how to wear a pocket square. You can either wear it corners down with the middle of the square puffed up and peaking out of the top of your breast pocket; or with the ends, or points, of the square showing.

JEWELRY

Flashy cuff links and rings may bring out the gypsy in your soul but they'll do nothing but detract from your corporate image. However, if you insist on wearing your elaborate gold treasures to the office, the key words to remember are "minimal" and "discreet."

Rings   Two rings are the maximum you should wear, assuming one is a wedding band. If one happens to be your college ring, fine, as long as it's not the size of a golf ball.

Cuff Links   Do not wear ornate cuff links studded with diamonds or other precious stones. Cuff links should be simple in design and made of plain gold or silver. There's one other alternative: Some of the better men's shops around the country are now selling cuff links made of corded silk knots in dark blue, black, silver, burgundy, and brown. They're quite elegant looking and surprisingly inexpensive.

Tie Tacs and Clasps   Although these items are not popular at the moment, they could become fashionable again. When and if they do, keep them simple. And never wear a tie tac or clasp so that it is visible above a buttoned suit coat. The only time these accessories should be seen is when you are in shirtsleeves.

Lodge and Club Lapel Pins   They're terrific little adornments for your suit when you are attending a lodge or club function. They're out of place when worn to the office.

Watches   Never wear the large, sporty or novelty watches with your office attire. Also avoid those expandable metal watchbands. A thin gold, or gold-toned, watch with a good leather band or a matching link band is always in good taste.

Pocket Watches   Pocket watches—particularly if they are real gold and antique—look truly elegant with suit vests. But it is imperative that the gold chain accompanying the watch be as fine in quality as the watch itself. After all, it's the gold chain hanging across the vest that is visible far more often than the actual watch.

ID Bracelets   NO!

BELTS

From a fashion standpoint, your belt should *not* make a statement about you. It should go unnoticed. A good quality leather belt in brown or black, wide enough to slide easily through the belt loops, and with a simple, unadorned buckle, is still your best choice for business wear. Belts require very little care. An occasional saddle-soaping and light waxing will keep them looking good for years.

WALLETS

Your best choice is a quality leather in soft calfskin, either burgundy or brown. The wallet you select should be slim, without a lot of transparent windows and compartments. Today, there is no need to carry a bundle of credit cards. Two or three of the most widely accepted cards will suffice. Besides, a bulging wallet will eventually stretch the back of your trousers out of shape—and it looks awful. Another image destroyer is a wallet with frayed corners, cracked leather, and a tattered lining. Before yours reaches this sorry state, replace it.

The rectangular breast-pocket wallet or card case is a cut above the popular folded, back-pocket model. Withdrawing this slim item of supple leather from an inside breast pocket is an impressive gesture. It implies power and authority and indicates that you are a man who *always* wears a suit.

GLOVES

I'm partial to lined leather gloves, especially for gripping the steering wheel of my car on cold winter mornings. In colder climes, lined leather gloves are practical besides imparting a dressy look to your business outerwear. They afford you freedom: You don't need to keep your hands stuffed in your pockets all the time for warmth.

If you are about to buy a pair of gloves, deerskin or pigskin are your best choices. Both of these leathers are soft, durable and conform nicely to the shape of your hands. With the exception of black, most other shades of leather are acceptable for business wear. These include all tones of brown, tan, and gray suede.

As practical and warm as they may be, save your fleece-lined mittens and knitted gloves for leisure or sports wear.

SOCKS

A celebrity friend of mine appeared on a late night television talk show recently. Impeccably dressed—so he thought—he greeted the host congenially, took a seat next to him, crossed his legs to get comfortable, and bared six inches of his leg above his ankle-length socks. All his sartorial splendor went "poof" the minute that flesh appeared on the screen. When he bared his leg, he broke the continuity of trouser leg to shoe. The hiked-up trousers exposing his leg and short socks gave him a fragmented look. This is a classic example of one of the most inexpensive accessories in your wardrobe destroying your entire look.

Calf-length socks are the only appropriate socks for business wear. Save your anklet, multicolored, and novelty socks for weekends in the country. The best material for socks are the traditional wool, wool blends, nylon, and cotton lisle. Sheer silk is only worn with formal attire. The natural fibers such as cotton are the most absorbent and comfortable but will require sock garters to keep them up. Socks made of blends—such as nylon/wool and cotton/spandex—are considered stretch socks and usually stay on the calf without the aid of garters. Solid black, navy, burgundy, brown, and tan socks will all coordinate nicely with your business suits.

SHOES

Shoes are a fast and accurate indicator of a man's social and professional lifestyle. Men who are self-confident and aware of the impact their image has on others are scrupulously attentive to the style, fit, and condition of their shoes. Shoes that are poorly fitted, scuffed with worn-down heels or turned-up toes label their owner as a careless and disorganized person, someone who does not pay attention to details.

Quality Skimping on quality and opting for a cheaper shoe is a mistake—often an expensive mistake since cheaper shoes don't last as long. True, quality shoes are expensive but they're well worth the investment. Besides looking better, quality shoes give your feet the support they deserve. After all, your feet support you during most of your waking life, so pamper them and treat them well. Investing in quality shoes will pay you back tenfold. If weli maintained, the better shoe, due to its more detailed construction and finer leather uppers, will outlast the cheaper models by years. This is primarily because the finer calfskins are more supple and less likely to crack than the thicker cowhide uppers.

Fit Let me put to rest that old wives' tale about having to "break in" a pair of new shoes before they become comfortable. Not so. A properly fitted pair of shoes should be comfortable the first time they are worn. If you are able to slide your heel about, or if your toes are being pinched and squeezed, you are wearing a shoe that is improperly fitted. All the breaking in in the world is not going to correct the problem.

Whenever I'm in a shoe store, I'm amazed at the number of men who buy the first pair of shoes they try on. This is the main reason why twice as many men as women are the victims of improperly fitted

FIGURE 5–8. The lace-up shoe still has the most traditional look for business. The plain oxford (lower left) works well with business or more formal attire. The wingtip (center) and cap toe models also give the wearer an understated elegance. (Art credit: Linda Tain)

shoes. Gentlemen, follow the example of the ladies! They never buy the first pair of shoes brought to them by the clerk. Try on as many pairs of shoes as it takes to give you a basis for comparison. Then and only then will you know what is comfortable and right for your individual foot.

Style   To be considered properly dressed, your shoes should complement your suit. They should be well styled with an understated look, making your feet look lean and trim. They should not be clodhoppers, thick of sole or heel. The soles should range between middle- and lightweight, but not be so thin that they'll wear out quickly. The heels should be no more than 1⅛-inch high.

FIGURE 5–9. It's only recently that slip-on shoes have become acceptable as appropriate business attire. The most popular slip-on models are the plain-toe monk strap (lower center), the loafer without tassels (middle right), and the loafer with tassels (top). (Art credit: Linda Tain)

Among the lace-ups (see Figure 5–8), the oxford is the shoe that best fits the needs of the well-dressed man. Whether you choose the wingtip or captoe models, any oxford works well with business or formal attire.

Not too many years ago, anything other than lace-up shoes was considered improper for business wear. Thankfully, that rigid stance has modified and slip-ons are now acceptable, although it is mostly the younger businessmen who are wearing them. The most popular slip-on models are the plain-toe monk strap, with its strap and buckle over the instep; the loafer with or without tassels; and slip-ons with plain, cap, moccasin or wingtip toes. (See Figure 5–9.)

Color   Your business footgear should be restricted to three colors: black, burgundy, and dark brown. For dark blue and gray suits, black shoes are the most appropriate, with the burgundy running a close second. The middle-blue and gray-toned suits look best with burgundy shoes. Dark brown shoes are a natural for suits ranging from tan to dark brown.

Care of Shoes   To extend the longevity of your shoes, follow these six suggestions:

1. Always use a shoe horn when putting on shoes.
2. Never wear shoes in the snow, slush, or rain unprotected. Invest in a pair of rubbers.
3. Rotate your shoes. Never wear the same pair on two consecutive days.
4. Use shoe trees. They keep the shoes in their original shape and prevent the leather from cracking.
5. Clean and polish shoes on a regular basis, ideally before or after each wearing. Mud, grime and dust can be removed with saddle soap. Polish shoes only when they are completely dry. And never dry shoes in the direct heat of a radiator, furnace or stove. Such treatment will not only remove the natural oils from the leather but permanently damage and crack both the sole and uppers.
6. Don't wear shoes with run-down heels. To find out if they are run down, place your shoes on a flat surface. Roll a plain lead pencil up to the heel. If the heel is so worn that you can fit the pencil under the worn part, it's time for a new pair of heels.

ATTACHÉ CASES

If you need a briefcase, can't afford a real leather one, and are tempted to buy a cheaper vinyl case, restrain yourself. Hold off any purchase and just go without an attaché case until you are able to afford the better leather model. It doesn't take a mental giant to know that vinyl is not only cheap but, worse yet, looks cheap! A good leather case broadcasts the message that you consider yourself and your business goals important enough to opt for the best.

When you are ready to make your purchase, keep in mind that simple is elegant. The case you choose should be free of designer emblems, initials and extraneous brass hardware. A deep brown, burgundy, or luggage tan is the most tasteful color for business wear. Avoid cases in gray or black.

If you are not comfortable with an attaché case yet you need something in which to carry your business papers, a zippered leather portfolio with leather handles is an excellent alternative. However, stay with the same color recommendations I just made for attaché cases.

LUGGAGE

Whether you travel extensively or just make an annual pilgrimage to your company's headquarters office, your luggage is still an integral part of your business wardrobe and, as such, deserves to be chosen carefully.

If money is no object and you are out to turn a few heads, by all means select a custom-made burnished leather bag, preferably crafted by a French or Italian designer. At the other end of the luggage spectrum are poorly constructed bags of leather-grained vinyl. They're a complete turn-off. Avoid them. There *is* an acceptable middle ground: bags that look good and won't require you to take a second mortgage on the ol' homestead to afford them. Waterproof nylon bags for example, are long lasting, good-looking, and reasonably priced. These nylon bags are available in soft-sided and rigid-shaped (i.e., the nylon is stretched around a metal frame) models. Either is acceptable. For such bags, my color recommendations are brown, blue, olive, or tan solids. The heavy molded plastic suitcases are also tasteful. They look best in shades of dark gray and brown.

Naturally, the length of your trips will determine the amount of luggage you require. Taking appearance and practicality into consideration, my choice for a short business trip would be:

1. A two-suit garment bag, with extra pockets, in leather; or a water-proof nylon garment bag with a shoulder strap.
2. A nylon carry-on bag specifically designed to stow under your plane seat.

UMBRELLAS

Since we don't have to endure the rainy climate of a country like Great Britain, an umbrella is not an accessory we carry with us every day. Nevertheless, it's an important and necessary wardrobe staple.

Quality   Unaccustomed as Americans are to carrying umbrellas daily, we tend to lose them easily when we do bring them along. With this in mind, you should probably opt for an umbrella on the lower end of the price spectrum, which ranges from the $6.00 sold-by-street-vendors variety to the elegant $125 model. However, do not sacrifice quality for price. There is nothing more ridiculous looking than an otherwise fashionably attired businessman wrestling with a cheap umbrella that's been turned inside out by the wind.

Style and Color   The oversized, sturdy black umbrella is traditional. But other equally acceptable colors are brown, gray, burgundy, and tan, as long as they are solids. Avoid those multicolored umbrellas that look more at home on a golf cart than on a businessman's arm.

6

SHOPPING SAVVY

by Stan Farb

It's a common belief that men hate to shop for clothes. This notion is so ingrained that a large publishing company recently put out a book aimed at women. The subject: How to dress the man in your life.

If you let your wife, girl friend, or anyone else select your clothes for you, you're making a mistake. Your wardrobe should reflect your personality—the man you are now and the man you aspire to be. Who understands you—your values, hopes, and ambitions—better than you? Certainly not the women in your life, who have their own subjective view of where you've been and where you're headed in your social life and career.

The goal of this chapter is to help men who hate to shop—perhaps because they don't understand *how* to shop—learn to like it, if not enjoy it. The information to follow will take the pain out of shopping trips and transform a chore into a pleasant experience. Who knows, it may even turn personal shopping expeditions into downright exciting experiences.

PRESHOPPING PREP

Advanced planning is a prerequisite for any successful shopping trip. In fact, I'd advise you to be as well prepared for a clothes-buying expedition as you are for any other important venture involving your finances. These days quality menswear is expensive. I estimate it will cost you about $1,100 a year to buy basic additions to your wardrobe: two suits, five shirts, five ties, two pairs of shoes, slacks, a sport coat, sweaters, and various accessory items. Clearly, it's in your best interests to shop carefully and avoid costly mistakes.

You avoid such mistakes by deciding what you need and want—which may be two different things—*before* you purchase any clothing item, even one as insignificant as a belt. Your objective is to build a wardrobe, one in which all the individual clothing items coordinate with each other.

Operation Closet Clean-out

The most crucial part of the shopping process doesn't even take place in a store. It takes place in your bedroom closet.

Set aside several hours and make a thorough inspection of your closet's contents—both what's on the hangers and what's on the floor or on shelves. When you're finished in the closet, move on to your bureau drawers. When you get through, you should have carefully examined every clothing item you own. I'm sure you'll come across many surprises, things you didn't know you still owned and haven't worn in several years.

Now it's time to make some decisions. Force yourself to discard any clothing item that is worn-looking or shabby. Clothing doesn't have to be threadbare to fall into this category. Also get rid of items that are out of style. Yes, fashion for men does change, albeit more slowly than for women. If thin ties are now "in" and you've got a fistful of fat ones from the old days, you'll be wise to throw them out unless you're lucky enough to have the space to store them in the hope that they'll be back in vogue one day during your lifetime. I wouldn't count on it, however. Clothing designers have a way of bringing old styles back in, but with a twist, some added dimension that makes that throwback style look contemporary. Thus, your old double-breasted suit with the gigantic lapels will never really be fashionable again. The double-breasted look and wide lapels may both stage a comeback, but probably not in tandem.

Another excellent reason for discarding an item concerns fit. If you've still got the clothes you wore five years ago when you were size

40 and you are now size 44 and likely to remain that way, throw them away—or, better still, give them away. But don't clutter up your closet—no matter what the reason—with clothes you don't wear.

Poor quality is the final reason for removing an item from your closet forever. Perhaps you always tried to save money by buying inexpensive clothes. The mere fact that you're reading this book indicates you want to spruce up your appearance. Wearing better-quality clothing is one of the best ways to attain this objective. Be completely ruthless if your wardrobe is filled with polyester fabrics, leisure suits, plastic belts, and cheap ties.

Clothing Storage and Arrangement

Once you've gotten rid of the unworn and the unwearable, the next step is to rearrange everything that's left. First, separate your clothing by season. Put your fall/winter clothes in one place and your spring/summer clothes in another, preferably in two different closets. If not, cover all your out-of-season clothing with a clean sheet or garment bag and push it into the back of your closet where you won't see it. Psychologically, this will prevent you from becoming bored with your clothing just because you have to see it every time you open your closet door.

Arrange this season's wardrobe by categories: suits in one group, dress shirts in another, formal wear and leisure attire in others. Within these categories, arrange shirts from the lightest shades to the darkest. The same principle applies to suits, sport clothes, slacks, and leisure wear.

List Making

With pad and pencil in hand, go through the contents of your closet once again, this time jotting down what's there. Be descriptive enough so that your notes will summon up a mental image of the item at some later date. For instance, state each shirt's collar style, color, and fabric.

Leave several lines blank under each suit you list. Now figure out what coordinates with those suits and write it in the blank space. You may find you only have one tie that goes with your gray pinstriped suit, for example, or only two shirts. Those gaps in your wardrobe should be noted on another list—your shopping list.

In addition, you may find you must add a major item to your wardrobe—a new suit, sport coat, or topcoat. When you shop for those items, bear in mind what you already own so you won't be forced to buy all new accessories as well. Occasionally, you may add a suit or other major item that starts you off in a completely new direction. For instance, you may want to change from a black-navy-gray wardrobe to a basically brown wardrobe. Such radical changes are expensive so don't even make that first purchase unless your succeeding purchases will continue to lead in that new direction.

YOUR BODY TYPE—WHICH IS IT?

There are three basic body types, or somatotypes: the endomorph, the mesomorph, and the ectomorph.

The endomorph man has rounded lines to his body. An extreme endomorph frame on a short man might be called "stocky," "squat," "fleshy," maybe even "fat." Weight, however, is not the determining factor when typing a body. Rather, it is the person's basic body configuration—his bone structure, the length of his limbs, and the appearance of his musculature.

The mesomorph man has a medium build. He's typically called "the athletic type" since his musculature is the most pronounced feature of his naked body. He might be referred to as "brawny," "well built," or "strong."

An ectomorph is lean; the lines of his body are vertical. An exaggerated ectomorph who is tall would be labeled a "stringbean."

Genes determine your body type, not the treatment you give your body after you're born. A mesomorph who is overweight, for example, does not become an endomorph. He's simply an overweight mesomorph. Nor does an ectomorph who works out and develops muscles move into the mesomorph category. In short, after puberty, one's somatotype cannot be altered appreciably by diet, exercise, or even age.

If you don't know your body type, take off your clothes and stand in front of a full-length mirror. What do you see? Do you belong in the rounded-build, medium-build, or lean-build category? Knowing your somatotype will help you when you're buying clothes. For example, an endomorph man may want to play down the rounded, broad-beamed look of his body by buying vertical-striped suits. Plaid suits, in contrast, would emphasize his broadness, hardly something he would want to do. A mesomorph man has the widest range of clothing style choices and will also find his clothes tend to fit him better since, theoretically, he's the ideal somatotype. The ectomorph man, on the other hand, should select clothing that emphasizes breadth or horizontal lines. A subtle check or plaid would look good on him.

WHEN AND WHERE TO SHOP

In the men's-wear field, there are two distinct selling seasons: fall/
winter and spring/summer. (Pity the poor women who must contend
with four selling seasons!) The fall/winter line arrives in stores in late
August. Retailers recommend September and October as the best
months for men to shop since the merchandise will be fresh and wide
ranging. The fall/winter clearance sales consume the month of January,
making room for the debut of the spring/summer line in mid- to late
February. The ideal months for spring/summer clothes shopping is April
and May; sales are held in July.

The best time to shop is during a weekday, when the stores are less
crowded and you can capture the maximum time and attention of
salespeople. Your second best bet is to shop on whatever weeknight
your local stores stay open. Weekend shopping is fairly hectic. If you
must shop then, at least make it early, ideally when the stores open
around 10 A.M. The only other alternative is to call ahead and make an
appointment with a specific salesperson at a mutually convenient hour.
But this kind of personalized service is usually only possible in selected
stores where you've established a long-term relationship.

There are four types of stores beckoning for your clothing dollar.
They are specialty men's shops, specialty department stores, department stores, and discount stores and outlets.

For quality business attire, I recommend the first two. Every community of reasonable size contains at least one fine quality shop specializing in men's attire, or "furnishings," exclusively. Give your business to
such a store or seek out a specialty department store (e.g., Saks Fifth
Avenue, Brooks Brothers, J. Press, Barney's, Giorgio's) in a larger city. A
specialty department store has fewer departments than a full-service
department store. Typically, it might restrict its merchandise to men's
and women's clothing and accessories.

I recommend these two kinds of retail establishments for several
reasons. Generally, the service is better in such stores. Also, the quality
of the merchandise is clearly defined because these stores cater to a
specific market—the middle- and upper-middle-level executive, for
example. Department stores cater to a much broader market. But worse
than that, department stores can be extremely confusing places to shop
because of their wide range of merchandise and assorted departments
where that merchandise is displayed.

Don't shop in department stores or discount stores unless you like to
shop, have an educated sense of style, and know quality fabrics and
workmanship when you see it. Department stores and outlets are

excellent places to shop for casual items, jeans, or active sportswear. But I wouldn't go there to purchase my business wardrobe basics. Also, outlets will probably charge extra for alterations.

It is true that prices are often higher in the specialty stores but I think it's worth it. A good specialty department store imports its merchandise from the fashion centers of the world. The sales staff has a sense of fashion as well as full familiarity with the merchandise. Neither the specialty department store nor the smaller quality men's shop can afford to be abrupt with customers, intransigent about returns, or uninformed about the latest styles. That's their business. Their reputation rests on those factors.

DRESSING FOR A SHOPPING TRIP

The Men's Fashion Association has a slogan: "Dress Right! When you look your best, you do your best." To paraphrase that slogan: Dress up for your next shopping trip. When you look your best, you'll feel more in the mood to shop and you'll get the best treatment from salespeople.

If you take my advice, you'll never shop for both business and casual wear during the same shopping trip. Why? The moods are different as are the types of stores you'll frequent.

When you are purchasing business or formal attire, dress for the occasion. Wear that suit you need to accessorize; or a handsome sport jacket and trousers. Like attracts like and the treatment you receive in the store will reflect the way you look when you walk through the door.

When you are shopping for leisure wear, you can be more relaxed in your appearance. Jeans or sport slacks worn with open-collared sport shirts or jerseys are fine. Bermuda shorts are even acceptable in the summer in the Sun Belt. Casual soft-soled shoes or running shoes could add to your comfort.

ESTABLISHING A RELATIONSHIP WITH SALESPEOPLE

A good salesman is an important link between yourself and a balanced, attractive wardrobe. The qualities you seek in a clothing salesman are a refined sense of taste, intelligence, a willingness to work within your budget and lifestyle constraints, a pleasant, soft-sell manner, a thorough knowledge of his merchandise, an awareness of current fashion, and expertise on fitting.

A good salesperson will help you coordinate what you already own with the items you are about to buy. He'll listen to your ideas, comment on them, and then make further suggestions of his own. This give-and-take relationship is the ideal one. Avoid the salesman who patronizes or bullies you; is impatient, rude, or pushy; acts as if selling clothes is a job rather than a vocation; and couldn't care less what you buy as long as the bill is fat. A salesman who knows a great deal about his merchandise and nothing about you, your taste, or your lifestyle—and, worse, is unwilling to learn—will do your image more harm than good.

When you do find a salesman you like, show your appreciation for his personalized service and let him know you intend to seek his counsel in future. By all means, give him your business card. Ask him to call you when new merchandise arrives, when the store has sales, or when he sees an item he knows you want. Once this salesman becomes your eyes and ears at store X, you'd be wise to thank him occasionally with a small gift or tip. Of course, this would be out of order should the man double as the owner of the store.

FIT AND ALTERATIONS

The most attractively styled garment of the best quality will lose its impact if it doesn't fit you properly. Never compromise on fit, even if the quality is tops and the styling is exactly what you want. Consider having your clothes custom made if fit is a perennial problem for you. Otherwise, follow these guidelines to make sure the clothing you purchase fits you correctly, or can be made to fit you correctly with minimal alterations.

The Tailored Jacket   I'd venture that about 50 percent of the suit jackets men wear today don't fit them properly around the neck and shoulders. This is a crucial area. When you try on a jacket, make sure the collar hugs the neck comfortably and fairly snugly. The jacket collar should lie about one-half to three-quarters of an inch below the top of your shirt collar. The fit is all wrong if the jacket collar stands away from your neck or gapes when you move your arms around. A collar can be altered if it gapes only slightly.

The jacket should lie flat on your shoulders, forming a smooth line. There shouldn't be any horizontal wrinkles just below the back of the collar; nor should there be any buckles or creases in the shoulder-blade region. Vertical wrinkles around the shoulder blades can often be removed during the alteration process, but horizontal wrinkles indicate the jacket is too small. If the shoulders feel tight or binding, try the next-larger jacket size, since suit shoulders cannot be made larger by alterations.

The distance between the bottom of the jacket's sleeves and the tip of your thumb should measure approximately 4¾ to 5¼ inches. When the sleeve length is right, about ¼ to ½ inch of your shirt cuff will show with your arms at your sides. Of course, this won't be the case if your shirtsleeves don't fit you properly, a subject I'll get to in a minute.

To determine whether the length of the jacket is correct, place your arms at your sides and bend your fingers to the second knuckle. If the bottom of the jacket comes to your knuckles, the length is fine. A jacket slightly longer or shorter (i.e. one-half to three-quarters of an inch leeway) is still acceptable, but no more. Jackets cannot be lengthened; and they can only be shortened slightly without throwing the general balance and proportions of their styling out of kilter.

The jacket should fit easily over the waist with a modest suppression to give some shape. Too much suppression, however, could make the jacket spread around the hips, causing the vents to open on the sides or in the back. Vents should always fall in a natural line perpendicular to the ground.

Finally, the front of the jacket should form a smooth line across your chest. Too much material at the chest will cause gaping; too little will make you look as if you've gained weight so your clothes no longer fit you. Neither is desirable.

Trousers   The same rules on fit apply to both suit trousers and sport slacks. The waist must be reasonably snug but never uncomfortable. It should be snug enough so that a belt is not really necessary to hold up the pants. (Incidentally, trousers and slacks are worn on the waist, not on the hips. Save the hip-hugger style for jeans.) The seat and crotch of the pants should follow the natural contours of your body and look neat and trim, never baggy and sloppy.

The bottom of your pants should gracefully touch the front of your shoes or even rest slightly on the shoe for a longer look. The cuff or hem of the trouser leg should be angled so that it is one-half inch longer in the back than the front.

If you don't like the way the trouser legs look on you, ascertain whether it's the style or because the legs don't fit you properly. If it's simply a matter of fit, have the tailor make the necessary alterations. If it's a matter of style, choose another suit or pair of slacks.

The Vest   If a vest comes with the suit, check to make sure the front points are 3½ inches below the top of your trouser waist. In the back, the vest should cover about one inch of your trousers. Your shirt should not show between the bottom of your vest and the top of your trousers.

The Dress Shirt   There are four considerations when you are checking to see if a shirt fits you: neck circumference, sleeve length, the height of the collar at the back, and the height of the collar in the front from the base of the neck upward.

The shirt's neckband should touch your neck all the way around but it should not be so tight that it chokes or binds. The sleeve should be long enough to extend one-quarter or one-half inch further than your suit jacket or sport coat.

The height and spread of the collar are always relative to the length of a man's neck and the shape of his face. Trial and error is the best way to decide what looks good on you.

QUALITY—HOW TO SPOT IT

The quality of a garment may be defined as its "degree of perfection." Perfection is measured by how good it looks, even to the untutored eye, by its workmanship or details, and by the texture and durability of the fabric.

Quality workmanship is evidenced by straight seams that lie flat and patterns that fit together at the seams. Also look for handsome buttons that are sewn on tightly, and for thread that is doing its job keeping the garment securely stitched together, rather than hanging loosely from hems. (Incidentally, plastic thread is one sign that a garment is of inferior quality.) When you are purchasing any garment you will wear open as well as closed, such as jackets, the collars of sport shirts, etc., check to see that they are nicely finished inside. In the case of jackets, linings are preferable. Avoid gaudy trim and stitching. It can make a clothing item look cheap or dated.

Fabrics of superior quality are generally resilient and hold their shape. When you touch them, they feel substantial. Unless a fabric is supposed to have a rough texture—tweed, for instance—it should feel smooth. But fabrics that are too soft to the touch could also be a problem since they tend to pill or ball up.

To develop an eye for quality merchandise, visit the most expensive men's store in your area and examine some suits by a designer known for quality in fabric and workmanship. If you can't afford that designer's clothes, at least try to duplicate the quality and workmanship in the clothing that you do buy.

THE ULTIMATE ALTERNATIVE

It is my hope that the shopping plan I have just outlined will cure you of your clothes-shopping phobia. If it hasn't, though, I caution you not to slide back into that comfortable old habit of letting other people shop for you—unless that other person is a professional dress consultant.

Hiring a dress consultant/personal shopper to help you select an appropriate wardrobe is like hiring an interior decorator to help you furnish your home, or like having a hairdresser help you choose a hair style and then cut and style your hair for you. Don't be afraid that a dress consultant—also called "image consultant" or "fashion consultant"—will make you look just like every other man who works in your industry. True, a good clothing advisor will take your industry, even your company, into consideration, but he will also ask you detailed questions that focus on what makes you unique. He will consider all these factors when he accompanies you on a shopping expedition. Sorry. Even if the dress consultant pre-shops for you, you'll still have to go into those stores and try on the clothes he's preselected. Devoting at least one afternoon in the fall and spring each year to clothes shopping is necessary—indeed, absolutely unavoidable! To locate a fashion consultant/personal shopper in your area, consult the *Directory of Personal Image Consultants* (available for $17.50 from Editorial Services Co., 1140 Avenue of the Americas, New York, NY 10036), which gives a complete profile—specialty, credentials, size of staff, and fees—of more than two hundred consultants in seventy-four cities, thirty-five states, and four foreign countries.

7

ABOUT FACE!

by Elaine Posta

When I counsel a client, I usually start with his upper body—his face, head, and neck area. No other part of the body has as much sustained image impact. After all, the face is the site of so many of our senses and signals of communication. We blush, we smile, we frown, we beam with pleasure. The face is a powerhouse of information. It can be more expressive than all the other body parts put together—the discovery of "body language" notwithstanding. It is also the part of our body most visible when we conduct business "face to face." As we talk to business associates, isn't most of our attention focused on our companion's face, and vice versa?

Women have traditionally had more face-changing tools at their disposal. Men enjoy less variety in their hairstyles, and few avail themselves of cosmetic techniques. Yet, as you'll see in this chapter, you still have a myriad of acceptable methods available for altering your facial looks. Most of them are based on the principle of establishing harmony with the rest of your body and your personal goals. For example, does your hair stand out too much because of its volume, style, or color? Are your teeth too prominent? Do you have such bad skin that it distracts other people from concentrating fully on your message? Is your neck very thick, necessitating a camouflage trick with a judicious choice of collar style? (See Figure 7–23.) Or perhaps you wear your collars too tight, so that the skin bulges out, giving you a "turkey wattle" look? (See Figure 7–28.)

You can do wonders to correct these imbalances. This chapter tells you how. I will discuss hairstyling and coloring, beards and mustaches, baldness and hair transplants, plastic surgery, cosmetic dentistry, skin care and shaving, and even how the right shirt-collar style can make a difference.

ALL ABOUT HAIR

The fashion look for men today is conservative—crisp, neat, and orderly. That includes hairstyles. The "in" style is short. In general, facial hair is passé. (See Figures 7–1, 7–2, 7–3, 7–4.)

FIGURE 7–1. The more conservative "corporate look" came in with the 1980s. This man epitomizes the look. His hairstyle is short and neat—no long sideburns or elaborate styling. (Credit: Men's Fashion Assn.)

FIGURE 7–2. This man's hair tends to be curly. Here it's been styled to look wavy. Note that his hair is combed naturally; it is not plastered down with spray or greasy hair tonic. The dark, no-nonsense eyeglasses add years and authority to his overall image. (Credit: Men's Fashion Assn.)

FIGURE 7–3. The grey enhances, rather than detracts, from this distinguished-looking executive's image. His hair is cut very short and worn naturally. (Credit: Jacqueline Thompson)

FIGURE 7–4. This man has naturally wavy hair. He wears it short in an easy-to-care-for style. For casual wear, he can practically comb his hair with his fingers. (Credit: Glemby International)

The perfect male hairstyle is one that looks natural. It looks as if it doesn't need attention and has not just had any special work on it. Once you've gotten a proper haircut, your hair becomes almost carefree. No more time devoted to "styling" your hair with blow dryers or sticky hair sprays, the bane of many men's existences in the longer-haired 1970s.

Cappellino, a top hairstylist for Glemby International at the Plaza Salon, welcomes the change. He thinks men are just emerging from an era when they had to spend far too much valuable time fussing with their hair. The end result was that it was too set-looking and, because of the process, many men actually damaged their hair. "Today," he says, "if any man spends more than three to five minutes in the morning fixing his hair, he doesn't have the right haircut."

Your Ideal Hairstyle

Until you find the right hairstyle—the perfect one for your face shape and lifestyle—I'd spend more and go to a top stylist. If your budget just won't permit high-priced hairstyling on a regular basis, you may be able to go back to your favorite barber eventually. A barber—if he is any good—should be able to duplicate the ideal hairstyling you received at the hands of experts.

Pre-Styling Consultation One of my favorite stylists is Arnold Zegarelli. He is a nationally prominent men and women's hairstylist for Seligman & Latz, the Horne department store salon in Pittsburgh; and also co-host of a local television talk show.

Like any good stylist, Arnold's own impeccable looks and grooming would make many men want to emulate him. He spends a considerable amount of time getting to know his new clients *before* they take off their suit jackets preparatory to the actual haircut. Arnold wants to see what a client is wearing, how he presents himself to the world at large. He will ask his clients about their occupation; what they like or don't like about their present hairstyles; how long they've had them; any difficulties they have maintaining their hair; and what they have in mind for their next hairstyles. Zegarelli encourages clients to bring in photographs of celebrities in hairstyles they like. At the same time, he'd never give such a hairstyle to a man whose type of hair and overall appearance don't warrant it. (See Figures 7–5, 7–6.)

While his clients are talking, Zegarelli is evaluating their hair. He takes note of its *texture* (fine, medium, medium coarse, or very coarse), *abundance* (thin, medium sparse, or heavy), *pliability* (straight, wavy, curly, very curly); and *length* at the nape of the neck, crown, around the ears and in the bang-area across the forehead. He also notices whether a man's face is narrow, broad, oval, or square, and whether he has a weak chin or other prominent structural liabilities or assets. Finally, Zegarelli asks his clients how much time they want to spend maintaining a hairstyle and how good they are at working with their hair.

With all this information, Zegarelli will offer his hairstyle recommendation for you, keeping in mind that men, unlike women, generally stick with slight variations of two distinct hairstyles their whole lifetime.

The Haircut Once you've come to an agreement with the stylist about the appropriate hairstyle, don't lay back, shut your eyes, and enjoy the sensation of being pampered. Stay alert! Watch the stylist as he cuts. His movements should be precise and controlled. If what he is doing mystifies you or seems in direct opposition to what you've agreed upon, by all means speak up. Never feel you're a stylist's puppet,

FIGURE 7–5.   This man's hair is styled appropriately for his large face and thick neck. (Art credit: Linda Tain)

FIGURE 7–6.   Everything about this man's look is wrong. His round face is accentuated by his "round" hairstyle and the bow tie. The end result is a "Simple Simon" effect. (Art credit: Linda Tain)

to be manipulated at will. After all, it's your hairstyle and you're the one who will have to maintain it.

Post-Haircut Consultation   When the stylist signals he's finished, look over his handiwork carefully. State your reaction. If you don't like it, say as much; but also explain why. The stylist may be able to do some more cutting to satisfy your objections.

Don't walk out of the salon without discussing hairstyle maintenance, especially if the style looks complicated or is a totally new look for you. Get the stylist to recommend a good shampoo and conditioner. Ask him whether to use a brush or comb on your hair and, if necessary, what blow-drying technique he would suggest. Finally, ask him how much time he thinks this maintenance regimen will take.

Depending on your hair, you should get a haircut every two- to six-week interval. "When it gets difficult to work with," says Cappellino, "you need a haircut." The better the haircut, the less often you'll need a new one.

Other Alternatives: Permanents and Straightening

If your hair is extremely straight and lank, you might consider a body wave to add fullness and style.

The difference between a cold wave or permanent wave and a body wave has to do with the size of the curler rod used to set the hair. A *permanent wave* uses a smaller rod, thus creating a curlier hairstyle. The *body wave* uses a much larger rod, giving the hair more fullness but less curl. Both types of waves are accomplished using thioglycollate lotion, which changes the protein bonds in your hair strands.

Permanent and body waves should be administered only by an expert. Permanenting must be done carefully to prevent damage to the hair; it should not be attempted at all if your hair is dry, has been colored, or is already damaged. Should you have a permanent anyway, your hair will become brittle and break easily.

In the old days, heat hair straightening methods were the only ones available. Today, there are three types of chemical hair-relaxers that make the straightening process easier, more efficient, and faster. Again, let an expert do the job. Chemical relaxers administered incorrectly can cause both skin and hair damage.

Bear in mind that straightening cannot work miracles. If your hair is so curly that it's kinky, the most you should aim for is wavy hair, not perfectly straight hair. Moreover, if your hair is bleached or has a permanent wave in it, the hairstylist must exercise special caution. Don't straighten your hair more than once every three to six months.

Daily Hair Care

Good-looking hair is *clean* hair. Greasy, dirty, or unkempt hair is not only unpleasant to look at; it connotes unreliability, disorganization, and lack of self-esteem.

Shampooing   The frequency of shampooing depends on several variables: your hairstyle, the season, the condition of your scalp, and your environment.

Daily washing is advisable if the air where you live or work is polluted, if you have oily hair, if the weather is hot and sticky, if you use hair sprays or other hair tonics, or if you have thin or fine fly-away hair. It's a myth that daily shampooing is harmful to the hair or accelerates hair loss, according to Dr. Herbert Feinberg, the New Jersey dermatologist and author of the book *All About Hair*. But for those who do shampoo often, Dr. Feinberg recommends a mild shampoo and one lathering. Less frequent washing calls for double lathering.

Always use a gentle touch while shampooing, and rinse thoroughly.

After washing, towel-dry your hair and run a wide-toothed comb through it to untangle it. Vigorous brushing is never particularly advisable, but it's especially bad for wet hair. Brushing when hair is wet and extremely elastic is liable to snap the strands.

Blow-Drying   There's been a lot of controversy about blow-drying: Does it or doesn't it damage hair? Done properly, it should not because blow-driers don't reach the 300° F. required to damage hair. But when done improperly, blow-drying can damage the hair.

Follow this regimen: Let your hair dry naturally until it's only damp. Then use the blow-drier. Don't hold the drier too close to your hair and keep the blower moving at all times, so that your hair and scalp aren't subject to prolonged, concentrated heat.

Eliminating Dandruff   Dandruff is the common cold of the scalp. Almost everyone gets it at one time or another—94 percent of the population according to one recent poll—but no one has as yet found a cure. Like the common cold, all we can hope for at this point is to control the symptoms.

"False" dandruff is due to improper hygiene. Your skin renews itself every twenty-eight days by shedding the old cells. Normally, this is a gradual process that goes unnoticed. But when you don't wash your hair often enough, there is a dead-cell buildup. The result is frequently mistaken for dandruff.

"True" dandruff is another matter. Dr. Feinberg admits that its exact cause is still a mystery. "It seems to result from a slight increase in the normal twenty-eight day turnover of skin," Feinberg says. "The fact that antiseptic shampoos work suggests that scalp bacteria, or the chemicals produced by their activity, may contribute to this scaling of the scalp."

Aside from wearing white suits all year round, what can you do about these embarrassing flakes? Dr. Feinberg says true dandruff responds to the therapeutic shampoos sold without a prescription, provided you don't use the same one indefinitely. There are four groups of specially formulated dandruff shampoos: (1) sulfur-salicylic acid (brands: Sebulex and Vanseb); (2) tar (brands: Polytar with a conditioner, and Vanseb-T); (3) zinc pyrithione (brand: Head & Shoulders); and (4) selenium sulfide (brand: Selsun Blue). Buy one shampoo from each of these four groups and alternate them every few days.

Dandruff that is accompanied by red, scaly, itchy patches is probably caused by either psoriasis, seborrhea, or some other skin disorder. If the above regimen fails to cure you, see a competent dermatologist.

HAIR COLORING—IS IT FOR YOU?

Does our septuagenarian president, Ronald Reagan, dye his hair? Only his wife, Nancy, and his hairstylist really know for sure, but his full head of brown hair definitely gives him a younger, more vigorous-looking appearance. To me, his even brown-hair tone, without *any* streaks of gray, looks artificial. But if it is natural as claimed, then perhaps we should all take to wood-chopping and get Reagan's vitamin list.

If Reagan does dye his hair, he's not alone. Many men are coloring their hair today for various reasons, not just to camouflage their age. The male stigma against it is fast disappearing. However, if a man does choose to do it, he should do it gradually and subtly, or people will notice the radical change.

Before you color your hair, ask yourself:

• Do I look the way I feel?

• Does my natural hair color suit me temperamentally or does it seem to contradict how I envision myself?

• If gray or white hair is my problem, do I work in a youth-oriented business or a field where maturity and seasoning are valued?

Also ask your wife or a few close friends before you do anything rash. Coloring your hair is an important image decision.

Why Men Color Their Hair

There are probably four major reasons why men color their hair. Men with mousy brown hair do it to perk up what they feel is a drab look. A colorist would add blond or red tones, depending on the man's skin coloring. The overall effect is to make such men look healthier, younger, and more energetic.

Some men are actually born with a natural hair color that does not complement their skin tone. For example, if a man has a ruddy complexion and his hair is a carrot-color red, he might want to tone down the red in his hair with ash tones or deeper brown tones.

However, the two most common reasons are simply because men don't like their hair color or feel it suits their personality; and to cover up gray or white hair, giving a more youthful appearance.

Vanity—A Good Enough Reason to Color Your Hair

I had a young executive client who was in the process of interviewing for a high-level position. Because he was relatively young, and looked even younger, I had him dress very conservatively. I also advised him to get a shorter, more mature hairstyle to give him more authority and seriousness. I didn't question his blondish-brown hair color because it seemed so "him"—an integral part of his personality. Later, he confessed to me that his natural hair color was dark brown; and he felt he'd passed the supreme test when I didn't question him about it. He got that high-level job, and since it is in a somewhat creative field, his new image was perfect for it. However, should he ever decide to move into a more conservative industry or job function where a man's veteran status is valued, I'd probably advise him to let more of his natural dark color predominate.

Eliminating That Telltale Gray

When less pigmentation, or melanin, is produced in the hair follicle, more noncolored spaces become noticeable on strands of hair. This creates the appearance we call "graying." When melanin production ceases entirely, a person is totally gray- or white-haired.

I find well-toned gray or graying hair dignified looking. It is extremely attractive on many men. If such men feel comfortable with their shock of white or gray hair, all the better. They've earned the right to that distinction.

However, many men feel gray hair detracts from their otherwise young and vital appearance; or they work in a company or industry where youth is highly valued. These men are candidates for hair coloring.

Nina Marino, a hair colorist in the Jean-Louis David salon in the Henri Bendel specialty department store in Manhattan, has had many Wall Street executives as clients over the years. One, a fiftyish lawyer, was all gray. Rather than enhancing his image, the gray made him look older. He had tried coloring his hair himself, but he wasn't particularly happy with the result. The problem was a lack of highlighting, an effect that requires a professional's skill. Highlighting creates a more natural look. Instead of a solid mass of one tone, hair that's been highlighted has strands of a lighter tone throughout. Highlighting has to be done with an artist's eye, so that there's no severe or distinct color difference. Nina Marino covered a major portion of the lawyer's gray hair but not all of it, achieving a more natural, and younger, look. This method of coloring gray hair isn't as harsh looking. It's softer on a person's skin tones and adds color to the skin as well.

Highlighting should be done every two to four months; or more often if a man wears his hair very short.

The important thing to remember in covering gray is never to go darker than your original hair color. Instead, go slightly lighter because a man's skin tone changes as he gets older. Your original hair color complemented your younger, deeper-toned skin. If you restore your original color when your skin has aged, you will create a harsh, unnatural, even eerie effect.

When coloring gray, you must consider your gray *shade*; it may be an unflattering yellow-gray, for instance. Instead of eliminating the gray, you may simply want to achieve a better-looking gray tone. You can do this yourself using a rinse or semipermanent coloring.

Hair Coloring Methods

There are three types of hair coloring: (1) permanent, which is best accomplished by a professional colorist; (2) semipermanent; or (3) temporary.

Tints Tints are the most commonly used permanent dyes. They are colorless chemicals that must be oxidized by peroxide before they are applied to the hair. Tints come in a variety of natural shades and are applied in a one-step process. They have the ability to lighten or darken hair only slightly, one of their great advantages.

Should you attempt to use a tint yourself, you must always test the tint on several strands of hair first, for two reasons: to make sure that the color is right and that you don't have an allergic reaction to it. Anyone who doesn't test first is taking a risk.

When you're doing your own hair coloring, consult the color chart on the outside of the package. But keep in mind that your natural hair color will influence the end result.

Henna This is a natural highlighter, used for adding a warm accent to drab brown hair. It also gives hair more body and shine and makes it look healthier.

Semipermanent Coloring Products Most of these products are applied when you wash your hair; they rinse out gradually in subsequent washings.

Men whose hair is less than 50 percent gray often use semipermanent hair-coloring agents. These products cover most of the gray and wash out gradually. As the hair grows out, more gray becomes apparent as well. Unlike permanent coloring, this method leaves no distinct line at the roots when the hair starts to grow out; thus continual retouching is unnecessary.

Temporary Coloring Agents These products are available in liquid, powder, or spray form. In liquid form, they are called rinses, and can only darken, not lighten, your hair. Rinses do not affect the structure of the hair, but merely coat each strand with a harmless dye that rubs or wears off easily or can be shampooed out.

FACIAL HAIR: BEARDS, MUSTACHES, AND EYEBROWS

Beards and mustaches have been popular at various times throughout history. This is not one of those times. The clean-shaven look is what's "in" right now.

The growth of facial hair has long been one of the most potent weapons in a man's personal-appearance arsenal. To downplay unfortunate facial features, women have endless permutations of hairstyles and makeup; men traditionally resort to growing beards and mustaches.

Facial hair creates a powerful impression on all who see you; so the decision to grow a beard or mustache should not be a frivolous one. If you want to present a hirsute picture to the world, be sure it is acceptable in your field. A distinctive or unusual mustache or beard is fine if you want to cultivate an aura of authority or eccentricity. Artists, musicians, actors, writers, and filmmakers can not only get away with whiskers, but their careers may actually be enhanced by them. Would Salvador Dali's face come to mind as easily as his paintings without that curlicue on his upper lip? The wildebeest look is also acceptable in most academic occupations, along with pipes, tweeds, and slightly rumpled attire. But is it acceptable in your field?

If you already have a beard or mustache or are thinking about growing one, consider these pros and cons:

Reasons for Growing Beards and Mustaches

Even if the hirsute look is unpopular in your industry, you might consider it anyway to correct a number of serious facial-feature defects—a weak or double chin; too-thin or too-thick lips; a harelip; crooked or stained teeth; an extremely youthful appearance. Facial hair can balance and compensate for a bald head. Sometimes, it is the only alternative to chronic ingrown hairs. Moreover, the right beard or mustache can showcase your good features, such as your eyes or high cheekbones. The psychological lift that a beard or mustache could give you to correct your liabilities or enhance your assets should be weighed before you let an unwritten proscription deter you. (See Figures 7–7, 7–8, 7–9.)

Other Considerations

In addition to the fact that facial hair is "out" right now, there are other reasons you may want to forgo the experience. For example, a large

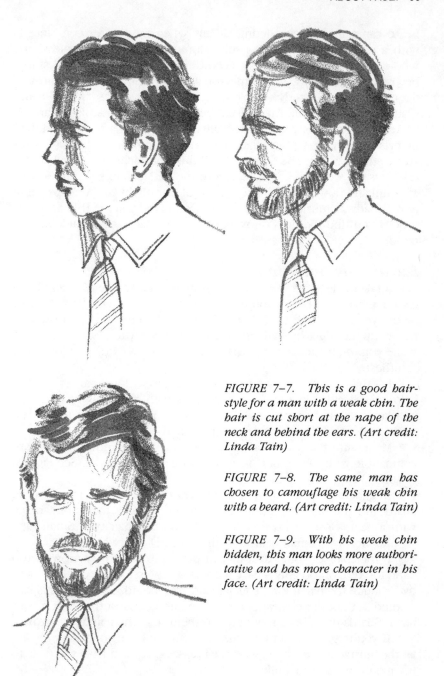

FIGURE 7–7.   This is a good hair-style for a man with a weak chin. The hair is cut short at the nape of the neck and behind the ears. (Art credit: Linda Tain)

FIGURE 7–8.   The same man has chosen to camouflage his weak chin with a beard. (Art credit: Linda Tain)

FIGURE 7–9.   With his weak chin hidden, this man looks more authoritative and has more character in his face. (Art credit: Linda Tain)

beard can send out conflicting signals when the wearer combines it with a conventional business suit. Moreover, a bearded professional who works with children may, according to one psychological study, be "creating problems in interpersonal relationships" because most of the children in the study sample felt a bearded face was "scary," Santa Claus notwithstanding. An unusual beard, such as the Amish beard or goatee, may express your individuality, but it could also have oddball or prissy overtones. Mustaches, too, can conjure undesirable images and even date you: the short, pencil-thin mustache à la Errol Flynn relegates the wearer to the late 1930s; the Fu Manchu style drips with evil; full and flowing styles like the handlebar might get you a part in a new Broadway musical, but probably won't land you the IBM account.

So if you find the pros outweigh the cons, keep these guidelines in mind:

Facial Hair Guidelines

• It takes at least six weeks for most men to grow a decent beard. No matter what style beard you're cultivating, don't attempt to shape it before you have three to four weeks of healthy growth. Then you can neaten up the edges by shaving. Needless to say, try to begin the project while you're on vacation, as growth in the first week or two looks the scruffiest.

• For the first shaping, it's best to go to a professional barber. He will help you decide on the final style and trim your newly sprouted whiskers better than you can. Thereafter, you can simply follow the shape and beard line that's been established.

• Make sure the style and shape of your beard and mustache are compatible with each other, as well as with your hairstyle. (See Figures 7–10, 7–11, 7–12.)

• In general, big, tall men have a better chance of carrying off a full beard and mustache. Tall, slender men accentuate their appearance with a neat, close beard coupled with shortish hairstyle. Small men should stick with small beards so they are not overwhelmed.

• If the *color* of your facial hair displeases you—it may grow in too dark, too red, or too gray—have it colored professionally. Ordinary hair dye is much too harsh for the facial hair. You should also have facial hair colored if it doesn't correspond to the natural color of the hair on your head. Beards often have more gray in them than the hair at the crown.

• If you're growing a mustache, let your smile be your guide. Don't let the mustache extend beyond the creases that form from the nose to the mouth when you smile.

FIGURE 7–10. This man has a long, narrow face. (Art credit: Linda Tain)

FIGURE 7–11. A neat-looking mustache adds width to the face's length. (Art credit: Linda Tain)

FIGURE 7–12. This mustache is the wrong style for the man's long face shape. The mustache droops, giving the illusion of dragging down his face and features. (Art credit: Linda Tain)

Beard/Mustache Maintenance

Your beard will stay clean enough with a soap-and-water washing during the growing-in period. Thereafter, you should use a mild shampoo to make sure both the hair and the skin under it stay clean. Beards can become a breeding ground for bacteria.

When a beard flakes, it usually means you haven't rinsed the shampoo out well enough or you've been drying it improperly; it doesn't mean you have dandruff. To groom your beard, don't blow-dry it because the process will dry out the delicate skin underneath. Instead, do a vigorous towel-drying. Once your beard is dry, comb it with a wide-toothed comb to untangle any knotted strands. If you follow up with a brushing, make sure it's a stiff-bristled one that penetrates the coarse hairs. When combing or brushing, make sure your strokes go in the direction you want the hair to go.

It's possible for facial hair to become dry. If this happens to you, try using a conditioning shampoo. Avoid hair creams, which will make your beard too greasy looking.

How To Avoid Eyebrow Errors

A well-groomed woman wouldn't think of going for more than a week without tweezing her eyebrows. But most well-groomed men never consider it. Well, do! It can make a big difference in your appearance. Bushy brows, particularly when they grow over the bridge of your nose, not only make you look unkempt but they may also give you a scowling, almost mean, appearance. (Anyone remember labor leader John L. Lewis's brows?) Note the before-and-after effect in Figures 7–13 and 7–14.

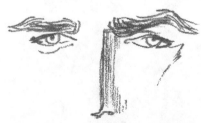

FIGURE 7–13. Incorrect: This man hasn't bothered to pluck the hairs growing on the bridge of his nose. As a consequence, he appears to be scowling and looks slightly unkempt. (Art credit: Linda Tain)

FIGURE 7–14. Correct: Note how much better this man looks after tweezing the hairs on the bridge of his nose. (Art credit: Linda Tain)

I'm not suggesting you overhaul your eyebrows; just pluck out the excess hairs growing where they shouldn't be. Tweeze any hairs growing across the bridge of your nose. To find out where your eyebrow should begin, place a pencil on the side of your nose straight up past the brow. The place where it crosses your brow is where the eyebrow should begin. Also tweeze any excess hairs growing above or below your eyebrow line.

THE TRAUMA OF HAIR LOSS

As men mature, their hair has the annoying habit of disappearing from the very area they most wish it would thrive (their scalp), while it sprouts merrily from those areas where it looks unsightly (their ears and nostrils).

Most baldness or thinning is due either to aging or an inherited tendency toward the condition. The inherited condition experienced by some 20 million Americans—mostly males—is called "male-pattern baldness," and it does most of its damage early, by age forty, sometimes even thirty.

Baldness—Accepting the Status Quo

To many men, baldness is a fact of life, like a large nose. At worst, they can learn to live with it. At best, they can turn it into an asset. There are many self-confident, sexy, and successful bald men: Yul Brynner, Telly Savalas, Sean Connery. Even macho Burt Reynolds recently decided to end his hair-loss coverup. Personally, I know several balding men who have adjusted to their new look quite well. On them, thinner hair or baldness is appealing; occasionally it even makes them look better.

If you, too, are self-confident enough to present yourself to the world as is, here are a few pointers to keep in mind. In general, men with bald or thinning spots shouldn't try to disguise the condition by combing the remaining side-hair strands up from one ear over their bald pate toward the other ear. They're not fooling anyone. However, a short haircut combined with the regular use of a protein or hair-thickening shampoo will help give the illusion of substance to thinning hair; gentle blow-drying to fluff it up also helps. If your profession allows it, a neat beard and/or mustache can complement thinning hair or a completely bald pate. One more drastic measure: If your personality or profession can handle a severe but dramatic look, try shaving off everything.

Hair Loss—Doing Something About It

To the men who regard baldness with dread and depression because the condition to them symbolizes age or unattractiveness or, thanks to

Samson, weakness, there's hope. There are cosmetic "cures" even though there aren't any genetic or patent medicine "cures" yet.

After reviewing all the so-called "guaranteed" methods of restoring hair, I can only recommend two with any enthusiasm. The first is a *quality, custom-designed hairpiece;* the second is a *hair transplant,* which is a surgical procedure. (*Hairweaving* is a third, remote possibility. A nylon base is secured to the edges of your existing hair and real or synthetic hair is woven into the nylon. The only problem is that as your real hair grows, the nylon base loosens. The periodic visits for re-tightening can give you headaches, a deflated bank account, and possibly more hair loss.)

Hair Transplants During a hair transplant, small plugs of your own hair-bearing tissue are removed from the sides and/or back of your scalp. Similar empty plugs are taken from your bald spot(s) and are replaced with the donor plugs.

Since a transplant is a surgical procedure requiring a local anesthetic, it may be performed only by medical doctors—usually either dermatologists or plastic surgeons. A personally recommended physician with his own private practice is best, especially if, like Dr. Feinberg, he or she performs the total procedure rather than delegating it to assistants. Most doctors, including Dr. Feinberg, consider going to a hair "clinic" for a transplant somewhat risky. On the other hand, I've seen some quality results at a few, such as the Hartford Hair Clinic in Pittsburgh. This clinic offers transplant surgery by well-qualified surgeons.

The obvious advantage of a transplant over a hairpiece is that, when

FIGURE 7–15   *FIGURE 7–16*   *FIGURE 7–17*

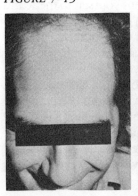 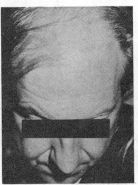 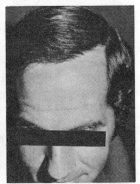

These three photographs show the stages of a hair transplant done by Herbert Feinberg, M.D. (Photos courtesy of Dr. Feinberg.)

done well, it is permanent and natural looking. Your own hair emerges from your scalp and can grow to any length once more. (See Figures 7–15, 7–16, 7–17.)

There are a few drawbacks as outlined by Joseph Ceremeli of the Hartford Clinic. A transplant is expensive, although perhaps less so than a lifetime supply of hairpieces. It *is* a surgical procedure. Moreover, it cannot be performed when too much hair is lost, the reason why Mr. Ceremeli opted for a hairpiece. (See Figures 7–18, 7–19.) The transplant process can be time consuming and it's somewhat painful, though only temporarily. During the treatment or "scabbing phase" (two to three weeks), your head won't be pleasant to look at. However, I think the long-term benefits outweigh such temporary disadvantages.

(Incidentally, don't confuse a hair transplant with an *implant*. Implants are not recommended under any condition. This process, whereby strands of synthetic hair are permanently sutured or im-

FIGURE 7–18. This is a photograph of Joseph Ceremeli of the Hartford Hair Clinic in Pittsburgh, before donning a hairpiece. (credit: Hartford Hair Clinic)

FIGURE 7–19. Here is Joseph Ceremeli wearing his hairpiece. (credit: Hartford Hair Clinic)

planted into a bald area, may lead to constant discomfort. In addition, Dr. Feinberg warns that rejection, infection, and terrible scarring are a constant danger, thus making frequent medical checkups necessary.)

Hairpieces   People have been wearing wigs and hairpieces for centuries. More often than not, the wigs were elaborate, obviously fake, and used to attract attention and convey status. Today, the opposite is true. Howard Cosell notwithstanding, hairpieces are meant to look real and undetectable.

Fred Zauder of Zauder Brothers, the manufacturers and wholesalers of fine hairpieces for some of the best salons as well as a handful of individual clients, feels that the only way to obtain a proper hairpiece is to have it custom made. I totally agree. As Zauder so rightly points out: "In ready-made hairpieces, you have to have the head to fit the piece, rather than have the piece fit the head." He also recommends that the wig be professionally styled and maintained, preferably by someone as expert as Mr. Anthony of Bergdorf Goodman in New York City.

Mr. Anthony, who wears a totally undetectable hairpiece himself, is understandably pro-hairpiece. When a man consults with him about buying a hairpiece, Mr. Anthony always cautions against unrealistic expectations. He, like any good stylist, will take into consideration the appearance of the client's original hair, as well as the client's lifestyle, profession, and head shape before recommending a specific style of hairpiece.

A few words about hairpiece construction. A hairpiece will either have a *silk gauze foundation,* which is light and comfortable and best for most people; or a *net base,* which creates a full look, affords maximum ventilation, and is best for the young, active person. Sometimes *lace* is used in certain areas such as the front, to create a more natural look when the hair is combed back. There are also fine nylon-net bases with *urethane* in the part and at the hairline; this creates the illusion of skin under the hair. Mr. Anthony wears the latter type and recommends it for experienced wearers who have more than one piece and don't mind the delicacy and frequency of repair. Nylon net is also the best base for those who only want a partial hairpiece.

Finally, a comment on hairpiece wear and maintenance. A hairpiece is usually secured to the scalp with doubled-faced tape. You may wear a hairpiece every day, even around the clock for up to three days on occasion. Mr. Anthony recommends that under certain conditions— sports, hot sunlight—it's more practical and comfortable to go without. A businessman should always wear his "piece" in business situations, but in his private life, he can let other considerations determine when others may see him *sans* his hairpiece.

A hairpiece that's worn everyday should be cleaned once a week, either by your stylist or by you. If you do it yourself, make sure you're well versed in the correct procedure. A dry cleaning solution is usually recommended.

A custom-made hairpiece costs between $650 and $1,000 and should last at least two years with the proper care. Maintenance visits cost about $30 and include a shampoo and trim for your real hair, plus a cleaning and styling for the hairpiece.

PLASTIC SURGERY: THE RADICAL ALTERNATIVE

I asked Dr. Gerald Imber, a noted New York City-based plastic surgeon and founder of The Institute for the Control of Facial Aging, how he decides whether a patient is a candidate for cosmetic surgery. He says that the first thing he does is analyze his patient's supposed "appearance problem," noting in particular whether the person has poor grooming or posture. Dr. Imber feels that sloppy grooming and bad posture are often indicative of a lack of self-esteem, and to perform surgery on such a person to correct, say, a less-than-perfect nose won't correct the true problem. However, when Dr. Imber is convinced that a facial feature is causing a patient real anguish and creating feelings of inadequacy, he sees plastic surgery as the best remedy.

Dr. Imber also evaluates whether a patient's problems are due to aging, poor skin tone, or poor texture. These can be corrected surgically. In addition, there are certain types of facial flaws for which plastic surgery is the only remedy. They include a receding or inadequate chin, a heavy neck, a permanent "double chin," and a "flat face."

About a so-called flat face, he says: "You have to have highlights on the face. If a face is flat and without prominences, then it has no shape. Without obvious cheekbones, a person looks completely bland and uninteresting. By creating cheekbones, the same person's whole visage will be transformed."

According to Dr. Imber, another correctable facial problem is the short, fat face caused by an inadequate chin or heavy neck. For the person with no discernible chin line, Dr. Imber suggests a plastic implant to give the chin and face more balance.

A rhinoplasty ("nose job") often requires some work on the chin as well. Why? Because the patient's chin may be out of proportion to the new nose. In such cases, Dr. Imber corrects the chin at no extra charge, because he feels strongly that the extra work is necessary to give the face the proper esthetic balance.

How do you go about locating a qualified plastic surgeon? Dr. Imber points out that the laws of most states allow any licensed physician—regardless of training or experience—to declare himself or herself a plastic surgeon. So be wary. Dr. Imber recommends contacting the American Society of Plastic and Reconstructive Surgeons (29 East Madison Street, Suite 807, Chicago, IL 60602) for a list of qualified, board-certified surgeons in your area. When you're considering a doctor, ask to see samples of his or her work.

COSMETIC DENTISTRY

An attractive smile can be one of your most important assets. For those of you who try to avoid broad smiles because you're ashamed of your teeth, take heart! Tremendous strides have been made in the past few years in cosmetic dentistry, which is now quicker and less expensive than the older method of tooth capping.

The Miracle of Tooth Painting

I discussed the process of bonding with resin—popularly known as "tooth painting"—with Manhattan dentist Dr. Jack Kern. I was sold. I went to Dr. Kern because I had noticed one of my teeth, which was slightly recessed, was looking darker than my other teeth in photographs. I didn't have the time to embark on the long, drawn-out project of capping, so I went to Dr. Kern for tooth painting. I was pleased with the results.

Before you follow my lead, consider the pros and cons fully:

Pros Tooth painting is excellent if you want to fill in the gaps between teeth, restore color to one or several teeth, or build up uneven, malformed, malpositioned, or chipped teeth—in short, get rid of that "snaggle-toothed" look. With tooth painting, you no longer need to cut down two perfectly good teeth to fill the space or improve tooth color as you do in capping. Suppose your teeth are pulling away from your gums. Now the dark line at the gum need only be painted to restore that natural look.

Tooth painting is a more conservative procedure than capping. Resin is simply painted over the tooth, saving the tooth, yet making it (or them) more appealing to look at. If you need several teeth painted, you can save time by asking your dentist to arrange one long appointment for you. I had four teeth done in about two hours. Each tooth takes approximately thirty minutes to complete, although some teeth are more difficult than others. Dr. Kern charges about $125 per tooth, considerably less than the cost of capping one tooth.

Cons There are disadvantages. Resin can stain over time and it fractures more easily than caps. Thus, it's not as permanent. Furthermore, a tooth cannot be shaped as well with resin as with a porcelain cap. Porcelain jacket crowns also match your natural tooth color more perfectly than resin, although you have to look closely. Resin does not have the translucence of porcelain so it reflects light differently. Resin lacks the strength to be used on back teeth, unlike a crown made of precious metal.

Dr. Kern is adamant about not giving anyone perfectly Chiclet-white teeth, no matter how badly they want them. He thinks they look too artificial. With the eye of an artist, Dr. Kern uses a person's skin tone as the basis for deciding the appropriate shade of the tooth.

THE IMPORTANCE OF HEALTHY-LOOKING SKIN

If you have bad skin, all my advice up to this point will do you little good. People will think of you as "the man with the bad skin." So pay close attention to this section if you suffer from skin problems.

First of all, the most important thing you can do for your skin is keep it clean. And for that I recommend plain old soap and water. Having worked with and been indoctrinated by Dr. Erno Laszlo, the famous skin-care specialist, I'm a confirmed soap and water advocate. Not just any soap, however. Use a good cosmetic soap that's been chosen especially for your skin type after consultation with a knowledgeable skin consultant. Though a new fad has started to get men to use cleansing creams instead of soaps, just when women are finally wising up and eschewing this expensive practice, Dr. Feinberg, as well as all dermatologists I know, agrees that soap and water is the only thing that makes sense.

Your Skin Type: A Self-Analysis

You cannot be an educated consumer about soap or any other skin-care or shaving product until you know your own skin type. Otherwise, you'll find yourself trotting home from the stores with expensive mistakes that will probably do you more harm than good.

To discover your skin type, answer the following questions. Be sure, however, that your skin is absolutely bare at the time you answer the questions. Also, don't answer the questions directly after washing, because the natural condition of your skin will not have had a chance to reassert itself. Wait several hours.

1. Do I have an oily shine over my entire face?
2. Do I have enlarged pores?
3. Do I have a scaliness or flakiness in my "T"-zone—forehead, nose and chin? (This is dead skin that doesn't flake off because it is encrusted with oil. It is not, as commonly supposed, dry skin.)
4. Does my skin have a thick, coarse texture?
5. Do I frequently have blackheads, whiteheads, or blemishes?

If you have answered yes to questions 1–5, you probably have *oily* skin. "Yes" to question 5 indicates problem skin. Although acne cannot be totally cured, it can be controlled for long periods, and many people outgrow it. Anyone with severe acne should be under the care of a competent dermatologist, not only for immediate benefit but to prevent future scarring. There are new ways of treating acne today: Oral antibiotics have been replaced by new topical antibiotics (applied to the skin) that seem to work well.

If you don't have oily skin, let's try another series of questions and see if they apply to you:

1. Does my skin have a smooth firm texture?
2. Does my skin have good color and tone?
3. Do I sometimes have flakiness around my "T"-zone?
4. Do I have slight oiliness in the "T"-zone?
5. Do I have relatively fine pores?

"Yes" answers to a majority of these questions indicate that you have *normal* skin.

If you didn't type your skin with that set of questions, let's try another:

1. Does my skin have a thin, parched texture and feeling?
2. Do I have fine lines around my eyes and mouth?
3. Is there scattered flakiness on my face (not just around my "T"-zone)?

If your answers are affirmative, your skin will feel dry without a moisturizer and cream because it's *dry* skin. If you have dry skin, I would guess you're forty or older. In contrast, men with oily skin are usually thirty or under.

If you still haven't discovered your skin type, let's try one more time:

1. Do I have deep expression lines on my face?
2. Do the contours of my face sag?
3. Does my skin have a thin, parched texture?

These characteristics generally describe the skin of a man over fifty. It is very dry skin and easy to recognize.

Now that you know your skin type, let me recommend a skin-care regimen for you.

Regimen for Oily Skin

Squeaky-clean skin is a must for you! Wash with a soap especially recommended for you and rinse with lots of hot water. Use an astringent at least three times a day. Use freshener in between to freshen up. (Note: An astringent is much stronger than a freshener. Because it is predominantly alcohol, an astringent has a drying quality, and it should only be used on oily skins—or in especially oily areas, such as the "T"-zone, of other skin types. A freshener or plain toner will do nothing to alleviate oiliness.)

On the controversial subject of moisturizers, I recommend that oily-skinned men avoid them. You have enough of your own natural facial oil, so why add to it? Does it make sense to use a drying soap and an astringent to remove surface oil and then add a moisturizer? Your own natural oil is better than any artificial moisturizer you could buy, and it's there (in excess!) at no charge.

However, I do recommend cream for the eye area. Eye cream is a necessity because the skin around your eyes—and on your hands—will get dry first as you age.

Heat stimulates the oil glands, so you'll have more of an oiliness problem to contend with in a hot climate. In fact, every skin type should be treated a little differently in the summer than in the winter.

Generally recommended for oily skin:
• A drying soap suitable for your skin
• An astringent
• Eye cream

Regimen for Normal Skin

Normal skin does not imply perfect skin, which is rare after age seven. But, obviously, normal skin is the best to have, even if it is slightly on the oily or dry side in patches. Don't forget the eye cream I mentioned for oily skin.

Generally recommended for normal skin:
- Oil, always applied immediately before washing your face (but not to be used if your skin is on the oily side)
- A balanced soap, neither drying nor oily
- Freshener
- Eye cream
- Throat moisturizer/cream

The man with oily or normal skin might consider using a water-based foundation, adding vitality to his look. Erno Laszlo's Shake-It, for example, offers light, transparent protection from the elements as well as giving a man's face a slight glow.

Regimen for Dry Skin

I recommend a good oil and a specially formulated soap for dry skin with lots of warm water to stimulate your oil glands. Make sure that your soap is an oil-base soap.

Generally recommended for dry skin:
- Oil, always applied immediately before washing your face
- Soap
- Possibly a light freshener
- Moisturizer
- Eye cream
- Throat moisturizer/cream
- Night cream

Regimen for Very Dry Skin

My suggestions for very dry skin are similar to those for dry skin:
- Oil
- Soap with oil specially formulated for dry skin, rinsed with lots of warm water
- Possibly a mild freshener
- Moisture cream or dry-skin lotion
- Eye and throat cream
- Night cream for very dry skin

Regimen for Combination Skin

Some men have oily skin on the forehead, nose, and chin, while the skin on the rest of the face is relatively dry. For these people, I recommend using an astringent on the oily areas, a freshener on the normal and/or dry areas, and a moisturizer on the dry areas. Then, for the oily areas, follow the regimen outlined above for that kind of skin, and do likewise for the normal and dry-skin areas.

Cosmetic Dermatology

Many defects of the skin that were dangerous if not impossible to correct a few years ago are now done much more simply and with more assured results by competent, board-certified dermatologists. (Check to see if yours is board certified.)

The newer dermatological methods have been refined considerably, are much less drastic, and the after-effects are reduced, if not eliminated. For example:

• Abnormalities of color (i.e., brown spots on the skin) can be lightened simply by applying liquid chemicals—bleaching agents called "hydroquinones"—to your skin. Such products should be used only under a doctor's care and direction, however.

• More severe brown spots, small red lines (i.e., visible blood vessels), and small scaly age growths can be removed from the skin by cauterization. Cauterization uses a freezing method to remove such skin defects. Moles and warts can be removed surgically.

Eliminating Wrinkles and Scars

Wrinkling and scars, which are really depressed portions of the skin, can also be removed. Dr. Feinberg uses two approaches. One involves removing some of the normal skin around the wrinkles or scar, thus bringing the whole surface of the skin down to the same level. The procedure is called "dermabrasion." The other method is just the opposite: it's done by elevating the depression(s) with injections of either silicone or collagen. The method your doctor uses will depend on the exact nature of your condition. Unfortunately, any large, craterlike scar, even a large chicken pox scar, cannot be eliminated with either of the above procedures. Another method, called "punch autograph," might be successful. Using this method, a dermatologist cuts out the scar and replaces it with a circular patch of skin from behind the ear.

COLLAR STYLES: HOW TO CHOOSE THE RIGHT ONE FOR YOU

Small as it is, the collar is an important aspect of your total look. It functions as a focal point, as a kind of pedestal upon which you present your face to the world. A collar is, in addition, probably the most important design element in a dress shirt. After all, it's often the only part of the shirt that other people see.

By the collar you choose, you can accentuate the positive and eliminate the negative features of your face and neck. Here's how.

Slope, Point, and Spread

In order to make sense out of any discussion of collars, you will need to understand their anatomy. The *slope* of a collar simply means the height on your neck; the slope may be low, medium, or high. The *point* indicates the distance from the neckband to the tip of the collar; it may be short, medium, or long. The *spread* of the collar is the distance between the tips; a spread is either narrow, medium, or wide.

The average point-size of collars is between 2½ and 3¼ inches. On the standard straight-collar shirt and some button-down shirts, the points measure approximately three inches, a medium length. However, you can buy special long-point-collared shirts whose points are up to 4½ inches long. On Windsor and French collars, the points are shorter and the spread wider; thus these collars require large-knotted

FIGURE 7–20.   Right: The pin collar looks good on this man. The shorter points and the horizontal pin give the illusion of width to the man with the long, thin face. (Art credit: Linda Tain)

FIGURE 7–21.   Wrong: This large collar with the long points accentuates the man's long, thin face. (Art credit: Linda Tain)

ties. The button-down and tab collars have narrower spreads while the narrowest spread of all is found on the pin-collared shirt (i.e., the tab collar worn with a pin).

The type of collar you choose should always have a harmonious and flattering relationship with your face shape and neck length. Here are some guidelines.

If You Have A...	You Should Choose...
Short neck:	collars with low slopes, narrow spreads, and moderately long points. Your collar should end about one inch above the collarbone.
Long neck, thin face	collars with high slopes—up to 3 inches above the collarbone. A moderate spread and relatively short points will also help downplay your vertical facial and neck lines. (See Figures 7–20, 7–21.) Should you want to play up your long, lean look to suggest elegance and aristocracy, choose a high collar with wide, flared points.
Wide face:	collars with wide spreads and low slopes in order to give your facial width some symmetry. Such collars will also emphasize a strong jaw.
Large face, thick neck:	collars that are large in all their dimensions. Small collars look silly on top of a large body. (See figures 7–22, 7–23, 7–24.)
Small face, delicate features:	collars with moderate to low slopes and moderate to short points. High slopes and long points will overwhelm you. (See Figures 7–25, 7–26.)

FIGURE 7–22. Wrong: This Windsor collar is too small and dainty for the man with the large face and thick neck. Rather than downplay these features, it accentuates them. (Art credit: Linda Tain)

FIGURE 7–23. Right: This large, long-pointed collar with an average-sized tie knot gives the man's large face and thick neck a symmetrical look. (Art credit: Linda Tain)

FIGURE 7–24. Wrong: Although the long-pointed collar looks good on this large-faced man, the oversized tie knot does not. (Art credit: Linda Tain)

FIGURE 7-25. Right: This collar with the moderate slope and shorter points looks good on the man with the delicate facial features. (Art credit: Linda Tain)

FIGURE 7-26. Wrong: This high-slope, long-pointed collar overwhelms the man with the delicate facial features. (Art credit: Linda Tain)

FIGURE 7-27. Right: This older man has age lines in his face and neck. This collar is the right style and fit for him. (Art credit: Linda Tain)

FIGURE 7-28. Wrong: This collar has too low a slope for this older man. Consequently, too much of the wrinkled flesh on his neck is exposed, creating a "turkey-gobbler neck" effect. (Art credit: Linda Tain)

Shopping for the Right Collar Style

The next time you go shirt shopping, look over a large variety of collar styles. During the elimination process, look only at white shirts, since patterns and colors will distract you. Ask the salesman to measure each shirt collar's slope and point for you. Once you've found your ideal collar size and style(s), make note of the manufacturer(s) since they probably make all their shirts with the same or similar proportions.

The Rest of the Picture

No discussion of collars would be complete without a mention of ties and jacket lapels. All three must harmonize with each other. Styles come and go, but the concept of balance and proportion stays the same.

For example, narrow lapels should be paired with narrow ties and smaller collars. When lapels are three to four inches wide, so are ties. (Ties are measured at their widest point, called the *blade*.) In the same way, collars with a narrow spread (e.g., pin and button-down) call for a small knot; and larger collar spreads (e.g., Windsor and French) require a large knot to fill the larger space. A man with a large, heavy face, however, should always avoid large tie knots and bulky tie fabrics. (See Figure 7–24.) These are the reasons why this year's shirt and tie seldom work with five-year-old jackets.

8

THE 10 MOST COMMON DRESS AND GROOMING MISTAKES

by Lois Fenton

Feeling inappropriately dressed can be a demoralizing experience. It is, however, a situation you can learn to avoid if you observe some guidelines. With a little forethought and effort, you can avoid those embarrassing dress and grooming mistakes that make you want to go home, get in bed, and pull the covers over your head.

As a speaker on executive dress—my seminar is called "Executive Wardrobe Engineering"—I travel a lot to corporate meetings and conventions throughout the country. Consequently, I spend a considerable amount of time waiting in airports, and my favorite airport game is pre-guessing who will be flying which class. Some travelers surprise me. But, more often than not, I can spot the first-class customers. Their dress and grooming are the giveaways.

In this chapter, I'll describe the dress and grooming mistakes of men I encounter most frequently in airports, in my audiences, and in the executive business environment. It would be wise of you to avoid the same errors.

MISTAKE 1: BARGAIN-BASEMENT THINKING

Bargain-basement thinking is false economy. It is what prompts men to spend too little for their clothes.

If you think buying quality clothing is an unnecessary extravagance, think about today's emphasis on image in business. In the past few years, the country's top business publications have been featuring stories on the booming image-consulting business; graduate business-administration schools offer seminars in business dress; and renting fine clothes to executives has become a growth industry.

Recently, a young man I know, after receiving his MBA, was hired by a highly respected management consulting firm. They gave him—company policy—$3,000 up front to outfit himself in a business wardrobe. They stipulated that he should spend at least $400 on each suit, and that they should be dark blue or gray. The shirts he bought should be white or light blue. He was to wear no jewelry except a wedding ring. That was one firm that didn't want its prestige damaged by junior executives wearing bargain-basement purchases.

Most people recognize quality clothes on other people. The men who wear them are thought of as winners. To step out of the business context for a moment, suppose you're an actor looking for a job. I'll bet you wouldn't drive to your audition in a beat-up old car. You'd borrow a car if you had to to make sure you arrived in a sleek model that suggested you were successful. Your clothes, in a business setting, should also emphasize your successfulness.

Another way to justify investing in quality clothes is the concept of "cost per wearing." If you were to buy a classic navy blazer or a gray suit for $350, you could quite conceivably wear such a basic, traditional item once a week for seven years. Figuring once a week for seven years, the cost per wearing would come to $1. And each time you wore it you would feel like a million dollars.

If, on the other hand, you were to walk past a store, see an $80 green polyester suit in the window, and buy it, here is what might happen: The first three or four times you wear it, no one compliments you; in fact, no one says a word. The fifth time, your wife says she never did like that suit. The sixth time, you look in the mirror and wonder what ever made you buy it. The seventh time, you decide you'll wear it even if you don't like it anymore to save money, and you feel low all day. The eighth time, the waiter at lunch seats you near the kitchen and you—wisely—decide to give it to Goodwill. Eighty dollars divided by eight wearings is ten dollars per wearing. *That's* expensive!

"Polyester dressing" is a prime example of Bargain-Basement Thinking. Since synthetics have a way of looking cheap, the man who insists on wearing polyester does himself a great disservice. The natural fibers—wool for suits, cotton for shirts, silk for ties, and linen for summer wear—are more impressive, more comfortable, longer wearing, and carry with them an aura of "success." When you do buy a blend, the more wool or cotton, the better.

Buying on sale is not false economy. What is wrong with getting a $300 blazer for $150? And buying merchandise from a fine store boasting the store's own label rather than a designer's name is likely to be a best buy. Just be certain before you go shopping that you know what you need in your wardrobe. Don't ever buy on a whim something you would not have considered without a sale. The old adage is still true: "A bargain is not a bargain if you don't wear it."

MISTAKE 2: IGNORING FASHION CHANGE

Although men's fashions do not change as often or as radically as women's, they do change. An aspiring executive should pay heed to them.

The pendulum of change for men's clothing swings slowly. It usually takes about seven years from one cycle to the next. By the time most men notice the change, it is about two years into the cycle—which still gives them about five years' wearing time for any new purchases.

During most of the 1970s, the trend had moved toward vested suits, wider lapels, wider ties, longer collar points, and a shaped silhouette. In the late 1970s and early 1980s, the classic look returned in force. Of course, some men have always dressed this way, but the man who had changed with the earlier trend now had several options. He could "refuse to be dictated to" and continue to wear what he had in his closet—looking dated; he could throw everything out and start over; or he could be realistic and make judicious changes. His new purchases could have more classic lines: suits with narrower lapels and less pronounced shoulder padding, shirts with shorter collar points, slimmer ties with small knots—all in proportion.

If you think changes in fashion are merely the whim of the manufacturers and have no rhyme nor reason, you are mistaken. Since balance and proportion are essential to designers, when one part changes, others follow—as in the domino theory. When vests were in fashion, less of the tie showed and so the ties needed to become wider. When vests became less common, narrower ties could stand on their own.

The pressure of change is compelling. When the fashion changes, stores carry different merchandise, men buy what is shown, you see more of the new and less of the old, your eye adjusts, and soon what is new is the only thing that looks right to you.

When change occurs, buying everything new is not necessary. Often the lapels are the only part of the suit that is out of date. A good tailor can narrow the lapels of a suit for about $35 or $40. Ties can be made narrower and shirt collar points made shorter by experts who specialize in this.* Now that shirts and ties have become so expensive, updating the ones you have and like is a wise, worthwhile investment. This is a good time to make changes; after the next seven-year cycle, you cannot make the lapels wider!

By its very nature fashion is confusing and transitory. What causes the change is a most inexact phenomenon. Even the strongest-willed man should not resist a major trend in fashion for too many seasons. This does not mean that a man of taste will jump on the bandwagon of every new twist of fashion or adopt styles unbecoming a gentleman; but he who insists on wearing wide ties, wide lapels, fuller hairstyles, and long sideburns when these have become passé risks appearing dated and unprofessional.

Knowing when new trends are coming—even if you're not quite ready to go along with them—can actually save you money. For example, when the "classic look" reappears strongly, you should know that trousers with cuffs will soon be returning. I've heard men say they would not ever consider wearing cuffs—"too old-fashioned." And, since cuffs are more trouble for the store's tailor than plain bottoms, you can be sure *he* won't suggest them for your new suit. Then, six months later, you may find that your $350 "investment" suit looks out of date and has lost its investment quality. This is information that I have given my audiences a full year before they learned it from their favorite stores. After all, it is to the *store's* advantage should you decide the next year that you need a more updated look—and another new suit.

Where do you find out what's "in"? You'll get a comprehensive picture of the direction men's fashion is taking by reading such publications as the *Playboy Guide to Fashion for Men;* "Fashions of the Times," *The New York Times* Sunday supplement issued twice a year;

For shirts: L. Allmeier, 119 W. 23rd St., New York, NY 10011 (212) 243–7390. They do a wide variety of shirt alterations: shortening and replacing collars, shortening and lengthening sleeves, etc. For ties: Tiecrafters, 116 E. 27th St., New York, NY 10016 (212) 867–7676. They narrow ties and professionally dry-clean them.

and *Gentlemen's Quarterly.* Further helpful information may be found in your own company's annual report. Your industry may favor a traditional Brooks Brothers look at all times. If so, it doesn't make much sense for you to be swimming against your company's tide.

The fact is that things do change in the men's fashion area. It is in your own best interest to be aware of the changes and decide which ones are suitable to incorporate into your overall image.

MISTAKE 3: ILL-FITTING CLOTHING

Even the finest clothes you can buy won't make you look good if they don't fit correctly.

Fit is 90 percent of the game. Any man who is rude to the tailor is a fool. Tip him, flatter him, ask his opinion, cajole—do whatever works to get him on your side. He may be able to perform near miracles by giving a $200 suit a $400 look.

The single most common mistake I see—particularly among well-dressed Ivy League types—is men wearing their trousers too short. The "high water mark" look is definitely out. Trousers should have a slight "break" in front. In other words, the front of your pants should rest on your shoe.

I realize the preppy, Eastern Seaboard look dictates a short trouser length. I know an excellent Italian tailor who was close to tears when a customer—one of the PYG set, otherwise known as the pink, yellow and green boys—made him shorten the trousers of an $800 Oxxford suit. The end result would be trousers two inches too short. The tailor found it so painful to do what the customer wanted that he had to alter the pants three times to get them short enough!

Another mistake men make is wearing their clothes too tight, probably because they think it will make them look thinner. The reverse is true. Too-tight clothes tend to look like sausage casing.

When Clark Gable was beginning to age and found his neck thickening and slightly wrinkling, he had his shirts made a quarter-inch larger so that *they* would look *larger* and *he* would look *thinner.*

Learn to take a critical look at yourself in the mirror and see what can be done to minimize your imperfections and maximize your strong points.

MISTAKE 4: COLOR CACOPHONY

One afternoon two men walked into a men's store to shop for clothes. They each spent the same amount of money and, in fact, bought the very same three items: a suit, shirt, and tie. The only difference was their choice of colors. The first man put together a combination that looked terrific; the second man bought a discordant threesome that was not only unattractive but unprofessional looking as well. Color made all the difference.

Color is free; using it well costs no more than using it poorly. But either way, its impact is tremendous.

Choosing colors for business wear is still a traditional game and is best played according to conservative rules. The guidelines need not be followed slavishly; but it's best to know the rules . . . then you can break them.

In my seminars I teach color coordination formulas that are easy to follow. Of course, if you are adept at combining colors, do what your instincts tell you to do. But if you don't trust your instincts, or would like some guidelines, here are a few rules you can use:

Begin with the color of the suit as a base. Suits are usually one of three colors: blue, gray, or brown. What constitutes a color? Blue is everything from the palest powder blue to the deepest navy. Gray ranges from the lightest gray through deeper shades of gray to charcoal and black. And brown varies from off-white through beige, tan, camel, and dark chocolate brown. For a variety of subtle and psychological reasons, the best use of the three fail-safe colors is to wear *dark* shades of blue and gray, and *light* shades of tan. These colors are always appropriate. Of course, there are other colors that some men wear, but I regard them as questionable judgments. A burgundy suit suggests a lower-class image, and men in green suits tend to look like leprechauns.

After beginning with the suit color as a base point, add a second, or accent color, for the shirt. Shirt colors come in a wider range than suit colors—yellows, greens, and reds are added to the blues, grays, and browns. "Reds?" you say! Yes, remember that all shades of a color are still called by the name of the color, so that a light pink shirt, a burgundy stripe in a shirt, and a deep wine tie are all reds.

With the suit as the base color and the shirt as the accent color, next consider the item that ties it all together—the necktie. No single item in a man's outfit makes as much difference as the necktie—or tells as much about the man. By its color, design, quality, and placement, it focuses the eye on your face and should call flattering attention to you. It should say many good things about you: that you have good judgment; that you know how to make the most of your best qualities; that you are a person of taste; that you have the strength of your convictions, but are not an exhibitionist; that you are successful. Yes, a carefully chosen tie can say all of this about you—a convincing reason for buying quality in this highly visible item.

If a necktie is patterned, it should include both the color of the suit and pick up the color of the shirt—making a harmonious combination of all three. For example, a favorite of mine is a dark blue suit, a soft yellow shirt, and a navy tie with a small yellow pattern. Or, when the shirt is not a second color, the tie can be the accent color. As an example, with a blue suit and a blue striped shirt (that's only one color so far) a burgundy tie would provide the second, accent color.

The shirt should be lighter than the suit, and the tie should be darker than the shirt.

Wear black shoes with blues and with grays. Wear dark brown shoes with beige, tan, and khaki. Wear socks that match your shoes—black with black shoes and brown with brown shoes. It couldn't be easier. (If you prefer, navy socks may be worn with blues.) Business socks should be dark, preferably a solid color.

And now for a suggestion that separates those who dress safely from those who dress with style: *Repeat colors* so that they appear more than once in your outfit. If shoes are brown, the belt should also be brown. If you wear a light blue shirt and a dark blue tie, you are repeating the color even though you are using different shades of the same color. Reds and yellows are so strong that they need not be (in fact, should usually not be) repeated. A yellow foulard tie and a yellow pocket square would probably be too much.

Men can learn what smartly dressed women have known for years— how to find their own best color. If you have blue or hazel eyes or light hair color, wear those colors often. With blue eyes, wear a lot of blues. What color do you suppose Paul Newman wears most of the time? The fact is almost everyone looks good in blue. But people with dark hair and sallow or olive (Mediterranean) coloring should contrast their coloring with light, clear, flattering colors near the face (white, ivory, pink, light blue). They should steer clear of most browns, grays, dark greens, rust, and mustard yellow—colors that are unflattering to their skin. With sandy-colored hair and green eyes, you can wear a tan suit, off-white shirt, and brown, gold, and green patterned tie and be handsomely put together; the tie will pick up the colors in your suit, your shirt, your hair, and your eyes. (Avoid wearing a red tie when you are "hung over." It is neither good business nor good judgment to emphasize your bloodshot eyes!)

MISTAKE 5: MIX-AND-MATCH MISTAKES

Some men have an instinctive sense of how to mix-and-match everything they wear. But the more typical man does not. He decides one day that he needs some new shirts, goes into a store, and buys six shirts. The next week he realizes he needs new ties, goes back to the store, and buys six ties. And nothing goes with anything.

Most men need help with mixing and matching. Their mistakes are usually in one of three areas: pattern, texture, and what I call "spirit." The man who masters the art of mixing and matching will get more pleasure than he ever thought possible out of wearing clothes.

Patterns

Books that have been written by experts on dress usually tell men that they should wear only one *pattern* in an outfit and everything else should be a plain or solid color. Yet the same experts, as well as other well-dressed men, often combine two patterns. The reason experts say not to wear more than one pattern is that they assume most men cannot learn how to do it. Certainly, when assembling the usual business trio of suit, shirt, and tie, wearing two solids and one pattern is always safest and sure to be right. You can even wear three solids for a very sophisticated look. If you think this sounds too dull, keep in mind that men generally look their best in "black tie," which has not only no pattern, but no color. When you feel venturesome and wish to go beyond the two-solids-and-one-pattern rule, you can do as the world's best-dressed men do—mix two patterns.

At my seminars I demonstrate the principles behind combining two patterns. Imagine a large, overscaled graphic drawing of a blue and white striped shirt. On this I place a solid navy blue tie. Everyone agrees that the tie is a correct and safe choice. But, now consider another selection—a navy background tie with close-together white polka dots. When I show this tie with the striped shirt, the audience groans. What is wrong with this choice? It is *not* that polka dots can't go with stripes, but rather that the close-together dots seem to fight with the stripes. By replacing the polka dot tie with another tie with the same size white dots that are more widely spaced, the eye is relieved and the combination works. The rule then is: when mixing two patterns, it is best to *combine one small pattern with one that is also small but more widely spaced.*

Now, picture the next step where I show a red, green, and yellow paisley tie on the same blue and white striped shirt. It looks terrible; but the mistake is *not* that a paisley tie is all wrong with a striped shirt. The problem is that the colors clash. When combining two patterns, you must give a little extra thought, and *make certain that the colors are exceptionally well coordinated.*

Never, *never* wear three patterns together unless you have impeccable taste...and unless you're not the only one who thinks so.

Textures

Don't underestimate the importance of texture when you're coordinating your clothes. Creative use of texture is a concept that is often overlooked. You can give yourself a lesson in texture by trying this experiment. Select two shirts of contrasting textures from your closet. One shirt might be a smooth cotton broadcloth, the other a rougher button-down oxford cloth. Now choose several different ties: your dressiest silk ties, a wool solid, a striped repp, or a knit tie, perhaps. Place each tie against the shirts. Your eyes will tell you which ones are too dressy for the oxford cloth and which go better with the elegance of the fine broadcloth. Note the difference texture makes!

The basic rule is: Combine smooth with smooth, like texture with like texture. Visually, the weight of the two textures you're combining should complement each other. With practice, you'll develop a second sense about which textures look good together.

Spirit

Sophisticated mixing and matching involves combining items compatible in pattern, texture and "spirit." The concept of *spirit* is simple. It has to do with suitability. You wouldn't wear sneakers with a pinstripe suit, would you? How about a Lily Pulitzer tie, with all its bright tropical colors and fanciful designs, with a navy blue solid suit, a strong authority symbol?

Here are three typical mix-and-match groupings where the patterns, textures, and spirit all go together perfectly:

For that perennial Dartmouth graduate look, a casual outfit might include a sports jacket, a blue oxford cloth shirt, a wool tie, penny loafers and argyle socks. A more formal, authoritative grouping could include a pinstripe suit, a white broadcloth shirt, a silk tie, fine cotton lisle hose, and wingtip shoes. This is the Boardroom Look! The spirit of the most formal group, the "black tie look," is elegance. You might wear a black tuxedo with satin lapels, a pleated shirt, a silk bow tie, silk hose, and black patent-leather pumps. (Odd, isn't it, that while patent-leather shoes are elegant and correct for formal evening wear, they have definite negative connotations on a man dressed for business?)

To further help you mix and match so the different parts of your outfit coincide in spirit, here are a few rules:
* *The smaller the pattern, the dressier the tie.* A small pin dot on a

dark tie is one of the most powerful choices. But a large dot on the same dark ground tends to suggest Nathan Detroit.

• *The smoother the texture, the dressier the tie.* Silk ties are the most imposing. Ties become more casual as they become rougher. The most casual are wool, Viyella, and knits.

• *The darker the color of the suit and tie and the lighter the color of the shirt, the more elegant the spirit of the outfit.* Navy suit, white shirt, and dark pin-dot tie create the president-of-the-bank look. Much more relaxed would be a medium-blue suit, blue striped shirt, red foulard tie. A white tie on a navy shirt imparts a Las Vegas look.

MISTAKE 6: ACCESSORIES TO A FASHION CRIME

Did you know that Tiffany's—the jewelry store accepted far and wide as an arbiter of taste—will not make, for any amount of money, a diamond ring for a man? It does not matter if you offered to pay $1 million for it; they still would say "no." It is their strong conviction that a gentleman does not wear a diamond ring.

A few years ago I was speaking at a bankers' convention in Palm Springs. In the evening following my program, I attended a large dinner and was seated at a table with several bankers and their wives. Everyone was introduced and, as often happens, I missed a few of the names. During dinner and conversation, something struck me as odd: one of the men was attractive and quite well dressed in traditional bankers' garb—navy suit, white shirt, and striped tie—but something was totally incongruent. He was wearing a large, ostentatious diamond ring. Normally, I would have assumed he just didn't know any better; but everything else was so right about his looks that this did seem peculiar. As the evening progressed, men came up to our table and asked for his autograph. Then I listened more carefully. It was Rocky Bleier, of football fame, and the ring was his third Super Bowl ring. I decided that in that case, the ring was just fine!

The wrong accessories can distract the eye and ruin the effect of a man's outfit. Simplicity is of the greatest importance.

Most experts agree that a man should wear very little jewelry, if any, besides a wedding ring, a fine watch, simple gold cuff links, and a collar pin with certain shirt collars. Fancy hardware on belts and shoes is generally inappropriate.

MISTAKE 7: SMALL IMAGE-DESTROYERS

Small image-destroyers are those little grooming no-no's that leave a bad impression. Most are careless mistakes and all are easy to correct—once you're aware you're making them. The following checklist of blunders is intended as a self-assessment test. Are you guilty of any of them?

_____ Greasy or unwashed hair.

_____ Curly hair that is not attended to each day with a brush or a comb.

_____ Bald men who comb their seventeen strands of hair across their bare scalps. (Somehow I always picture them running in the wind with those strands blown over the opposite shoulder.) Bald men are *not* unattractive.

_____ Unflattering or out-of-date hair styling. Look at men's fashion magazines; if you don't see even one man pictured with your length hair or sideburns, it's time to consider changing yours.

_____ Eyebrows that grow right across your nose in a single sweep. Shaving the center section works.

_____ Hair untrimmed in ears and nostrils. A good barber will trim it for you, or do it yourself.

_____ Five o'clock shadow.

_____ Untrimmed facial hair. Beards and mustaches require care. They should be an element of your personal style, not a sign of being too lazy to shave.

_____ Chewing gum.

_____ Frayed collars and cuffs or polyester pilling on collars.

_____ Wilted collars. *Spray* starch on collars is not as stiff as starched shirts and is also non-irritating. Remember to replace collar stays after laundering.

_____ Dandruff shoulders.

_____ Lint on dark clothes. Use a clothes brush or adhesive lint remover.

_____ Unpressed suits.

_____ Spots on ties.

_____ A gap between the bottom of the vest and the top of the trousers, with shirt showing.

_____ Shabby belt.

_____ Buttons loose or missing.

_____ Wearing jacket sleeves too long or wearing short-sleeved shirts with no shirt cuff showing beyond the edge of the jacket sleeve.

_____ Wearing short socks, allowing skin to show when you cross your legs.

_____ Shoes in need of repair.

_____ Unpolished shoes.

MISTAKE 8: OLFACTORY OVERKILL

When some people enter a room, you don't need to look up to know who it is. Their scent has preceded them.

In the same way that smoking assaults many people's sensitivities, so too does too much or the wrong cologne. Think of it this way: It's unfair to surround others with your fragrance whether they like it or not. Used in abundance, cologne can be an invasion of other people's territory.

One way to tell if your fragrance choice is the best one for you is by learning what others think about it. The tipoff is someone's asking, "What is that cologne you're wearing?" Usually they want to know the name so they can avoid buying it. One or two negative remarks should be enough to send you looking for another. Naturally, fragrance preference is highly personal; it should be one that you are comfortable with.

More important than the scent itself is the intensity. Can you remember being in a crowded elevator and almost made dizzy by the combined scents from all those people? Think of what it must be like in an office all day long with several different heady fragrances wafting through the air. After-shave, which is lighter than cologne and more of a skin-treatment product than a scent, is fine for an office setting. Reserve cologne, which is stronger, for evening, social situations.

In my opinion, unless you are dancing with someone (or just closer to a person than is appropriate in business) you should not be able to smell his scent. As the advertisements suggest, the whole concept of wearing fragrance is based on encouraging intimacy; obviously, using a strong come-on scent during business hours is inappropriate and unprofessional.

MISTAKE 9: BODY ODOR/SMOKER'S BREATH

Far worse than the affront to our sense of smell made by too much fragrance is the attack on our senses made by offensive body odor. It is difficult to imagine anyone being unaware of body odor in this day of television advertising.

A tennis court or locker room is the only place where body odor is conceivable—and then only until the offending person reaches the showers. Deodorant soaps for all-over help, drying yourself thoroughly, antiperspirants, spray or roll-on deodorants for underarm "protection," talcum powder for those parts of the body where you can't use deodorant—all work.

Stressful situations can increase perspiration and necessitate temporary measures. Between showers, splash quickly and rewash underarms to freshen your body, or use a small roll-on kept in your desk—you'll feel better. Wearing cotton T-shirts and all-cotton shirts also helps. Synthetic fabrics are notorious for increasing perspiration and retaining odor.

Another form of body odor often associated with nervousness is bromidrosis, or foul-smelling feet. It is caused by perspiration in the warm, dark environment of most shoes. The one thing that helps most is wearing cotton socks, which absorb perspiration better than synthetic ones. Foot powders also help to keep the feet dry. Of course, there are not many business situations where you would remove your shoes; but, who knows, you could be taken to lunch in a Japanese restaurant!

Most women agree that the most attractive odor a man can have is a clean, freshly scrubbed natural smell.

Smoker's breath is a bit trickier, because you don't know if you have the problem. But everyone else does! My guess is that if you are a heavy smoker, you can be sure you do. Brush your teeth more often, use a mouthwash, floss your teeth. It would also help if you could refrain from smoking before appointments. If that is asking too much, use a breath freshener after smoking.

Incidentally, everyone, not just smokers, should use dental floss after meals, followed by thorough swishing with water. This removes the food that accumulates in spaces between the teeth—the most frequent cause of bad breath.

After dressing well and paying attention to all of those other small grooming details, you wouldn't want to turn people off like a fire-breathing dragon!

MISTAKE 10: NASTY NAILS

Your hands are always on display, and nails tell a lot about a person. Don't ignore them.

A blue-collar worker will have difficulty keeping his hands looking good. He needs abrasive soaps and a pumice stone—and hand cream to counteract the harsh cleansers. On the other hand, a business or professional man has no excuse for hands and nails that look less than perfect.

Nails look their best when kept all the same length—short—and scrubbed clean. All the equipment a man needs is a pair of clippers and a nail brush. Bitten nails tell people you are nervous and not in control. They are guaranteed to detract from an executive's image.

I recommend an occasional manicure just so you can see how short to clip your nails, how far to push back your cuticles, and how good your hands can look. However, do not under any circumstances allow anyone to put polish on your nails. Even clear nail polish has a dreadful new-rich, or *worse* connotation. What's worse? A well-groomed-mobster look!

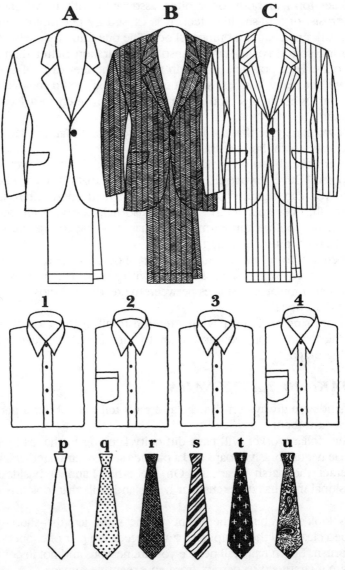

(Credit: Reprinted with permission from the Donnelley Record, *Issue 1979 No. 1 by Reuben H. Donnelley.)*

The Mix-and-Match Quiz

These suits, shirts, and ties have been combined as indicated—suit (A) with shirt (1) with tie (p), for example. On the line after the combinations, put a "yes" if you think it is a well-coordinated look and "no" if you don't. Then check your opinion against the opinion of men's wardrobe consultant Lois Fenton.

* A 1 p ____	C 1 t ____	C 3 s ____	A 1 u ____
B 3 t ____	B 2 r ____	C 3 r ____	A 4 p ____
C 1 q ____	A 2 p ____	A 3 r ____	B 1 s ____
A 1 q ____	A 2 r ____	A 3 p ____	A 1 r ____
	A 1 t ____	A 3 t ____	

*Match suit (A) with shirt (1) and tie (p) and answer "yes" or "no."

ANSWERS TO QUIZ

A 1 p
Yes, can be *very* sophisticated when color is used well.

B 3 t
No, too busy.

C 1 q
Yes, the "diplomat or chairman of the board look." Elegant. Too formal for some situations. Can be made less dressy by substituting a foulard (r) for the polka-dot (q) tie. A striped suit is limiting, in terms of where you wear it and what you wear with it.

A 1 q
Yes, one of the most handsome, elegant looks, particularly when the polka dots are small and light-colored on a dark tie.

C 1 t
Yes, you'll knock 'em dead in this one.

B 2 r
No, never. Well, hardly ever. If the pattern of the suit is very subdued, such as a subtle herringbone or tweed, rather than a bold plaid or check, it *could* work. But it is generally best not to combine any three patterns. Since every rule has an exception, the exception to the never-wear-three-patterns-together rule is: a small, silk, pocket square may introduce a third pattern. This is true because the item is so small, but it is not easy to do well.

A 2 p
Yes, the safest and surest combination. With reasonable care in selecting colors, you should *always* be able to do this well. Solid-color ties are most useful in navy, brown, and wine.

A 2 r
Yes and no. This is easy to do poorly, which is the way you usually see it. But annual reports are full of pictures of men in this combination. Harmonious color coordination is the important difference between unattractive and highly distinctive.

A 1 t
Yes, even Johnny Carson couldn't do it better.

C 3 s
No, you've got to be kidding!

C 3 r
No, no, no. Almost as bad as C 3 s.

A 3 r
No, this shirt requires a solid-color suit and tie or a spaced club tie (t).

A 3 p
Yes, a safe, smart way to be a bit bold and distinctive.

A 3 t
Yes, another way to be bold and distinctive, but more difficult to do than A 3 p.

A 1 u
Yes, the paisley tie is a great way to spark up a too-dull combination.

A 4 p
No, even though it is correct to combine one pattern with two plains, this type of shirt is *never* appropriate for business or professional wear—except for a formal luau.

B 1 s
Yes, particularly handsome when the shirt repeats the second, or less dominant, color in the suit. Example: with a subdued brown glen-plaid suit with a blue line in the design, wear a blue shirt with a brown-and-blue tie. Brown and blue is a "successful"-looking color combination, particularly in dark brown and light blue or navy and camel. Avoid dark brown and dark blue.

A 1 r
Yes, a guarantee comes with this one. Though it is not particularly distinctive, it is always right. Almost every famous and successful man in the world has been photographed in this one.

PART III

PERSONALITY AND PRESENCE

9

FOR EXECUTIVES:
The 17 Fatal
Business Faux Pas

by Jacqueline Thompson

They say manners are the body language of a culture, a manifestation of its soul. The more civilized a society, the more its citizens observe the social niceties.

Etiquette means knowing how to move through a sometimes hostile or indifferent world with ease and grace. It is the code that elevates human beings above a dog-eat-dog existence. And it is a code that is no less important in business than in one's personal life. In fact, it is courtesy, more than any other single element, that greases the wheels of commerce and makes them turn smoothly.

Below, I have isolated the seventeen gravest business faux pas committed by far too many men in the course of doing business each day. If you don't want your business associates to come away from an encounter with you feeling awkward, annoyed, or even angry, make sure you aren't guilty of any of the following breaches of etiquette:

FAUX PAS 1—AUTOMATICALLY ADDRESSING ALL BUSINESS ASSOCIATES BY THEIR FIRST NAMES

In a small office, the use of first names among employees is generally decided by the owner or highest-ranking corporate officer. Take your cue from him. In a large company, expect to be on a first-name basis only among your peers.

If you have subordinates, you, as boss, dictate the forms of address in your department or division. For instance, you may wish to call your subordinates by their first names although you prefer to be addressed more formally as "Mister." If this is your preference, you have the law on your side. The jobless-pay board set a precedent on this issue by denying unemployment compensation to an employee who insisted on calling his boss by his first name after repeated requests to the contrary. The board ruled that the employee was guilty of insubordination.

If as boss you invite your subordinates to call you by your first name, make sure, however, that you specify the occasions when that's *not* appropriate. Otherwise, you'll find yourself in the same sticky position as one company president. He was meeting for the first time with officers of another company to discuss a possible merger. It was an important initial encounter requiring the utmost delicacy on everyone's part. When the guests arrived, the president went out to the reception area to greet them. The receptionist, in her most formal voice, introduced the guests to the president as "Mr. So-and-So," and introduced the president to the guests as "Charlie." The moment she got the word "Charlie" out of her mouth, everyone froze. The guests looked puzzled and the president looked horror stricken. Gone forever was that president's ability to negotiate from a position of strength.

FAUX PAS 2—MISTREATING BUSINESS ASSOCIATES' SECRETARIES

By mistreatment, I mean any behavior that might cause a secretary to dislike you. You should always strive to make secretaries into your allies. Their mere proximity to their boss give them an edge over you. If they say something disparaging about you to their boss, you'll never know it and won't be able to defend yourself. All you'll know is that suddenly their boss stops returning your telephone calls and breaks an important appointment with you. Remember, on a subconscious level, many an executive adheres to the old adage: "Anyone who insults my secretary insults me."

FAUX PAS 3—DISPLAYING A CAVALIER ATTITUDE ABOUT BUSINESS TELEPHONE CALLS

When you make a business phone call, always identify who you are and what company you represent. (If it's a personal call, say so.) If you are calling a close business associate, you can drop the mention of your company, but you must still identify yourself by name no matter how many times a day you speak with this person. To do otherwise invites confusion and a misunderstanding that could prove embarrassing.

When you answer the telephone in your office, you should also identify yourself.

If you are calling a stranger long distance and he or she is not in, don't ask that person to return your call unless the individual stands to benefit from your subsequent conversation. A journalist might ask a stranger to return his long-distance call if he was going to give that stranger some favorable publicity, for instance. A salesman, on the other hand, would show a decided lack of manners if he expected a stranger to call him back long-distance for the purpose of getting an unsolicited sales pitch.

Avoid putting anyone on hold because "an important call just came in." That diminishes the importance of the person to whom you are speaking. In fact, don't put anyone on hold unless it's just for a moment to transfer a call.

I also advise against the installation of the Bell System's "Call Forwarding Service," which allows a second caller to "beep-in" on phones which don't have hold buttons. If your line is busy, the second caller will try again later. And the person with whom you are talking will not be made to feel second rate by being placed on hold for another caller.

Never—I repeat, NEVER!—simultaneously talk with someone at your desk while trying to keep up your end of a telephone conversation. If you absolutely must speak to someone in your office in the middle of a telephone conversation, excuse yourself politely and cover the phone. And be brief about it.

The best policy is to have your calls held when someone is in your office. In fact, instructing whoever answers your phone to hold your calls in the presence of your visitor will make that visitor feel very special. It also gives the impression you care about common courtesy.

When answering the telephone for someone else, never give nebulous or untrue reasons to explain why that person cannot come to the phone, such as "He's in conference" when he's not. A simple "I'm sorry. He's not available. May he call you back?" will do. Then make certain the call *is* returned, within the same hour if possible. If someone has taken a call for you, make sure you get back to the caller promptly. Some busy executives block out thirty-minute to one-hour periods twice daily to return morning and afternoon calls.

If you've got a secretary, don't have her place your calls for you unless they are complicated long-distance calls that will take time to complete. The Hollywood movie moguls are famous for using the telephone to play the kind of one-upmanship games that you should avoid. In that industry, secretaries place most phone calls, even local ones. The power play starts once one secretary succeeds in getting the other person's secretary on the line. Then the big question is: Which mogul will come on the line first? The mogul who succeeds in keeping his opposite number waiting is the one who wins—that round at least.

These kinds of games are not only silly, they're offensive and a waste of precious time. Don't engage in them. Remember, the telephone is a medium of communication. It is not a toy to be used as a way of establishing your authority. Besides, your authority must be pretty shaky if you find such tactics necessary.

FAUX PAS 4—SMOKING IN THE WRONG PLACES

Most smokers know enough not to light up in elevators. Unfortunately, too many smokers do light up in reception areas and in people's offices where there are no ashtrays. Don't start smoking and then look around for a receptacle. If there's no ashtray in sight, assume that smoking is prohibited—or at least not encouraged. And just because it is obvious you can smoke in the reception area, don't assume you are equally welcome to smoke in someone's private office. Extinguish your cigarette *before* leaving the waiting room. If there is an ashtray in your host's private office, ask if he or she minds if you smoke. If there's no ashtray, don't even bother to ask permission. Just refrain from smoking.

FAUX PAS 5—LAXITY ABOUT MAKING AND KEEPING BUSINESS APPOINTMENTS

Never drop in on a business associate just because you happen to be passing by. Arriving on someone's office doorstep without an appointment is rude, to say the least. By making an appointment in advance— and arriving promptly—you are granting your business associate dignity by assuming that he or she leads a busy, *orderly* existence.

Consistently being late for appointments creates a bad impression. Your tardiness says to the person kept waiting, "My time is more valuable than yours." Viewed from this perspective, tardiness is an insult.

FAUX PAS 6—FAILING TO SAY THANK YOU IN WRITING

People who fail to show proper appreciation for acts of kindness on the part of their colleagues are generally people who feel the world owes them a living. They are selfish people, incapable of seeing things from the other person's point of view. It never occurs to them that other people's time is valuable, for instance. They don't realize that an executive who has granted them an interview to discuss general employment prospects in his industry, for instance, has done them a big favor. Thus, they don't bother to acknowledge the favor with a thank-you note.

Since the advent of the telephone as the principal form of business communication, the practice of writing thank-you notes has waned. This is a pity. In my opinion, a written expression of thanks is far superior to a two-sentence aside slipped into a telephone conversation. A letter is concrete; a spoken "thank you" is ephemeral and easily forgotten.

Thank-you notes are the one form of business correspondence that can be handwritten, if that is your preference. If you do write in longhand, monarch-sized stationery is the most appropriate. Again, it is imperative that you use the highest-quality stationery.

FAUX PAS 7—SENDING OUT SLOPPY-LOOKING BUSINESS LETTERS

You'll cancel out all the goodwill that a thank-you note—indeed, any business letter—may engender if that correspondence is filled with typos. Mistakes of this kind brand you as unprofessional. Mailing such letters is tantamount to walking into somebody's office for a business appointment dressed in jeans and a T-shirt. By your carelessness, you are saying to the addressee, "I'm not concerned with details or surface impressions." Unfortunately, success in business is largely attributable to details and surface impressions.

FAUX PAS 8—FINGERING OBJECTS IN OTHER PEOPLE'S OFFICES

Expressing interest in the knickknacks, photographs, paintings, plants, and other objects in a person's office is one thing. Picking up those objects or running your fingers over them without explicit encouragement—verbal or nonverbal—from your host is impolite.

Reflect, a moment, on what you must look like to your host when you do this. There you are, walking around his or her office, picking up objects and scrutinizing them as if you just got off a spaceship from Mars. Your host will think, "What's with this guy? Hasn't he ever seen a paperweight before? Are the contents of my office so unusual or is this guy just extremely naive and unsophisticated?" Even worse, your host may interpret your actions as pushy and aggressive.

I doubt you want to give anybody either impression. Restrain yourself the next time you get the urge to let your fingers do some walking. Fingering objects—whether they belong to you or someone else—is a common method of releasing nervous energy. There are better ways. A more productive rechanneling of energy is to use more gestures when you speak than you might ordinarily. Strong gestures make you appear to have a high energy level. Futhermore, they help you emphasize important points, and they tend to add inflection to an otherwise monotone voice.

FAUX PAS 9—ROCKING IN CHAIRS AND BALANCING ON THE BACK LEGS

Nothing destroys chairs—or your image—faster than this childish back-and-forward motion. Didn't you get enough rocking as a child or are you still trying to relive the experience?

Chairs were made with four legs on purpose. Each leg is supposed to support one quarter of the weight situated in that chair. If two legs are forced to carry the burden, those two legs are gradually going to dislodge themselves from the rest of the chair. Even if you don't mind ruining your own chairs in this manner, I doubt your host will share your feeling.

Whether on your own premises or someone else's, never, *ever* let anyone catch you rocking back and forth in what is intended as a stationary chair. The next time you are tempted, remind yourself of the following true episode, involving a consultant from a large and highly respected management consulting firm.

The consultant had just completed a high-priced assignment for a nationally known company. At the concluding meeting in the client's austere, mahogany-paneled boardroom, the consultant presented his final report, amid much praise, and then tried to sell those assembled on engaging his firm for an even more expensive follow-up assignment. The consultant sat down at the conference table with the corporate officers and encouraged them to ask questions. Everything was going splendidly. The more he fielded their questions with ease, the cockier he became. Also, unconsciously, he began rocking on his chair legs. The client was intrigued enough to ask, "How much will all this cost?" At that very moment, the consultant lost his grip on the edge of the table and the chair fell backward all the way to the floor. The client looked down at him and, with a mixture of amusement and disdain, said, "That much, huh?" While the chair survived the incident, the consultant never got any more business from that client.

FAUX PAS 10—SPITTING IN THE STREET

Obviously, you don't find this habit disgusting or you wouldn't do it. Maybe you don't do it in front of women because you know it turns them off. But you don't hesitate in front of men, both male business associates and friends.

Don't do it in front of anybody—unless you're Marlon Brando playing the part of Stanley Kowalski or you want to look like a construction worker. That's what you will appear to be, by the way. Blue-collar workers don't have to worry as much about their image. As a businessman or professional, you do. No matter how well dressed you are, spitting in the gutter will create the impression you just recently emerged from the gutter and haven't quite polished off all the rough edges yet.

FAUX PAS 11—GIVING CONFLICTING SIGNALS ABOUT WHO IS GOING TO PAY THE BILL WHEN YOU LUNCH WITH A BUSINESS ASSOCIATE

The words "Let me take you to lunch at Restaurant X" indicate that you intend to host the meal. The person who chooses the restaurant usually pays. Taking command at the table is another indication you intend to pick up the tab. For example, if you are the one who gives the order to the waiter throughout the meal, your luncheon partner has a right to be chagrined if you don't insist on paying at the end.

If your idea is to go dutch treat, the correct way to phrase the invitation is: "Let's have lunch together. Where should we go?"

FAUX PAS 12—NOT KNOWING HOW TO CHOOSE AND COMMENT ON FINE WINES

If you live in terror of restaurant wine lists and order the most expensive bottle on the list merely to hide your ignorance, do something about this gap in your knowledge right away. The ability to converse about wines is important and will be noticed by peers as well as executive recruiters and others in a position to move you out and up.

Sorry, knowing that red wines are served room temperature with red meats and that white wines are served chilled with poultry and fish is not enough. You'll remain a "vincompoop" until you know such basics as the broad categories of wines (e.g., Beaujolais, Bordeaux, Burgundy, Rhine, Moselle, Cognac, and champagne) and the characteristic shapes and colors of their respective bottles. You must also know which wines improve with age and which don't. (Yes, some wines should be imbibed while still "young.") Wine terminology is another must. For example, "bouquet" refers to a wine's smell. "Body" is a word used to describe its texture, weight, and flavor intensity. "Finish" means aftertaste. "Magnum" and "jeroboam" are both oversized wine or champagne bottles. Finally, you should be familiar enough with popular oenophile phrases—"a regal nose"; "pleasantly unassuming"; "an amusing impudence"; "rich and full bodied"—that you don't wince when they're uttered. Ideally, you should be able to utter similar descriptive phrases of your own when you taste the wine you selected so carefully.

You can squeak by with the above smattering of knowledge. But you won't qualify as a true connoisseur until you can discuss vintage years, the relative merits of the wines of different countries and of different vintners, and the contents of various restaurants' wine cellars.

FAUX PAS 13—FLUBBING A TOAST

Even if you aren't a card-carrying wine snob, you should know how to offer a toast. It's a basic social skill. Toasting is a ritual that marks a special occasion. You can make any libational meeting into a special occasion merely by the act of offering a toast.

What or to whom you toast is limited only by your imagination and powers of recall. By all means, recite a well-known toast if you know you can't match it for wit and style. Every writer of note from Milton through Mencken has left us with at least one memorable toast. Commit several to memory and have them at the ready during festive gatherings. The more you practice the art of toasting, the better toastmaster you'll become. One day you might even rival one of America's greatest—Benjamin Franklin. Impromptu toasts-to-end-all-toasts were his speciality, such as the one he, in the role of emissary to France during the American Revolution, delivered at Versailles.

The British ambassador spoke first: "To His Britannic Majesty,

George III, who, like the sun in its meridian, spreads a luster through-out and enlightens the world." The French minister parried: "To His Christian Majesty, the illustrious Louis XVI, who, like the moon, sheds his mild and benevolent rays on and influences the globe." Finally, Franklin: "To George Washington, commander of the American arm-ies, who, like Joshua of old, commanded the sun and the moon to stand still—and both obeyed."

FAUX PAS 14—TALKING SOLELY ABOUT BUSINESS ON A BUSINESS/SOCIAL OCCASION

This is a grievous error in the United States. But abroad, it could be fatal. In Europe and many other parts of the world, managers like to restrict their business dealings to people with whom they feel comfort-able. Most foreign executives would rather do business with a person who shares their lifestyle and values than with a stranger, even if the stranger does offer them a better deal.

To a great extent, this is also true in this country. You remain a stranger to your business colleagues if, for instance, you refuse to engage in small talk and voice your opinions on various nonbusiness topics. If you have no opinion on any topic other than business, or have no outside interests, I suggest you develop some. Start paying attention to something other than just the business sections of the newspapers and magazines you read, and take up some hobby. Executives who advance steadily are invariably well-rounded people, comfortable in all circumstances.

When you lunch with a business associate, it is customary to discuss nonbusiness matters initially. The person who is hosting the meal generally indicates when the small talk ends and serious discussion begins.

FAUX PAS 15—INVITING YOUR BOSS OR OTHER SUPERIOR OUT SOCIALLY BEFORE HE OR SHE HAS ISSUED ANY SUCH INVITATION TO YOU

While it is perfectly acceptable for a boss or other authority figure to invite a subordinate and his spouse to dinner, the reverse situation is tricky. Many bosses do not like to be indebted in any way to staff members, because such indebtedness makes it harder for them to treat their employees objectively. Thus, you should not extend a social invitation to your boss unless he or she has entertained you first—or at least made it abundantly clear that you are friends in addition to being business colleagues.

If you do socialize with your superiors, business subjects are *verboten* unless the person with the highest corporate rank brings them up. If the talk turns to business, make sure your wife or girl friend doesn't sound off about your company's problems, which will indicate to your superiors that you are indiscreet and gossip freely after hours. Nor should a spouse or girl friend use a social occasion to try to promote your business advancement.

If you have entertained or been entertained by your boss, never try to take advantage of the situation by acting unduly familiar in the office the next day.

FAUX PAS 16—MISTREATING YOUR WIFE OR GIRL FRIEND—OR REFERRING TO HER DISRESPECTFULLY—IN FRONT OF BUSINESS COLLEAGUES

In the Neanderthal era of business history, such behavior may have been condoned as a form of male bonding. But it certainly isn't acceptable today in this age of female liberation and equal employment opportunity.

Maybe you still believe that women belong in the home, barefoot and pregnant, or even elegantly dressed and waited on by servants. Either way, keep your anachronistic views to yourself. Just because your boss's wife is also a homemaker is no proof that your boss is pleased with that arrangement or shares your old-fashioned opinions.

On the other hand, suppose that even if you do entertain the current enlightened perspective on the place of women in the work force, you've still got a hot temper and occasionally give your wife or woman friend a piece of your mind in public. Don't do it. If ever there existed a person whom you should love, honor, and cherish in the sight of other people, it's the woman in your life.

A business or professional man who mistreats his wife in front of others is a man bucking for a fall. Such behavior is guaranteed to bring out the Sir Lancelot lurking in every man witnessing your actions. If your wife or girl friend has stepped out of line, a quick remonstrance and change of subject or venue is the most you can do and keep your otherwise flawless professional image intact. But delivering a full dressing-down is a surefire way to lose friends and shock other people.

Even business associates who dislike your wife or girl friend are liable to avoid you after witnessing such a performance. Why? Because any mature adult recognizes that arguments between a man and his wife (or woman friend) are delicate and private matters. Onlookers don't want to get involved or caught in the middle. In short, when you start ranting at your wife or speaking disrespectfully about her, other people don't know how to behave or what to say. They don't know what's appropriate in such an unusual situation. All they know is that they feel extremely uncomfortable and they're going to blame you for making them feel that way. Remember what I said in the beginning of this chapter: Good manners are defined as putting others at ease.

FAUX PAS 17—INVITING A WOMAN BUSINESS ASSOCIATE TO MEET YOU AT A PLACE WHERE SHE MAY FEEL DEMEANED

If you want to insult a female colleague, invite her to lunch at an exclusive men's club where women must enter through a side door and wait for their member-host in the powder room so their presence doesn't contaminate the lobby. I can think of few better ways to deliver a put-down. It's swift, wordless, and efficient. Your message to her is: I'm a member of a privileged class of people while you're a second-class citizen.

Granted, there may be insufferable women who deserve this blow to their ego. Fine. But don't subject women business associates whom you like to this type of subtle ordeal with the mistaken idea that you're impressing them. Quite the reverse. You'll be alienating them. Put yourself in their place for a moment. How would you like to be told— by a doorman, no less—that you're not good enough to enter this esteemed institution by the front door? No, the side door is reserved for the likes of you, just as servants always enter through the back door into the kitchen. Once inside, another pompous male lackey informs you that, "The powder room is around the corner to your left, madam. If you'd be kind enough to wait there, I'll ring you on the telephone when Mr. _____ arrives." I think you get the picture.

Other public places to avoid with women business colleagues are the Playboy Club or any nightclubs or cabarets featuring female nudity, and pubs or restaurants where the waitresses are overly familiar with you for whatever reason.

10

LIBERATED MANNERS: The Etiquette of Male-Female Business Encounters

by Phillip Grace

Whether you like it or not, women are playing an increasingly important role in the business world. But you don't need me to tell you this. Maybe you have a female boss or a major client who's a woman. Then there are the women still engaged in the traditional female jobs: secretaries, office managers, Gal Fridays, clerks, typists, receptionists, switchboard operators. You're surrounded by women every day on the commuter train, in your office, in restaurants, perhaps even in your formerly all-male club.

What should you do about this distaff swell in the business population? First of all, accept it. Women in business are here to stay, no matter who gets into the White House or how many states fail to ratify the Equal Rights Amendment. Second, learn to interact with these women in an appropriate way.

Despite the message you may have gotten from the radical wing of Women's Lib, chivalry is not outmoded. It should be updated, perhaps, but it's a mistake to think that good manners toward women are relics of the past. Quite the contrary. While deep bows and kisses on the hand went the way of the dinosaur, opening doors and helping women into their coats will never go out of style. Why? Because it's etiquette based on common sense. Doors are heavy and men are stronger than women; coats aren't easy to get into, so men *and women* should help each other with the task. The rule of thumb in dealing with women you meet through business is: Behave in a way that engenders mutual respect. Do not do anything that will downgrade or demean the woman. Of course, in this liberated age, it may take some hard thinking and sensitivity to other people's feelings to decide what behaviors, drummed into you as a child, to retain and which to discard as hopelessly *passé*.

HOW TO BEHAVE TOWARD YOUR SECRETARY

Office etiquette has changed in recent years as drastically as office equipment. Women now represent 52 percent of the work force compared to a mere 34 percent in 1950. While women have made remarkable inroads into the executive suite, a majority of them are still sitting outside that suite at a secretary's desk.

There may be no male-female relationship today more enduring—and, in some ways, more intimate—than the relationship between a male boss and his female secretary.

Let's begin with the title, "secretary." To many young women, that word has negative connotations. It represents a "pink-collar ghetto," an entry-level job, a place where they dump educated women who should, rightly, be in managerial training programs along with their male college classmates. Since your objective is to get work done and your secretary's job is to assist you by expediting your ideas, you might want to rethink the title "secretary" if you know it irks her. Good manners, as I've said, mean making other people feel comfortable both with you and themselves. If the title "secretary" makes someone uncomfortable, why use it? Personally, if addressing my secretary as the "Queen of the Marketing Department" would make her happier and more efficient, I'd start shopping for the coronation robes. Consider that the title, "administrative assistant" may be a more descriptive label, anyway. Titles are cheap. If a certain title makes a woman feel better or work better, why not adopt it? It's good business as well as good manners.

The phrase "working *with*" rather than "working *for*" is another subtlety that could pay dividends in improved worker morale. Seldom does anyone profit when superior-subordinate relationships are strongly articulated. If you sign a person's paycheck or employee evaluation form, that person knows for whom she works and to whom she owes her allegiance. Working *with* her will make her feel less inferior and more like a member of a team.

Additionally, I recommend limiting your assistant's duties to tasks that are strictly in the line of professional duty. Serving you coffee and buying gifts for your wife or friends are not. If your assistant or secretary offers to bring you coffee every morning, fine. Just don't *expect* it. On the other hand, I believe a polite secretary or assistant *should expect* to perform this task when you have visitors, or when you're absolutely swamped with work and can't spare a moment. You should have discussed such matters with your secretary before you hired her. If, during the interview, she resisted the idea with the same fervor your cleaning woman manifests when you mention washing windows, you never should have hired her to begin with. Good manners are reciprocal. If a secretary or assistant doesn't have them, get rid of her.

Although no secretary should be asked to buy her boss's personal gifts, it may be appropriate for her to select gifts for business associates or clients. If she has good taste and you value her judgment, by all means send her out shopping one afternoon.

As the boss, you also have a right to tell your secretary how to answer your phone. Make sure, however, that what you tell her is correct. And consider any suggestions she may have without dismissing them outright. After all, she may know more about telephone etiquette than you do. By all means instruct her not to grill your callers. There is nothing more irritating than having a strange voice insist, "Please tell me the nature of your call." The very most your secretary should say is, "Mr. Jones is unavailable right now. I'm his administrative assistant. May I help you?"

Remember, National Secretaries' Day is like the Fourth of July to some. If you happen to have a "patriot" for an employee, it's not just good manners but good sense to extend a special thank-you to her in the form of flowers or a lunch in a good restaurant.

DEALING WITH FEMALE BOSSES

From all I can garner from research and the many interviews I conducted with male managers for this chapter, female bosses are pure gold. By and large, they are ladies—in the most constructive sense of the word—or they wouldn't have gotten where they are today. Therefore, it shouldn't be hard to play the role of gentleman with them.

Women—especially women bosses—are people first and female second. When dealing with women bosses, keep your dialogue and body language on an asexual plane.

Even if you couldn't resist that once-in-a-lifetime wink at your secretary or the receptionist, make sure you never engage in anything remotely resembling flirtation with a female superior. Such behavior is out of order, insubordinate, and grounds for dismissal.

In the highly unlikely event that a woman boss flirts with you, make light of it and carry on in the same neutral way you always do. If, because of some beguiling change in the sequence of the moon, your boss should make an overt pass that you foolishly accept, my advice to you is: Resign or get a transfer—immediately. Even if the encounter is never repeated, the mere fact that it happened will, henceforth, confuse your role identities hopelessly. The next time she tries to reprimand you for a job poorly done, the mental image of her submitting to your physical advances may flash before your eyes. Instead of accepting her criticism as a vehicle for self-improvement, you'll act like a betrayed lover. It will never work. The relationship can never be recast in its former mold.

The only occasion that warrants some show of maleness on your part is when you find yourself acting as your boss's escort on a business trip. In this situation, you should be more chivalrous, the rigors of travel being what they are. Carrying luggage when porters aren't available and hailing cabs simply become extensions of your regular job. Fulfill such duties graciously. Be formal and polite, never fawning and unctuous.

BUSINESS ROMANCES

Since it's already come up, something more should be said about the controversial subject of sexual relationships with women you meet through business.

Suppose you have an appointment with the account executive at your company's advertising agency. Waiting in the lobby, you strike up a lively conversation with the receptionist. You've talked to this woman on other occasions and, as usual, you have a friendly, easy rapport. Somehow, the chat evolves into a discussion of rum drinks and daiquiris for which you've recently developed a passion. The receptionist finally screws up her courage and suggests you drop by her apartment tonight and try her special rum concoction. She adds, "Surely, your wife won't mind if you're only one hour later than usual."

What do you do?

I wouldn't categorically advise you to refuse the woman's offer just because you met her in a business context. After all, sociologists claim most of us meet our mates in everyday encounters—at the office, in supermarkets, at the laundromat. I wouldn't even tell you to refuse her offer because you're married. This is no place to debate the pros and cons of extramarital affairs. What I will do is give you a checklist of issues to consider the next time you're confronted with such a tempting invitation. The checklist will force you to weigh the risks you'll be taking should you opt to plunge ahead:

• The marital status of both parties. (In our hypothetical example, let's say you're married and she's not.)

• The strength and importance of your business relationship. (Your business ties are practically nonexistent.)

• The frequency of your encounters. (Say infrequent.)

• Your business status relative to each other. (Your status as an executive far exceeds hers as a receptionist. Even in this supposedly enlightened age, it's less complicated psychologically if the man's status is greater than the woman's.)

• Mutual business relationships that mitigate against your budding romance. (Few in this case. As a receptionist, she neither works on your company's account nor knows well any of the people who do.)

• The woman's reason for transforming your business relationship into a social one. (It appears to be sexual, since she assumes you're married.)

• Your reason for transforming a business relationship into a social one. (Also sexual, since you love your wife. It's always best when both parties' goals are the same.)

Those factors plus the usual male-female considerations—mutual attraction, common interests, rapport—are the types of things you should ponder before you do anything you'll both regret. Keep uppermost in your mind the trade-offs: What will I be gaining to compensate for possible damage to my professional image? Will a one-night stand with my boss' secretary be worth it if the end result is a strained relationship with my boss and office gossip that brands me a "womanizer," "cheater," or, worst of all, a man guilty of sexual harassment.

THE SEXUAL HARASSMENT DILEMMA

Getting involved with a female business associate who shares your enthusiasm for the idea is one thing. Trying to wrest sexual favors from a totally disinterested or hostile female colleague is something else. In this day and age, it's downright suicidal!

In case you haven't heard, sexual harassment on the job is now against the law. It's a violation of many state laws as well as Title VII of the 1964 Civil Rights Act; and there is a growing body of case law where women have recovered damages from employers under these laws and guidelines.

What is sexual harassment? According to the federal Equal Employment Opportunity Commission, sexual harassment is "unwelcome sexual advances, requests for sexual favors and other verbal or physical conduct of a sexual nature." Such actions become illegal if a woman's response to "such conduct is made, either explicitly or implicitly, a condition of employment . . . is used as the basis for employment decisions . . . or when such conduct has the purpose or effect of substantially interfering with work performance or creating an intimidating, hostile or offensive working environment."

When working women are asked to define sexual harassment, the definition is even broader and more specific. It includes male conduct ranging from simple leering and vulgar remarks to outright physical attacks. They also mention sexual propositioning, the most typical form of harassment, as well as spreading rumors that women who resist are lesbians.

The large number of working women sensitized to this issue, together with the laws on the books, combine to make for an extremely volatile contemporary office environment. Since most of the lawsuits so far have been instituted by women, it's hardly surprising that working men and women disagree on the extent of the problem. Two thirds of the men surveyed in the 1981 joint *Redbook Magazine–Harvard Business Review* study thought the amount of sexual harassment in the workplace is "greatly exaggerated." Only one third of the women agreed.

This may be changing. A *Time* magazine survey concluded that it's becoming harder and harder to tell who is chasing whom around the desk, a theme underscored in a current TV sitcom, "Bosom Buddies," in which a female executive was the sexual aggressor. Either way, sex in the office is no laughing matter.

THE MIXED-SIGNAL MORASS

Clearly, it's unrealistic to depict the majority of modern working men as sexual aggressors and the majority of modern working women as their innocent victims. "Innocent" is hardly the word to describe a number of career women today. "Confused" would be more accurate.

There are ambitious career women who can't decide how to relate to their male colleagues. They behave as if professional ambition and femininity are, somehow, mutually exclusive. They give off one set of signals with their bodies and another with their mouths. Beware! Women who give off conflicting signals are dangerous, especially if they're your professional peers or co-workers. In my opinion, such women should be required to wear scarlet letters spelling T-R-O-U-B-L-E on the lapels of their tailored suit jackets. Since they aren't, it's up to you to spot them. If you develop any sort of sixth sense in business, it should be the sense to steer clear of these latter-day Jezebels. I have nothing but contempt for the businessman who harasses, blackmails or otherwise pressures businesswomen for sexual favors. In contrast, I have nothing but abject pity for the businessman who gets caught in the pseudo-liberated businesswoman's web of mixed signals.

THE GENTLEMEN'S GENTLE PUT-DOWN

No matter how rude or bewildering you find a female business associate's behavior, my advice is to remain the gentleman always, even in this *un*gentlemanly age. Don't attempt lectures on consistency in thought, word and deed; don't throw temper tantrums. Both tacks are bound to backfire. If you can't rise above the incident, I recommend the gentle, rather than the strong, rebuff.

True Davis, the U.S. Ambassador to Switzerland in President John F. Kennedy's administration, is one of the most courteous individuals I know. He remains a gentleman even when he encounters a woman who is not a lady. One day when the elevator doors opened, he stepped aside as usual to allow the women in the rear of the car to exit.

"Mumble, grumble," said one woman, with a sneer on her face as she pushed by him to get out first.

"Pardon me," he said as he stopped her. "I didn't hear you."

"Mumble, grumble." She repeated her indistinguishable, but obviously nasty remark.

"Oh, I'm sorry. I thought you said, 'Thank you,' " was Ambassador Davis's only comment as he turned and walked away.

BEING A GENTLEMAN WITHOUT BEING A CHAUVINIST

Chauvinism is patronizing behavior toward women. Don't be guilty of it. Do continue to observe many of the following tried-and-true points of general etiquette toward women, whether they're businesswomen or women you date.

Entrances and Departures If anyone—male or female—approaches you when you are seated, you must stand. Standing is a form of greeting and makes the person approaching feel invited and welcome. Standing when they leave is also expected, particularly if the setting is a social one—a restaurant, cocktail lounge, or living room—or if the departure is in the nature of a long goodbye. In office settings, obviously men cannot be bounding out of their chairs every time a female passes. Nevertheless, it's courteous to get up for any person whom you do not see frequently.

The Handshake A gentleman never offers his hand to a woman unless she offers hers first. And when and if a woman does offer her hand, the compliment shouldn't be returned with either a limp wrist or death grip. A firm handshake somewhere between the two will do just fine.

Elevator Etiquette What True Davis did is still correct male behavior. Because he was standing in the front of the elevator, he stood aside to let the women in the back of the car exit first. However, if this is awkward for some reason, by all means exit first. The rule of thumb is to do what is most expedient.

Doormanship Again, it's a matter of expedience. I think whoever reaches a door first should open it, unless it's a heavy door that requires a strong shoulder. Then, the man must shoulder the burden. Also, if a woman arrives at a door and waits, she's clearly signaling her male companion to do his manly duty. Some women still expect this courtesy. Others don't. Take your cues from the woman in question.

The same advice applies to car doors. If it's convenient and obviously not out of your way, good manners dictate that you open the car door for your female companion. If you're already seated in the car as she approaches, you should reach across the front seat and help open the door, just as the polite woman reaches over to unlock the door on your side if she is already seated inside. However, it's a different matter when exiting. Here, men and women should get out of the car on their own. Anything else places you in the role of "doorman" or "chauffeur," both undignified and unnecessary.

On the Street Good news, men! It is no longer *de rigueur* for you to walk on the outside nearest the curb. Carriages no longer splash mud on ladies' frilly frocks. Nor do servants throw slops out of overhanging, casement windows into the gutter.

I once knew a man so indoctrinated to this outmoded principle that he would actually take flying leaps to reposition himself properly. He would fall behind his female companion for a brief moment, then rush to catch up with her on the opposite side. Watching this maneuver, one got the impression that the woman was a parade leader and the man a drum majorette doing a twirling routine in her wake.

Coats   Yes, help her on with hers. She may even return the favor and do the same for you.

Chairs   It's still polite for you to help a woman with her chair in restaurants, or any place where the chair poses a problem for her.

Cigarettes   It's the rare woman today who waits helplessly for a man to light her cigarette. However, it's still a gracious gesture when a man offers. Most women will be delighted to take you up on it.

If you are in a restaurant or other public place with a woman and you take out a pack of cigarettes, offer one to your companion. If she declines, ask her if she minds if you smoke. Only the woman with severe allergies will ask you to refrain. Save your cigars for stag parties.

WHEN A BUSINESS RELATIONSHIP TURNS SOCIAL

When the occasion for meeting a woman is purely social, you may find that the assertive colleague you know from the office has suddenly adopted a more feminine/passive posture in her relationship with you. Her softer demeanor must not be misinterpreted, at least initially. It's not a signal for you to become Harry He-Man or start condescending to her. Remain civilized and polite and observe the social niceties.

When calling for her, it is polite for you to go to her door. (I'd do this even if I were picking up a male friend.) Never honk your horn for her to come out. Incidentally, it's perfectly all right for your date to pick you up in her car. Don't be threatened if she offers. Take her up on it if it's more convenient.

Although it's courteous to ask your date if she has any preferences about the evening's activities, don't leave the decision to her. Many professional women spend all day making decisions and are relieved when their date takes the initiative after hours. If she has no preferences, outline your suggestions. She may want to make further suggestions or modifications. Let her, then come to some mutually agreeable plan of action.

If a formal dinner party at someone's home or a club is the evening's fare, make sure you inform your date well ahead of time so she can dress appropriately. Keep in mind that protocol is still more old-fashioned and rigid at such affairs than in other circumstances.

Escort your date or the woman nearest you into the dining room and wait until all the women are seated before you seat yourself. The woman to your right is considered your dinner partner. Thus, you are responsible for holding her chair when she approaches or leaves the table. If the woman to your right is the hostess at the head of the table, then the man to *her* right, in the guest of honor's seat, should attend to her chair. The guest of honor is also responsible for the woman to his right.

Toasts are common on such occasions. If you're proposing one, you should stand erect and hold your glass high. If you are the person being toasted, neither drink from your glass before or after the toast nor stand during the toast. You'll cut a dashing figure if you can reciprocate with a toast of your own.

If you're attending a dance, be sure to ask your date or wife to dance first and then your hostess. It is no longer necessary to ask every woman present to dance unless you genuinely wish to do so. When walking to the dance floor, the man precedes the woman. (This type of "leading" is also expected when you are accompanying a woman to theatre seats.) When dancing, lead your partner around the floor with the subtle pressure you exert from your right hand at the small of her back. Don't crush your partner in a close embrace unless she's signaled her willingness. Take your cues from her.

THE ULTIMATE GENTLEMAN

You have achieved the nirvana of gentlemanly behavior when you are capable of being a banker with bankers, a mechanic with mechanics, or even a thief with other thieves. In effect, I am advocating being all things to all people.

While most of you will simply adapt the etiquette rules I've laid down in this chapter, a few of you may be able to achieve that rarefied plateau where you become totally sensitive and responsive to what the other person expects in the way of manners. The professional and business worlds are so large and heterogeneous today that ideas about appropriate behavior run the gamut. With the woman's movement still very much extant, what is in or out, expected or not expected, courteous or chauvinistic changes constantly. Therefore, you will be prepared for all situations when you've developed the kind of sensitivity which allows you to use as grand or as bland manners as the other person wants or expects. This could even mean affecting what you would normally consider bad manners to please the people you're with. But if this out-of-the-ordinary (for you) behavior is expected, you'd be correct.

Marjorie Merriweather Post, the Post cereals heiress and doyenne of high society, was the ultimate gentlewoman in this regard. At one of her many formal dinners for foreign dignitaries, her guest of honor committed the audacious faux pas of drinking from his finger bowl as if the warm water were soup. What did Mrs. Post do? Why, she followed suit, of course. The guest of honor never knew he'd done anything wrong.

Etiquette for the 1980s demands that you make others feel comfortable and never out of place. Working with the principles I've outlined in this chapter, maybe you can help bring chivalry out of the doldrums of the 1970s, and, once again, the words "gentleman" and "lady" will emerge from the closet to become synonymous with the care and concern so vital to our individual and collective future success.

11

MAKING YOUR BODY LANGUAGE SAY WHAT YOU MEAN

by James G. Gray, Jr.

"**B**ody language" is the popular term for nonverbal communication. It refers to a wide range of silent techniques for communicating—facial expressions, posture, hand and body movements. This category of nonverbal communication is called "kinesics." A second category is called "proxemics" and refers to the ways in which a person uses space; how he or she arranges and interacts with the environment.

In the last twenty-five years communication experts have increasingly emphasized how much people depend on both kinesics and proxemics to get a message across—or, conversely, to interpret a message from someone else. With all this emphasis on nonverbal communication, you may have the idea that the ability to read other people's body language and manipulate your own is the magical key to success in all interpersonal situations. While I'm not willing to go that far, I do think an understanding of body language is important to ambitious people, particularly people in jobs requiring them to interact constantly with others.

The business world—indeed, everyday life—provides a laboratory for studying people engaged in all manner of nonverbal communications. Daily we encounter people who are communicating feelings of power and submission, affirmation and negation, truth and deceit through their body movements and use of space. We also give out such information by the way we move and use space. An understanding of nonverbal cues is important because it enables us to interpret more accurately the behavior of others. It augments people's verbal messages, providing us with insight into their true attitudes, emotions, personality, and status. An understanding of nonverbal behavior also helps us give off accurate signals as to our own feelings and attitudes. If a knowledge of nonverbal behavior can help you "read" others, the reverse is also true: it can help others "read" and manipulate you.

Ray Birdwhistell, a respected authority on nonverbal communication, estimates that in a typical two-person conversation, the spoken message conveys *less than 35 percent* of the total message, while the unspoken message conveys *more than 65 percent* of the total message. Moreover, in a business setting such as an interview, nonverbal cues may carry as high as 80 percent of the total meaning. That's why a thorough understanding of body language is important.

Having said that, let me interject two disclaimers. First, body language, or kinesics, does not exist in a vacuum. Pop sociology books and articles on the subject tend to describe and interpret people's body language without any consideration of the verbal message or environment in which the communication is taking place. Body movements are usually accompanied by spoken words and take place in settings that also influence the total message being conveyed. Interpreting someone's body language out of context, that is, without considering the verbal and environmental cues as well, is to *mis*interpret what is being communicated.

Secondly, there is no correct or incorrect interpretation of body language or proxemics. What is correct is largely determined by the persons involved, the setting, and the specific situation.

The suggestions made in this chapter are merely an attempt to guide you to cues that you can put to effective use in your professional and everyday life. They are based on nonverbal-communications theory, as well as on my experience as a professional image consultant working with ambitious people who are concerned with appropriate public presentation.

LEADERSHIP: SILENT POWER IN MOTION

Deciding whether leaders are born or made is like debating which came first, the chicken or the egg. Although that question has no definitive answer, we can observe the qualities that make a leader. One obvious characteristic is the ability to communicate, a trait in which body language plays a major role.

Who in your company or organization or purview projects a leadership image? Note that the people you single out project that leadership image not only through their body language (facial expressions, posture, gestures) but through the way their offices are arranged, the way they dress, and through their ability to command attention upon entering a room. It's an awe-inspiring image of authority and control, and nonverbal behavior plays a major role in it.

Perhaps the most readily distinguishable characteristic of a leader is deportment—posture, stance, and movement. The military, long aware of the importance of good posture and bearing, goes that extra mile to instill erect posture in all new recruits. A steady, even stride when a person walks is another silent indicator of confidence and power. To earn other people's respect, an alert, responsive posture when greeting others or leading a meeting is extremely helpful.

Dr. Dave Archer, the author of *How to Expand Your S.I.Q. (Social Intelligence Quotient),* delineates a cluster of behaviors he calls "the power script." This power script dictates how a person acts in certain settings with certain people. For example, a boss interacting with a subordinate in an office might put his arm around the underling's shoulder. The subordinate, however, wouldn't dare do the same and put his arm around his boss' shoulder. Both parties know and understand the gesture and what it conveys. They don't even think about it on a conscious level. It conveys the message that the boss has power and the underling doesn't. A boss is also more likely to interrupt a subordinate in midsentence while the reverse seldom occurs.

The dominant-subordinate relationship is similarly demonstrated in spatial distancing. The boss—or any power holder—is afforded more latitude in the way he uses space, and may actually crowd a subordinate to get him to change his opinion. Yet, very few subordinates would ever get very close to their boss—or someone with greater authority— during a conversation in an attempt to persuade. Instead, the subordinate would probably stand away from the boss and maintain rigid eye contact while he talks. The boss, on the other hand, may or may not maintain eye contact with the subordinate during the subordinate's monologue or when he delivers his own monologue. Because he has more power, the boss does not have to look the subordinate in the eye or even listen attentively.

The foregoing gives you examples of power transmitted through both kinesics and proxemics. To help you learn to use nonverbal signals to your advantage, the next section will deal with the separate components of body language—your facial expression, eye contact, head movement, arm and hand gestures, and posture.

YOUR FACIAL REACTION IS WORTH A THOUSAND WORDS

Of all the body signals, facial expression rates among the most revealing. Your face is your ambassador to the world. While a stone face may be perfectly acceptable for the four U.S. presidents carved in perpetuity on the side of Mount Rushmore, it won't do for you. In this age of executive informality, a stone face in a professional setting would be lethal.

Ideally, your face should be mobile and reflect your character, credibility, and emotional well-being. People who do have mobile faces find that their facial reactions are a dead giveaway to their true feelings. And their overall facial expression when they walk into a room gives others important clues as to their general emotional condition. How often have you heard someone comment, "Are you all right? You look pale"; or "You look puzzled"? A shuffling motion of your feet didn't tell them that. Your face did.

While a mobile face is an asset in today's world, it is only an asset if you can control it. Your goal should be to showcase your positive feelings on your face, but to disguise your negative feelings unless letting them show will help you get something accomplished. In short, know your goals in any situation and use your facial expressions—and other body movements which we'll discuss later—to achieve those goals.

Unless you have an immobile, expressionless face, you'll find controlling your facial reactions isn't easy without some practice. Retaining a calm look during a stressful situation (such as meeting a new boss or speaking before a gathering of angry stockholders) or a direct one-on-one confrontation (say a heated discussion about a raise) is difficult. Your reaction is involuntary. Your lips tense, your forehead wrinkles, your brows arch, and your eyes glare.

Understanding the reflexive muscular structure of the face is the first step toward controlling your facial expression. The lower half of the face is striated with muscles. Just like muscles anywhere else in the body, facial muscles, without regular exercise, tend to lack coordination and strength. Actors know this and attend facial-exercise classes to learn to control their reactions, as well as eliminate sagging chins and unsightly jowls. As a professional, you are something of a performer too, and should also learn how to emote with your face.

Making grotesque contortions helps relieve facial tension and increase muscular resiliency. Open your mouth wide and stretch your face. Move your mouth from side to side. Clamp your mouth shut and raise your chin high. Such movements will strengthen your facial muscles and afford you more control over them. A brief facial-muscle workout immediately before a speech or tough interview works wonders for tension release—as well as for making you look more alert. Tense lower-facial muscles contribute to a stilted look and garbled speech. Neither will make you appear dynamic or credible.

Nothing creates easy rapport like a smile. Not a smirk, nor the wide grin of a clown, but a natural, comfortable, ordinary smile. To find the smile that's best for you, stand before a mirror or video monitor and move your lips in various smiling positions until you find the one that looks natural and feels right to you. The smile is your passport to open communication with others. Practice it until it becomes second nature, the warmest gesture you can muster.

The upper face is more difficult to control because the muscles around the eye and brow tend to work involuntarily. For instance, when you get a sudden jolt, notice how your eyelids close or your brow furrows automatically.

Again, a mirror is your tool for better upper-facial control. Spend some time in front of a mirror studying your face as you assume various expressions. When you find an expression you like and would find useful in your everyday interactions with others, hold it. Memorize the way it feels. Then practice that expression when you are alone, in the shower, or reading in your study. A repertoire of effective facial expressions that you can summon forth literally in the wink of an eye will be very useful as a managerial tool, particularly in communicating with subordinates.

Eye Contact

"Shifty eyes can't be trusted".... "I gave him the job because I felt I could trust him; it was there in his eyes."

These are oft-repeated expressions that bear an element of truth. We make value judgments about honesty and trust from a person's eyes.

Did you ever notice how strangers glance briefly at one another but then quickly look away? This is particularly noticeable in elevators where everyone stares at the floor-number indicator and not at anyone else. Eye contact among strangers defines their willingness to open up to others or, conversely, to avoid them entirely.

Eye contact in the business and professional world among peers, superiors, subordinates, and acquaintances is also very telling. For example, a direct, blank stare from a boss may freeze an employee in his tracks. As a rule, it's up to the superior to make and break eye contact. Should the low man on the totem pole take the lead in establishing and maintaining eye contact, he is liable to get a retort from his boss: "So what's the matter with you, Harvey?"

Appropriate eye-contact patterns vary with the situation. When you are talking to a group of people, direct eye contact reflects sincerity and credibility. It increases your trustworthiness. The opposite effect is created when you stare at the back wall as you talk or glance quickly from face to face. Jerky eye movements in any situation destroy credibility.

During a one-on-one interview, I recommend maintaining a high degree of eye contact, perhaps as much as 95 percent of the time, with momentary glances away. If it is a job interview and you are the interviewer, lead the interview by creating rapport through eye contact. Signal your interest in what the interviewee is saying with an easy, direct gaze. But be careful not to stare or overpower the potential employee with your eyes, particularly if you know you have piercing, J. Pierpont Morgan-like eyes.

As a job seeker, follow the employment interviewer's lead. As you answer questions, lean slightly forward and maintain direct eye contact. Avoid blinking your eyes constantly or, just the opposite, not blinking them enough in a fixed stare. A stare may be interpreted as an attempt to dominate. When posing a question, sit erect or lean forward and maintain eye contact to convey a message of control mixed with professional curiosity.

Head Movement

A young woman who participated in one of my seminars wondered why she wasn't coming across well in job interviews. We role-played an interview to find out. When she saw the video playback, she knew why: she was constantly throwing her head back in an attempt to get her long hair out of her eyes. Her bobbing head created the impression of a woman who was tense and overly agreeable. Her image lacked authority and confidence.

As a general rule, holding the head down—or looking down, especially to the left—signals submission. In contrast, holding the head up and steady signals just the opposite: you're your own man. If you tend to adopt a submissive head posture, change it by eliminating any excess movements, particularly downward movements. The reference to Britishers' stiff upper lip refers as much to the high, steady carriage of the chin as it does to the way they hold their lips.

FRAMING YOUR BODY IMAGE WITH ARM AND HAND GESTURES

Arms and hands, as extensions of the central body, have the ability to shape and frame your entire body. For example, arms or elbows held too close to the body signal tension. Arms folded across the chest may indicate an unwillingness to communicate, to open yourself to other people's ideas. And flailing arms while speaking or walking can signal awkwardness, even hostility.

The key to using your arms is to be natural. Hold both arms above your head, then let them fall naturally to your sides. The elbows will usually land six inches or so away from your rib cage. Now begin to move your arms as if to gesture. Look at yourself in a mirror. This exercise will help you develop free, flowing gestures that appear natural rather than contrived.

Your hand movements, subtle though they may be, make a startling impact on others, an impact that's usually subliminal, however. Hand gestures can signal openness, receptivity, determination, tension, scolding, and pugnacity.

For instance, exposing the palm of the hand is a gesture recognized the world over. Rock stars and international leaders hold their hands high above their heads, palms open, to greet admiring crowds. The gesture indicates openness and receptivity. We shake hands by offering our palms, don't we? In contrast, the back of the hand is a negative signal. We use the back of the hand to strike others, literally or figuratively, or to push unpleasant information away. The verbal command "go away" is reinforced when the back of the hand is held up. Celebrities, politicians, and other public figures use the gesture to keep fans or admirers at a distance. Other hand gestures—clenched fists, a hand held rigid in a slicing movement—are strong and should only be used to reinforce your most important points.

Avoid pointing your finger, even to emphasize a major point in your speech. Pointed fingers are the gestures of schoolteachers or parents who are scolding a child. In general, keep your fingers together when gesturing. A cupped hand gesture is sometimes effective, provided the fingers are bent at the same angle and remain together. Open fingers, whether open and stationary or moving independently, connote weakness, lack of control, possibly even frenzy.

Speakers often use too few gestures. Learn to use gestures to telling effect to drive home your important points. But never use gestures constantly like an orchestra conductor or your audience will start watching your hands and missing your words.

STAND TALL: POSTURE AND BODY MOVEMENT

Shuffling your feet and slumping when you walk give the impression that you are a nonentity, that you lack both confidence and self-discipline. One of my clients—a consultant in international affairs with an advanced degree from one of the country's most respected universities—had this problem. Even with his Ivy League background, he had never absorbed the value of walking tall and sitting erectly. And he wondered why he was having trouble commanding the respect of his peers. A short walk in front of my TV camera and a video playback gave him part of the answer.

By good posture, movement, and stance I am not suggesting you look like a West Point cadet. In fact, posture that is too erect and rigid will also create a problem for you—a bad back problem. When searching for the right posture and walk, let comfort be your guide. Do what feels right for your body structure. To get an idea about what looks good as well as feels good, stand in front of a mirror or video screen and shift your body weight until muscle tension in your back and neck is at a minimum. Then gently pull your shoulders back (think of making your shoulder blades meet in your back) and elevate your head slightly. You should have a sense of adding an inch or two to your height as well as feeling more comfortable.

Now practice walking by taking a few steps. Watch your stride in the mirror, keeping your pace deliberate, not halting. Deliberate movements reflect confidence and control. That's the image you want to project. Always walk with your head up, looking ahead, not at the sidewalk or floor.

Whether you're a job seeker or a manager trying to resolve an employee grievance, an inappropriate sitting posture that gives off a conflicting message can be a serious barrier to achieving your goal. Shifting feet, slumped shoulders, a bowed head will make you look nervous and submissive, quite the opposite of how you want to look in situations calling for sound judgment and assertiveness.

If crossing your legs feels comfortable, by all means, go ahead. Acceptable seated posture for men includes crossing one leg over the other at the knee or even placing an ankle over the knee. When both feet are on the floor, keep your knees apart.

TOUCHING

Cultural considerations generally determine who touches whom. For example, Muslim culture places a great deal of emphasis upon touch between men. Many business transactions among Arabs are conducted with the men seated very close to each other, perhaps with their bodies touching. When the Mideast peace negotiations were in progress, the news footage of Begin, Sadat, and Carter hugging and kissing each other gave ample expression to cultural differences on this delicate matter of touch between men. In many cultures, including the Muslim, men clutching arms as they stride along talking is a typical gesture.

However, touching in the American business and professional world follows a different scenario. It is either played down or avoided entirely. Perhaps it's a leftover influence from our Victorian heritage, but, as a general rule, males in business do not touch each other. The pat on the back for a job well done or a warm handshake when greeting someone are the exceptions.

Doctors counseling patients, a consultant with a client, or a boss with an employee usually don't touch the other person except as a strong signal of reassurance, confirmation, and agreement. Occasionally, one man may touch the upper body of another to break into his monologue in order to interject an important point. When this happens, the contact is made, most appropriately, on the arm or shoulder. When a male touches a female in a business context—other than to pat her on the back to signal good work or to shake hands—the obvious negative connotations can be placed on the gesture. Don't go around touching the women in your office. Given the current controversy over sexual harassment in professional situations, it's a dangerous thing to do.

THE TERRITORIAL IMPERATIVE

The term for how we use space and perceive the territorial movements of others is "proxemics." Much has been written about "the territorial imperative," how animals stake out and protect their space or territory. Humans engage in some of the same behavior but, with us, it's done on a subconscious, nonthinking level. The people who consciously think about such matters are the architects and urban planners who design buildings and lay out cities.

Status and authority are demonstrated in business, not only through a person's body language, but through the arrangement of offices, the furniture within an office, the wall hangings, the layout and design of conference rooms and reception areas. Whether employees in an office communicate effectively with each other and management and meet productivity goals partially depends on the crucial matter of office layout and design.

Surely you're aware of how status is demonstrated through the allotment of office space. The president's office is usually on a corner with windows on two sides. It's roomy and well appointed. Supervisors' offices, in contrast, are often in the middle recesses of the floor; many others are small and airless with no windows.

Similarly, the interactions between people in offices are, in part, dictated by the office layout and furniture arrangements. A man who arranges his office so that his visitors' only choice is to sink into low, overstuffed chairs more than ten feet away from his desk is a man who wants to dominate in any and all encounters. A training session conducted with students seated in a circle or semicircle, rather than in straight, rigid rows, is more conducive to creative interaction and feedback. A huge, open office where a pool of 250 clerks work side by side all day long is, clearly, a place where progressive ideas and individuality are discouraged. This is one reason why modern office planners insist on modular offices with dividers and screens. Such space planning makes a point: even the lowest clerk is a person with a distinct identity in this company.

SPACE STRATEGIES

You've probably heard people use such pop psychology phrases as "invading your space" or "give you your space." While they probably intended those phrases in the figurative sense, these phrases can also be interpreted literally. When a person invades someone else's space, he moves too close, or at least closer than is appropriate under the circumstances.

Good manipulators and deal makers are often people who know how to use space as a weapon, either to crush the opponent or bring him around to their own way of thinking. Here are some space strategies you should be aware of as an ambitious businessman or professional.

One-on-One Encounters

When you are interacting with acquaintances or relative strangers, closeness is seldom interpreted as a sign of warmth or friendliness—at least not in America. On the contrary, very close body distances may bring conversation to a startling halt as one person steps back and looks alarmed at the "invasion" by the other party.

Close distances are sometimes used by persons of high self-esteem but low authority to reinforce their own feelings of self-importance. An example is the man who sits next to you on a bus and tells you his life story even though you continue to read your newspaper. In the same way, people seeking approval often approach the boss, teacher, or other authority figure too closely, alienating rather than impressing them in the process. Salespeople often invade this intimate distance between people, thinking such closeness breeds a positive atmosphere. It may work if the person can be induced to buy through intimidation. Otherwise, such an invasion will probably backfire and make the potential customer angry and offended.

An employee who understands status demonstrates it in his use of space when he's interacting with an authority figure. When he approaches the authority figure's office door, he may stop outside next to the secretary's desk and try to catch the man's eye. When he does, he abides by the signal he gets—either to come in or wait there. Once inside the office, he waits again for a signal. Should he remain standing or sit down? The authority figure decides and chooses the chair. If the subordinate feels the authority figure has suggested too close a seating arrangement—signaling a closer relationship than the subordinate feels exists—the subordinate may, subconsciously, fidget in his chair or even move the chair a foot or two away.

The subordinate who ignores the spatial protocol of superior-subordinate interactions does so at his own peril.

Small-Group Encounters

Understanding nonverbal group communication is especially important today because so much work is now done in groups, committees, and work teams. Perhaps no other encounter better exemplifies how people display leadership, dominance, subordination, competitiveness, or cooperation through proxemics than the small-group get-together.

How could anyone over twelve years old in the early 1970s forget the extended discussions about the size and shape of the conference table to be used for the Vietnam peace negotiations in Paris? The haggling lasted almost six months. Why the big deal?

The size and shape of a table and how people are seated around it is more significant than most people realize, even if the subject to be discussed is trivial. The table's size and shape and the seating arrangement have a great impact on the actual meeting—how it is conducted and how it is resolved.

The Paris peace negotiators finally resolved their "table talks" by choosing a large, oval table. Would that savvy office planners followed their lead. But, unfortunately, most business conference tables today are still rectangular in shape.

An oval table creates a sense of equal status and open communication while the positions of authority and leadership at either end of the table remain intact. With an oval table, it's easier for all participants to see each other and make eye contact. Communication flows and there's less chance that any one person will dominate the discussion. On the other hand, this shape may encourage the group to engage in too much aimless banter, and force the meeting leader to exercise a greater degree of control to keep the conference on course, so as to cover the planned topics on the agenda.

Typically, business meetings are conducted around rectangular tables in the company's conference rooms. Where people sit around a rectangular table says a lot about the role they will probably play in the forthcoming meeting.

Seating positions around a table are culturally ingrained. In occidental countries, the father or other authority figure sits at the head of the table. The second in command sits at the other end.

Figure 11–1 depicts a rectangular conference table. The people seated in positions 1, 3, 5, and 7, around the table are likely to participate more in the proceedings and be more dominant because they are in the "power seats." Those in seats 2, 4, 6, and 8 are in the weaker positions, thus are less likely to contribute and demonstrate feelings of status and control.

This power scenario is played out regularly in corporate boardrooms. Board members almost unconsciously sit according to the unwritten power pecking order. The same is true when a U.S. president calls a staff meeting. President Jimmy Carter, however, often disregarded the expected conference-table proxemics. In an attempt to make meetings more informal and open, he'd often sit in position 3 at the table. Because he was the American president, perhaps the most powerful man in the world, his show of democracy, his stab at being "one of the people," didn't work very well.

What position should you select when you enter a conference room? If it's someone else's meeting, let the occasion and the status of the other participants be your guide. If the meeting is formal (a board meeting, say), bringing together a group of high-status people, you'd do well to choose a nonthreatening, lower-status seat, unless you intend to use the meeting as an opportunity to make waves. Otherwise, avoid especially the high-authority end seat directly opposite the leader. If

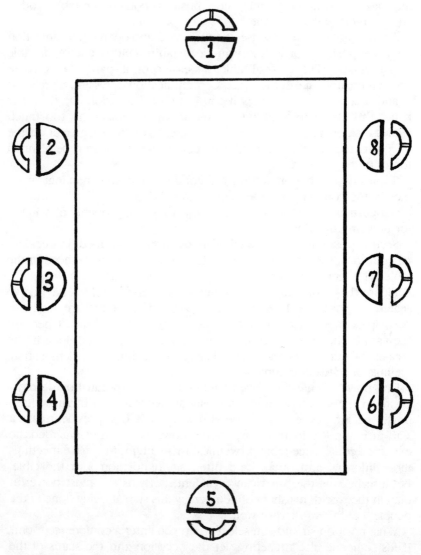

FIGURE 11–1. The people seated in positions 1, 3, 5, and 7 around this rectangular conference table are in the "power chairs." Those in positions, 2, 4, 6, and 8 are in the weaker chairs. (Art credit: Linda Tain)

you select this seat, you may find yourself cast in the devil's advocate role. When the leader wants some feedback, he'll seize on you as the most likely person with a well-thought-out opinion. But if you proceed to act out the role of "yes man" from that particular seat, you'll look ridiculous. One of the problems with rectangular tables is that communication flow is generally across, rather than around, the table. Thus, meetings frequently deteriorate with opponents debating viewpoints back and forth across in lateral Ping-Pong game fashion.

If you're leading the meeting, or among peers, feel free to take the high-authority end seat. Other participants will simply follow your lead. Like chickens, human beings also seem to have an inherent sense of pecking order. For example, if you are a member of a group that meets regularly, notice how the members tend to retain the same seat each time you assemble.

As meeting leader, you must be aware of the problems presented by the rectangular table. Draw out—with frequent eye contact or direct questions—the people seated in the low-status, low-participation seats. Calm down the more aggressive status-seekers in the more powerful seats by less direct eye contact, or by stating diplomatically, "Your ideas are always valuable and appreciated but I think we should give someone else a chance to offer some input." Then turn to a low participator and ask for his or her opinion.

Even if you find yourself seated in a weak position, you can insist on being heard by responding to and giving off appropriate verbal and nonverbal signals. People who assert themselves in such situations might interrupt, override an interruption, invite deference cues from others, or talk more often and at greater length than most other participants. Ideally, your goals would be better served if you behaved like this from a position of strength—seats 1, 3, 5, and 7—than from positions of weakness. In contrast, submissiveness cues include the following: allowing interruptions; being largely ignored by the meeting leader and doing nothing about it; or, when you do talk, saying less than most other participants. Unless you have a good reason for acting submissive, don't.

Interviews

Space cues are especially pronounced in job-interview encounters.

If you are being interviewed, enter the interviewer's office confidently. Walk tall and shake hands firmly—no limp or bone-crushing grips, please. Let the interviewer indicate where he wants you to sit. If he's got a huge, mahogany desk and indicates he's going to sit in his imposing desk chair and you are to sit in the chair facing the desk, do so. If there is a living-room seating arrangement in another part of his office and he chooses *not* to sit there with you, that tells you that he considers his status much greater than yours; or that he intends to give you a hard time.

Either way, stay composed. Avoid shifting in your chair, twiddling your fingers, frequent crossing and uncrossing of your legs, foot tapping or twisting, hooking your foot on a chair rung, or rocking in the chair. Every one of these movements makes you look nervous.

Should a man with a large office ask you where you would like to sit, choose the living-room arrangement. It's more informal, less threatening, and will open up channels of communication. Sit on the sofa or overstuffed chair accompanying it. Avoid a sitting arrangement where you are facing each other across a coffee table, if possible. This arrangement may work well for television interviews but I don't recommend it for job interviews. As the interviewee, you are liable to feel too exposed, on display, when there is only a low coffee table—or nothing at all—between you.

12

SMALL TALK IN BUSINESS-SOCIAL SETTINGS

by Catherine Gaffigan Nelson

One of my favorite cartoons shows a husband sitting in an armchair with a newspaper while his wife sits in a nearby chair, frowning deeply. The room is half filled with water. All the objects in the room—tables, lamps, bookcases—are floating. The husband is looking up nonchalantly at his wife and saying, "Of course, it will get you down if you keep thinking about it."

Rather than let you drown in worry about conversational limitations, this chapter will propose solutions to some typical small-talk problems. It will give you techniques to retrain yourself in handling social situations that might cause you difficulty. What it will *not* do is provide you with a list of snappy comebacks to repeat like a parrot. That's a mechanical, false approach to conversation, akin to painting by numbers. Within the framework I will give you, I encourage you to invent your own conversational rules.

SMALL TALK DOES MATTER

But why, you may ask, does it really matter whether I'm a good conversationalist? I have an excellent professional track record and

173

that's what *really* counts. This is true, especially if you are an engineer or other technical specialist who does *not* aspire to rise through the management ranks. Then you can remain tongue-tied and it probably won't affect your career. But if you are a manager of other people, or aspire to be, the ability to engage in light banter and make other people feel at ease is important. The ability to make small talk is also important if you want to impress executive recruiters. Many recruiters make a practice of placing candidates for any senior management job in tense social situations just to see how they handle themselves. Consider this: three minutes of awkward conversation, punctuated by long silences, is enough to make anyone feel uptight and uncomfortable and determined to avoid being alone with you in future. If that "anyone" happens to be an influential person who can promote your career, you just found out why small talk is not only important, but *very* important.

BE TRUE TO YOURSELF

The hallmark of comfortable communication with other people is *flexibility:* the capacity to listen, comprehend, and respond appropriately. In acting, this is called "being in the moment."

In order to achieve this flexibility, a man must be at one with himself—for better or worse—at any given moment. He must acknowledge to himself how he really feels, and not pretend to be stalwart and strong when he actually feels worried and vulnerable.

In short, *you have a right to your feelings.* During conversations—even with strangers—there is no need to allow your true feelings and opinions to be preempted by those of others. Nor should you try to alter what you say to conform to social convention. On the other hand, I do not recommend that you start an argument with everyone who holds views opposed to your own. After reading this chapter, I hope you will learn the art of conversational diplomacy—the ability to express even the most radical views while ruffling the fewest feathers. I will also give you pointers on how to steer conversations toward relatively neutral topics when this is warranted.

DO YOU LIKE YOURSELF?

A man's ability to engage in small talk is correlated to his self-esteem. In fact, strangers can get a pretty good idea of how you feel about yourself just by paying close attention to how you express yourself—in both form and content—in somewhat awkward or stressful small-talk situations. Surely, you've evaluated other people in the same way when you happen to meet them at a crowded beach or cocktail party, or during a convention.

In such situations, how do you come across to others? Ask yourself, "Am I poised? Do I appear relaxed and in control of myself? Are my comments appropriate or out of context? Do I express myself in a manner that is stimulating, interesting, and satisfying?"

If you answered no to a majority of these questions, perhaps your self-esteem, your confidence, is flagging.

BOLSTERING YOUR SELF-ESTEEM

Obviously, the more accepting you are of yourself, the more positive a person you will appear to be. Recall how you feel when you feel really good: rested, confident, alert, enthusiastic, energetic. When you're feeling that way, aren't you much more tolerant of others, much more secure around them, and don't you have better rapport? Clearly, then, your first priority should be to maximize the likelihood of feeling good about yourself all of the time.

So how do you go about transforming your negative feelings about yourself into positive ones? The first step is to plant some healthy intentions in your subconscious. Healthy intentions are ways of "talking to yourself" that will enable you to talk more positively with others. Healthy intentions make you buoyant and poised during conversation, not shrinking with fear, or hissing like a firecracker about to go off. (These are extremes, but not so uncommon as you might think.)

To aid you in doing this, buy a package of 3 X 5 index cards, plain or lined. Below is my list of healthy intentions. Write one on each index card. You can write your own intentions if you wish, but be specific and be brief.

1. I will not say (or do) anything that undermines my self-esteem, my professional standing, or my personal integrity.
2. I do not want to feel inferior, worthless, trapped, like someone else's pawn, anonymous, or devoid of human feeling.
3. I will not play any kind of role that minimizes my intelligence and/or my self-image.
4. I will ask for an explanation rather than allow myself to be intimidated, embarrassed, or ignored.
5. I will learn from my conversational mistakes.
6. I will accept the fact that every encounter is not a matter of life and death.

7. I will take more chances and try out some new conversational techniques.
8. What I most want to do is _____ .
   (Fill in the blank.)
9. If I had my way and anything were possible, I would like _____
   _____ .

(Fill in the blank and add three more intentions of your own.)

Take a blank card and write "Golden Dozen" on it. Place that card on the top of the pack. Carry these cards with you at all times. Look at each one individually and read the statements to yourself at least three times a day for the first week. If you look at them faithfully for a week, you will have memorized them without trying. Once memorized, you can review all or some of the statements in your mind without the aid of the cards.

Before long, you won't even need to think about these intentions on a conscious level. Your ultimate objective is to have your "Golden Dozen" take root in your subconscious, at which point they will become second nature, a part of you. That's when your feelings about yourself and your behavior will begin to change.

WORDS—THE BUILDING BLOCKS OF GOOD CONVERSATION

Conversation is accomplished through the use of words—words strung together in sentences that can be understood by other people. Obviously, the more words you have at your command, the better you will be able to express yourself.

You can test your vocabulary by doing the crossword puzzle in *The New York Times* Sunday edition or—if you're really brave—*The Times* of London puzzle. If these are unavailable, you can buy a book of *New York Times* puzzles. Another way to test your vocabulary is to watch some of the more erudite talk shows on PBS, the educational Public Broadcasting System. The nightly "MacNeil/Lehrer Report" is a good example. Listen carefully and write down all the words people use that you don't understand. If your list is long, you should consider doing any of the following: enrolling in an English composition class; getting a vocabulary book and learning five new words a day; doing the daily newspaper puzzle to get your brain working; or taking a reading comprehension course at a local university.

WHEN MEN TALK TO WOMEN: SOME DOS AND DON'TS

In conversations with women, particularly women who are strangers, many men revert to the traditional male role of decision maker. The man, not the woman, decides *what* they will discuss, the *depth* to which the subject will be discussed, and *how* it will be discussed.

For example, many men use conversation with women—both business acquaintances and perfect strangers—as an opportunity to adopt a courtly, condescending role. Such men add a sexual dimension to all encounters with women, no matter who the women are or what the situation calls for. When these conversational Romeos encounter a plain woman or one who is old enough to be their mother, they may try a patronizing mode of conversation: "How are you, Young Lady?" Believe it or not, I once heard a man in his mid-forties say this to an 85-year-old woman. On the other hand, when such men meet an attractive woman, they inject sexual innuendoes into the conversation even if the discussion concerns a serious subject: "You say your boss laid down the law with you. I wouldn't mind laying down with you myself sometime."

Another type of man may be overly concerned about projecting a masculine, invincible, knight-in-white-armor image when he is talking to women. He may try to police the subject matter of conversations with women, out of fear of revealing the chinks in his armor, his vulnerabilities. Or he may try to avoid showing any emotion, even when a show of feeling would be appropriate. He does this by keeping the conversation on an abstract, objective, or impersonal level. For example, a man who is afraid a recession may cause him to lose his job may open a conversation with the query, "Did you read the *Wall Street Journal* story about the layoffs in the automobile industry?" instead of saying, "I'm worried that this recession may hit too close to home...."

The conversational postures I have just described are nothing more than protective devices or insurance. They provide a man with protection against a display of vulnerability, and insurance that he measures up to some imaginary masculine ideal.

If you see yourself in any of the above examples, I suggest you read several recent issues of *Ms.* magazine. *Ms.* will acquaint you with the feminist point of view and related issues. You may view *Ms.* as the voice of the more radical feminists and, therefore, not worth your time and brainpower. Let me assure you that there are far more radical feminist views than those expressed in *Ms.* Also, you should be aware that a certain amount of feminist philosophy pervades most women's magazines today—even at the most fundamental level, in so-called home-maker magazines like *Woman's Day.* You are behind the times if you think the average woman still expects to be dealt with in a condescending, patronizing, or flirtatious manner just because she was born a woman and you a man. On the other hand, there are still women who trade on their sexuality, women who manipulate men by relying on all the traditional male responses and attitudes I've just described. Do you want to be manipulated in this way? If you don't, I suggest you stop manifesting sexist behavior and conversational patterns.

WHEN MEN TALK TO OTHER MEN: SOME DOS AND DON'TS

The conversational picture changes markedly when men talk to other men, however. Here power, competition, and one-upmanship come into play. Gloria Steinem, in an article "The Politics of Talking in Groups" (*Ms.,* May 1981), points out that in conversations with other males, many men use words as a kind of verbal swordplay. Some men, for example, see a conversation with another man as a competitive sport—someone wins, someone loses. They feel they must have the last word (literally) on a subject; or that their point of view must prevail. An open and democratic exchange of differing opinions for the purposes of general enlightenment, says Steinem, is *not* what such a man has in mind when he engages in a discussion with his peers.

Another male conversational mode is equally counterproductive. Again, men tend to do it only in the presence of other men. Here, a man takes the position that any conversation with his male peer group is a serious matter, even if the subject under discussion is the weather. Suddenly, this man's sense of humor vanishes (if he had one to begin with), his voice becomes monotone, and he restrains his body language, possibly by keeping his hands in his pants pockets as he talks. He may resort to "bureaucratese," or formulate his sentences in the jargon of his trade, or start substituting six-syllable words for one- or two-syllable words, all in an obvious effort to sound more important. This artificial display of importance is not only a waste of energy, it is also somewhat ludicrous when the subject of the conversation is the latest baseball scores or John McEnroe's epithets on the tennis court.

If you suspect you adopt either of the above practices in your informal chats with other men, you should immediately resolve to do something about it. Awareness of one's conversational defects is always the starting point for change. Try to stand outside yourself the next time you and your buddies meet for a drink after work, or when the men in your department talk informally before a staff meeting. Notice whether there is an ease and natural camaraderie among the group members; or if the tenor of the discussion is far more serious than the topic deserves. Check your own feelings as a participant in the discussion. Are you comfortable? Relaxed? What approach do you take to the subject? Super-serious? Moderately amused? Poking fun? Always adhering to either extreme—the very somber or the outrageously comic—indicates that you tend to hide behind a verbal pose rather than let the subject matter and the situation dictate how you will react. By following the advice and practicing the exercises in this chapter, you will find yourself becoming more comfortable in such all-male conversational situations.

HOW TO MAKE GRACIOUS INTRODUCTIONS AND REMEMBER NAMES

If you find introductions a trial, there are three things you can do to make them easier:

• First, recognize the purpose of introductions. They are simply one of the ways of bringing order to social exchanges. With introductions, we pass along information, establish bonds, and acknowledge respect for the individual: "This is Marie—she runs our office in Pomona"; or "George here is my brother-in-law from Connecticut; he's a skydiver."

The protocol for this exchange of information is easily learned and comes down to one guideline: The "lesser" person is presented to the "greater" person. For example: "Grandma [she's older], this is Charlotte [she's younger]." Or "Mr. President, may I present the mayor, the Honorable Mr. Koch." When you are introducing a man and a woman of about the same age and status, however, do whatever common sense dictates: "Mary, this is Edgar"; or "Edgar, Mary is the colleague I've been telling you about who is doing such a great job." Usually, it's simpler to name first the person who is standing closest to you.

• Second, when someone is introduced to you, *hear* what is being said and then immediately implement it. Whatever it is you think you heard, repeat it immediately as you shake hands firmly.

"Glad to meet you, John."
"Gene," he replies.
"Glad to meet you, Gene. Isn't the music loud!"

• Third, find a means of remembering what you just heard. You can associate the name you just repeated with another person you know with the same name—your college roommate, for example; or with a movie star, say Gene Kelly; or with some incongruous but very vivid image, the more ridiculous the better. Example: "George, meet Stephen." George then visualizes a gigantic hen taking huge steps around the chicken yard. From this mental picture, George can reconstruct the name Step-hen.

BREAKING THE ICE WITH A GOOD OPENER

A few years ago I was working for a film production company. One of the producers returned from lunch looking dazed and delighted. She sat down, sighed, and described how a handsome stranger had stopped her on the street and said, "There are a thousand questions I want to ask you." This statement flattered her enormously. Then, with her encouragement, he asked her a few of these questions—including whether she would be willing to meet him for lunch sometime.

Asking a question is the definitive, all-purpose icebreaker. The simplest way to initiate a conversation is to ask a personal question (not nosy—we'll get to that later). The possibilities are limitless, but basically you are saying to the other person, "What's going on with you?"— NOT, "How do you like *my* suit?"

Some more examples:

- Do you like it here?
- Are you enjoying your work?
- Do you look forward to these meetings?
- How has your family adapted to the move?
- Where are you from?

In acting we call this technique "putting your attention on the other person." What's good about it is that it completely eliminates the need for you to *think up* something clever. The other person is there as a source; for example: "Your outfit is really sharp looking"; "That's a terrific briefcase"; "You look bored."

On the other hand, you risk being a bore if you start telling stories in which you are the hero. Conversely, anecdotes in which the joke is on you have the opposite effect. Royal Little, an investor and entrepreneur for over sixty years, wrote a book called *How to Lose $100,000,000 and Other Valuable Advice,* which is replete with stories of his epic business failures. Little, a frequent lecturer, states that these stories are enjoyed by audiences much more than stories of his successes (which were also many). Self-deprecating humor can be extremely effective, *if the stories are true and you emerged triumphant in some way.*

As Barbara Walters warns in *How To Talk with Practically Anybody*

About Practically Anything, avoid "ponderous questions designed to demonstrate your penetrating intellect; the 'How do you feel about Book Four of the *Iliad*?' sort of thing."

Definitely do *not* say, "Tell me all about yourself," or "Tell me your life story." This has the unfortunate effect of putting the other person on the spot. Unless he or she is a total egoist, the question is more likely to inhibit conversation than encourage it.

PHRASES TO BOOST YOU OVER THE CONVERSATIONAL HURDLES

Theoretically, at least, you don't need any magical phrases to start a conversation—just an acute awareness of what's happening at the moment. However, it takes time and practice to develop this skill, and, realistically, you may be paralyzed by fears of various sorts in certain social and business situations. Or, a newly chosen conversational technique may not yet be an integral part of your vocabulary skills. Therefore, I've listed some phrases to help you over the initial hurdle. You can write them on a set of cards labeled "Phrases to Stay Afloat By." If you go over the cards regularly, these phrases will come to you automatically when you are under pressure.

- That's a wonderful dress.
- Do you enjoy big parties (like this)?
- What an unusual watch!
- You look very interesting (or appealing, mysterious, nervous, elated, etc.).
- What do you do for a living?
- Have we met before? You look familiar.
- I'd like to get to know you better. Can we have coffee (or lunch, dinner, brunch) next week?
- Could you give me the time?

Make up some of your own stay-afloat remarks—just be sure they are appropriate to the circumstances and reflect your true feelings at the moment.

SCRIPTING EXERCISE

Write yourself some "scripted" statements for the troublesome situations that are part of your daily routine. These mini-scripts need not be extended lectures but merely key phrases that will fit on your 3 X 5 cards. (Of course, for telephone conversations, you can actually have the "scripts" in front of you as you talk.)

Here are some samples:

- I see we disagree. Tell me your point of view.
- Your interest is very flattering, but unfortunately I'm just not available.
- Let's review the research because I've come to a different conclusion.
- I'm trying to maintain my sense of humor throughout this tirade, but, believe me, it's difficult.
- You've done a terrific job.
- Let's review the job description since we can't seem to agree where your job leaves off and someone else's begins.
- I can see the effort you've already put into this, but I'm afraid it will have to be reworked.
- What is your opinion?
- Please give me your ideas on how to make this work more smoothly.
- I want to discuss *my* financial needs for a moment.

RESPONDING TO NOSY QUESTIONS

The challenge of responding diplomatically to questions that you regard as inappropriate and rude may be met easily with some prudently prepared replies. Such questions might include: "How old are you?"; "Do you enjoy kinky sex?"; "How much did the Mercedes set you back?"; "What's your salary?"; "What's your rent?"; "Why don't you have any children?"

All-purpose replies include:

- I don't care to discuss that.
- Oh, I got a bargain.
- Are you with the FBI?
- (As a last resort) It's none of your business.

Mary Sanford, the leader of Palm Beach society, uses this comeback: "If you'll forgive me for not answering your question, I'll forgive you for asking it."

RECASTING YOUR CONVERSATION

A new behavior—in this case, a new way of responding in small-talk situations—is never acquired unless it is practiced. In fact, psychologists claim it takes twenty-one days of constant practice and reinforcement before a new behavior becomes a habit. So simply reading this chapter and understanding theoretically how you should change is not enough. Practice!

As you read plausible suggestions and listen to other people whose conversational skills you respect, pay close attention. Try out new conversational gambits. But don't try out everything at once. It's important that you arrange your new verbal responses in order of difficulty and experiment with them in that sequence: easy ones first, harder ones later.

Active participation—improved gradually through practice—is the only way to reshape the conversational patterns of a lifetime.

13

SUREFIRE WAYS TO MINIMIZE YOUR NERVOUSNESS AND RETAIN YOUR POISE AT ALL TIMES

by Dr. Shirley E. Potter,
with Helga Kopperl

People are always concerned about how they come across to others. For most of us, it's frightening to stand up in front of an audience in demanding situations. We are afraid that our "real selves" don't deserve the audience's rapt attention. When we wish to be our most interesting and engaging selves, we are paralyzed by the fear that, in relation to the audience, somehow we don't measure up.

There is no quick cure for nervousness. A leading magazine reported on a so-called miracle drug that is supposed to alleviate nervousness by regulating the heartbeat. The use of drugs or palliatives of any kind is extremely risky. They may be habit forming, and in no way do they equip you to find your own path to self-confidence. Most likely, in the long run drugs will only increase your feelings of inadequacy or awkwardness in stressful situations.

Like other methods of dealing with stage fright and anxiety, mine requires faithful practice—first while you are alone and then in an actual stress-producing activity. In brief, I believe that the best antidote to the poison of nervousness is to shift the focus of your attention away from self-defeating thoughts to:

1. yourself
2. the other people you are with
3. your surroundings

Most people have a limited view of themselves, as well as a narrow perception of their surroundings and other people. However, it is on these three areas of human experience—yourself, other people, and your environment—that you need to focus your full attention if you are to overcome self-consciousness, that painful sense of being looked at and judged.

FOCUSING ON YOURSELF

The following exercise will help you learn to focus on yourself. Work on it and make it your own. There is no one correct way to do this exercise—there is only the way that works best for you.

Exercise 1

The object of this exercise is to get you to take a careful inventory of what you are feeling in all parts of your body, and to describe which sensations are the strongest. This exercise can be done anywhere—before an important meeting, before you step onto the podium to give a speech. It can also be done in a standing as well as seated position. If possible, I recommend the latter.

1. Find a comfortable seated position in a straight-backed chair.
2. Arrange your clothing so that nothing is binding or distracting you. Close your eyes if you like.
3. Bring your attention to each part of your body, beginning with the head. Mentally scan your body, section by section—eyes, nose, lips, neck, shoulders, torso, buttocks, thighs, calves, feet. If you are alone, answer these questions out loud; otherwise, "think" the answers in your mind:
   • What is the most obvious sensation in my body?
   • Where are the tensions?
   • Are my muscles tight or relaxed?
   • Where is my body most relaxed?
   • How would I describe this sense of relaxation?
   • How do my clothes feel against my skin?

- Where are my clothes constricting?
- Where does the chair come in contact with my body?
- What parts of my body are supported by the chair?
- What part of my back is supported by the chair?
- Where is the bulk of my weight?
- Which part of my foot is touching the floor—the ball, the instep, or the heel?
- Is one foot touching the other foot? Where and how is it touching?

The more you focus on details the better. Too often people generalize about their bodies and concentrate on the theoretical rather than the specific. By doing that, they miss what is actually happening in their bodies and tend to dwell on negative thoughts such as "I slump a lot and that's bad," or "I'm so nervous I can't think straight."

These are interpretations of your sensations rather than statements of fact. In making interpretations of your experience rather than sticking to the specific reality of your experience, you bring on just the kind of self-consciousness you are trying to avoid. To interpret is to make judgments.

Rather than interpret, it is more constructive to "state the obvious" about your body. This means stating the impressions made upon the body by the five senses at the moment of perception. For example, "My stomach is rumbling," or "the sun feels warm." You will notice that when you focus on the concrete—the specific details of what you are actually experiencing in your body—you begin to relax and also quiet your mind.

By doing this exercise you learn to acknowledge what is going on in your body and to get in touch with what you are truly feeling. To be comfortable in your body you need to be aware of what is going on at all times. This exercise will also show you how to focus your attention when and how you wish. Knowing where to put your attention reduces feelings of helplessness and anxiety.

As I mentioned earlier, focusing on yourself is an excellent exercise to do before a stressful meeting or presentation. It can help you to locate areas of the body where you may want to work out tension with simple physical exercises.

HOME POSITION

"Home position" is the posture that people fall into when they are in a comfortable and familiar setting. Imagine yourself on a street corner having a casual chat with friends. The position that your body has taken naturally—without your consciously thinking about it—is probably your home position. Think of it as a kind of resting place for yourself.

While most of us fall into home position unconsciously, here is an exercise to help you find a comfortable home position consciously. Read the instructions carefully so you can remember them when you put the book down.

Exercise 2: Home Position While Standing

1. Find a comfortable place to stand.
2. Look carefully around you and notice your surroundings.
3. Ask yourself what is particularly pleasant about this spot that you have chosen.
4. Relax your body position until you are comfortable.
5. Out loud or to yourself begin to state the obvious in each part of your body. Be completely honest in your observations. Start with your feet and move slowly up to your head.
6. Focus your attention for a moment on the position of your body. At this point, you'll find that you've automatically found home position.
7. Memorize the posture by going over your body and noticing how each part is positioned. The greater the detail you attend to in your observation the better. Focusing on the details of home position locks the posture into "muscle memory" so that you can find home position rapidly even in times of stress. And, as in the first exercise, you are training your ability to focus on yourself without judgment.
8. Rehearse finding home position so that you no longer have to think about it.

You can use the standing home position to minimize self-consciousness whenever you're in a group situation. For example, most of us have at some time found ourselves among strangers at a cocktail party where we felt like a lion tamer who, without benefit of chair or whip, has been pushed into a cage full of lions. You can avoid this desperate feeling by simply taking the time to find a pleasant place for yourself in the room and then allowing your body to find its most comfortable position. This encourages a sense of ease that transforms all those "raging lions" into nonthreatening fellow partygoers.

Exercise 3: Seated Home Position

A seated home position is also invaluable for parties and informal meetings. The following exercise will help you find one:

1. Find a chair that looks and feels just right when you sit in it.
2. Put it in a place in the room where you feel most comfortable.
3. Sit in the chair.
4. Focus on all parts of your body in turn. How have you placed your legs? Is your back against the chair? Where is your neck in relation to the chair? Be complete in your examination.
5. Now get up and reenter the room. Before you sit down, focus on how your body was seated in that chair before. The more details you can remember the better.
6. Settle into home position in the chair. Notice how natural your position makes you feel.

FOCUSING ON OTHER PEOPLE

The second area of focus is other people—what they are saying or doing, their appearance, their attitude, the total impression you have of them.

As with focusing on yourself, the most important thing is to observe other people without interpreting what you see. With each encounter, keep a completely open mind, and you will be far too busy discovering new stimuli to worry about your nervousness.

Focus on those human characteristics of a person that you find most intriguing, whether it is the person's wild red hair, a direct gaze, or a generous mouth. The strongest stimuli for you might be the weakest for someone else.

STATING THE OBVIOUS IN OTHERS

Stating the obvious about your impressions of the other person is an easy way to begin a conversation with a stranger. No one can object to your interest when you are stating a fact: "I see you have a tan."

A more aggressive approach for the more secure is stating the obvious with your own point of view or opinion added. However, your opinion is an interpretation, so I don't recommend it. For example, you might say, "You have a tan. It's very attractive. It looks as if you spend a lot of time in the sun. I love the way a tan looks, but don't you think too much exposure to the sun can be dangerous?"

The other person's response might lead to an interesting conversation about the effects of the sun—or the person could turn his or her back on you and walk away. That's why it's safer to avoid making any judgment concerning the other person's way of doing things—at least at the beginning of a conversation, before you get a "feel" for the person.

State what is obvious to you; then, as you begin to feel more at ease, you can begin to ask innocent questions—"I see you have a tan. How did you get it?"—before venturing your own point of view.

EYE FOCUS

Looking into another's eyes is an invitation to intimacy in our culture. Thus, a more comfortable place to focus might be somewhere in the neck area so that, with a less sharply focused gaze, you can see the entire body of the person you're talking to. From time to time, you can switch from generalized focus on the other person's body to looking directly into his or her eyes. Alternate your focus so you don't become locked into a rigid focusing pattern. Experiment to find the style of focus that best puts you at ease.

FOCUSING ON YOUR SURROUNDINGS

Like focusing on yourself and on others, focusing on your surroundings is yet another tool to help you control nervousness. It directs your attention away from judgments about yourself and onto some useful stimulus in your environment. Also, a shared stimulus from the environment is often the only point in common that you have with a stranger.

Exercise 4

Here is an exercise that will help you focus on your immediate surroundings: State the obvious to yourself as you observe the room you're in right now. For instance, "I see the fruitwood chair with the flame-stitch upholstery. It casts a shadow against the wall. The window by the chair appears rose colored. The sunlight is dappling the curtains...."

This exercise should be pleasant and absorbing. Relish all the details. Do not make judgments about the condition of what you see, because this might lead you to think you have to do something to correct any defects—which will, in turn, lead to mental tension.

You should be able, with little difficulty, to apply this exercise to various real-life situations. For instance, let's say that you're at a cocktail party. After focusing on your surroundings during a tour of the apartment (which you made to make yourself feel more comfortable), you find yourself face to face with the hostess. She happens to be your boss and it's important that you be congenial.

In the dining room, you noticed a large photograph of a sun-drenched wheatfield by an artist whose work you admire. You state the obvious: "I see you have a photograph by Steichen. I really like his photography." Now you have something in common to talk about, something in your immediate environment.

A client of mine, who was raising money for a project to encourage the teaching of the arts in public schools, had been trying to interest an executive of a major corporation in the work of his foundation, to no avail. Leaving the executive's office, my client noticed some glorious photographs of a racing sloop hanging on the wall. Deciding to state the obvious, he said, "What beautiful sailboats! Are you the sailor?" The executive's face lit up. The esthetics of sailing could then have been an excellent starting point from which to convince the executive of the value of arts in education. However, it was too late in the conference for my client to use that technique, so he tucked it away in his mind for their next meeting.

As we look for the obvious in our surroundings, many interesting topics present themselves. I advise you to pick only those things in the environment that give you the most stimulus, since you will naturally be your most convincing and engaging self when talking about something that truly excites your imagination. Pretending something interests you when in fact it doesn't will make you feel uncertain of your ground and awkward in your presentation. When you talk about something that involves you, it acts as a tonic for both you and your audience. This is why it's important to present a topic at a business meeting that excites you or, if that's not possible, to find something in the discussion that you can make interesting to yourself. Never be afraid to show enthusiasm!

LETTING IN THE WHOLE PICTURE

"Letting in the whole picture" means looking at your environment and taking it in in a general way, eyes unfocused but resting in one place. (Eyes that dart around make you appear furtive and nervous.) This pleasantly passive way of gathering information allows stimuli to play on your sensory awareness. It enables you to notice things about the moment that you might overlook if you were focusing only on details. For instance, on a fishing trip, are you always the last person who tends to focus on details rather than the whole picture (for in order to see a fish jump out of the water you have to look at the whole lake with your full field of vision). If you put your entire focus on one area of the water, undoubtedly the fish will pop up somewhere else. The fish is a "detail." The lake is the "whole picture."

Letting in the whole picture gives you a truer sense of "feeling" about a place. In such a state of diffused perception, it is possible for the obvious to "jump up" and present itself.

This awareness of what is really going on can be particularly useful when you are speaking before an audience. Through it, you can get a sense of how your audience is responding. You will be more likely to notice people's body language and facial expressions. For instance, if the audience is paying attention, they may be sitting very still. Alertness is also displayed by a cock of a head or the forward thrust of the shoulders. To relieve boredom, people fidget.

A noted scientist friend of mine was addressing a group of pacifists about the advantages of nuclear power. Halfway through the speech, she sensed she was losing a large portion of her listeners because they were experiencing frustration at not being able to disagree with her immediately. In order to recapture her audience, she said to a large, restive woman in the third row who was fanning herself vigorously with a program, "I can see this is a hot issue, so I would appreciate it if you would remember just what you're feeling now so that you can bring it up during the question period."

By "letting in the whole picture," this speaker caught the fish as it jumped, so to speak. She then relieved audience restlessness by stating the obvious. It would probably have been pretty sticky going for the rest of the speech if she hadn't voiced the majority feelings of the audience. She also kept herself from becoming increasingly tense, flustered, and defensive.

STATING THE OBVIOUS TO AN AUDIENCE

If you feel you are losing an audience's attention, remember to state what is obvious in that situation. Observe without judging either them or yourself. Then act on your observation.

A former client of mine, a financial analyst, was giving a talk to a group of Wall Street executives at the end of a long working day. Everyone was tired and restless. Here is how my client described the situation and how he dealt with it:

> I arrived at five P.M. The businessmen were obviously keyed-up and weary. I knew I couldn't top their day or override their exhaustion, so I chose to acknowledge it. "Perhaps some of you

would like to loosen your ties and take off your jackets," I suggested. A few of them did. I also asked them if they wanted a few minutes to stretch their legs. They did, so we decided to postpone my talk for five minutes. The energy level started to pick up. I was so busy thinking of ways to help them be more comfortable that I forgot to get nervous or think about myself. I also found something in common with them and let them know I was very tired at the end of the day too, after my long flight from the West Coast. I felt I was bringing all of us in touch with the present moment and therefore that I was in control of the situation.

Another client of mine, an actress, was asked to be a panelist at a writers' conference. But she wasn't told the subject—"What's Happening in the Contemporary Theatre"—until the very last minute. As a consequence, this otherwise poised, self-assured woman was overcome with panic, although she managed somehow to say a few words on the subject despite her terror that the audience would discover she knew nothing about it. Her terror was actually irrational, since she had a sound knowledge of the theatre.

Later, I suggested to her several ways she might have stated the obvious in that situation, alternatives that would have put her—and everyone else—at ease. She could have said, "We were just given the topic of this discussion a few minutes ago. Let me see if I can share with you a few random observations about the modern theatre." Or, "I was just asked a few minutes ago to speak about what's happening in contemporary theatre. I haven't had a chance to think about it, but perhaps some of you have. What do you think is a common observation we can make about the theatre these days?"

By stating the obvious to an audience, we remove our own sense of remoteness from the situation and ask the audience to share what we have to say on a more personal level.

You can diffuse your own tension and nervousness by sharing it with an audience. You can state the obvious by saying, "I'm surprised to find that after all these years I'm still nervous!" Or, "This is my first speech and I'm a little nervous." Many in the audience will be familiar with your experience. They'll give you their attention because your admission makes you more real and human to them. You'll have used your feelings to establish a point of universal connection with the audience.

A universal connection is an experience that most people have had in their lives. It acts as a common denominator. For example, most people have fallen in love. Most people have forgotten someone's birthday.

Most people have been embarrassingly late, at least once, for a very important meeting.

How many speeches have you heard that start, "The funniest thing happened to me on the way here tonight," and continue with a personal yet universal anecdote that the audience can relate to immediately? "I was going down Main Street and I saw two taco stands. I had to stop at both and, of course, I ate too much. Now I have indigestion. But were they great tacos!"

If the story is true, if allows you to bring yourself into the present without trying to conceal what may have happened to you. Remember, your audience is human too and will empathize if you share honestly with them. Humor in which the joke is on you is often effective. After all, how many people with a facade of infallibility are fun to listen to?

Universal interest can unite a group of people who are distracted by the personal agendas they are running in their heads while you're talking. To shut off these interior monologues and bring the focus back to the podium, find a subject the group can identify with. For instance, if you're giving a speech at Christmastime, when everyone is rushed, you might acknowledge this seasonal pressure in your introduction. By doing so, you'll probably be articulating what a large number of people in the audience are thinking.

Universal interest can also be established if you know something about the town where you are speaking—assuming it isn't your hometown—and the people in it. You might also look for things in your life that are important to you and may be of general interest to your audience. But be specific, and select only those things that excite you enough to want to share. Have you just rented a new apartment in a town where apartments are hard to get? Found an offbeat way to beat inflation? Been stuck in traffic for several hours?

PREPAREDNESS

Preparedness is half the battle of avoiding nervousness, even if you never use a large part of what you've prepared. Whether the event is business or social, rehearse for it. Gather information. Find out as much as possible about the background of the place and the people you will be meeting. Before a party, your host or hostess no doubt will be glad to tell you a little about the composition of the guest list. You might even ask if there will be guests whom you might especially enjoy meeting. Every hostess likes to think she is bringing together her most interesting friends so that they may discover each other. Knowing something about a person beforehand will help you start a conversation.

If you are going to give a speech, check out the room where you will be speaking, beforehand if possible, and make sure that it has a table, a chair, or a lectern—whatever you need to make the space your own. Ask the maintenance people to place the lectern and/or microphone where they will work best for you. If you know what props make you feel more relaxed and know you'll have them available, it will be a great comfort to you. As you familiarize yourself with the space, practice walking into it and finding home position.

THE AGENDA

In order to be fully prepared, every speaker should have an agenda. An agenda is a plan, an outline of things to accomplish, a list of objectives. In preparing an agenda you decide what information you want to give to an audience and how you want to give it.

Bear in mind, however, that an agenda can't be effectively delivered if an audience or listener is not receptive. Thus, a good speaker is one who can time the delivery of his or her agenda so that it will be well received.

Here's an example of timing the delivery of an agenda in everyday life. An insurance saleswoman has just won the top selling award for the month. It's a trip to Italy for two. She rushes home to share the news with her twelve-year-old daughter. But her daughter, upset over a quarrel with friends, meets her at the door with tears streaming down her face. At the sight of her mother, she races upstairs to her room.

The mother goes upstairs immediately to deal with her daughter's problems. Of course, she will try to cheer up her daughter by telling her they're going to Italy together. But knowing when to introduce the good news is the mother's challenge. If she springs the news on her daughter too early, the unhappy girl will still be too preoccupied to respond with enthusiasm.

You face the same kind of challenge daily in the business world. You must prepare your agenda—or topics to be covered—carefully, and then allow the circumstances of each moment of the presentation to dictate when and how that agenda is to be delivered.

PUTTING IT ALL TOGETHER

There is, of course, no substitute for experience. In the following account, a client of mine—a Metropolitan Opera baritone who only felt comfortable when hiding behind a role—tells how he learned to use the foregoing techniques for controlling nervousness while being himself on stage.

> I was playing an engagement in Los Angeles in an outdoor amphitheatre, and just when I settled into my first song, an airplane flew directly over me, drowning me out completely. So I stopped singing and made a decision to say something to the audience, since we were both captives of the situation. I said, "Everywhere I go these planes seem to follow me and fly over just when I sing my high notes."
>
> It was such an absurd thing to say under the circumstances that everyone—including me—started to laugh. I felt a lot better and so, it seemed, did the audience, and I was able to finish the set of songs. But as I was leaving the stage, I tripped over a potted plant. This made it awkward for me to leave the stage, so I said, "I can't leave you after a performance like that, so I'd like to sing you another song."
>
> At that moment I happened to look up in the sky, just checking on the flight patterns, and I saw the most extraordinary sunset. Without thinking this time, I said, "Would you look at that sunset!" There was a moment of concentrated silence as they gazed at it, and I had a deep sense of communion with an enormous number of strangers who no longer seemed faceless. Then I sang my song.
>
> This time as I left the stage, I felt that the audience and I were a single organism, and I wanted to walk right out among them and shake all their hands. So I did. Several people had tears in their eyes. An old gentleman wearing a beret even gave me a big hug. I will never look upon an audience as something to hide from again.

All that I had taught him came into play in that one marvelous encounter. See if you can assign the following techniques their proper place in his story:

- Focusing on the self, the environment, or other people
- Letting in the whole picture
- Stating the obvious
- Choosing the right time to present an agenda
- Focusing on the strongest stimuli
- Using universal interest to build commonality

SHORT-RANGE TECHNIQUES FOR DEALING WITH NERVOUSNESS

Of all the techniques I know for overcoming nervousness and distraction, "reaching for details" is one of the most effective. When we reach for details, we examine an object or limited space acutely for its tiniest details. In the process, we exclude all distracting stimuli, whether external or internal in origin. For example, when you "reach for the detail" of a pencil, you notice its shape, texture, and varying shades of color. The more you look at that ordinary pencil, the more extraordinary it becomes. Stating the obvious to yourself, you may notice the yellow paint on the shaft of the pencil, the dent of teeth marks near the eraser, the way the light shines on the metal band holding the eraser.

As you're reaching for details, you become more and more involved in experiencing each concentrated moment fully—too involved to allow your thoughts to wander off to past or future happenings. Reaching for details can thus be used to steady your mind before and during an important presentation.

Next time you are waiting to "go on," focus on your hands in your lap. Look at your hands as if you were truly seeing them for the first time. The more you become absorbed in the details of what you are seeing, the less energy you will be putting out in the form of anxiety about your turn at the podium.

LONG-RANGE TECHNIQUES FOR DEALING WITH NERVOUSNESS

You would not try to read a book on natural childbirth while you were going into the delivery room with your wife, so don't try to learn these techniques the day of your presentation.

• Make two mental lists. First, list all the mishaps that could possibly happen, and then make a list of all the things that easily excite you any time you think of them: a sexual fantasy, for instance, or a favorite place. Now do this exercise: Practice making the transition from all the negative images on your mishap list to the positive ones on your second list. Do this three or four times in a row. It will take time to build up a ready bank of strong images that you can call up at will. Examine your positive images in great detail. Your goal is to replace negative images with positive ones, so work toward greater and greater richness of detail in your positive images.

• Sharpen your ability to focus by stating the obvious in yourself, your surroundings, and other people. You can do this anywhere—on a plane, at home, in the office. Practice five minutes a day.

• Practice the difference between "reaching for details" and "letting in the whole picture." Try combining them. To practice "reaching for details," pick an object or place and examine it with all your senses. Let one detail lead you to another so that your absorption is totally within the cosmos of that object or place. To practice "letting in the whole picture," fix your gaze anywhere and leave it there. See how much you can let in, using your full field of vision and your peripheral vision.

Practice all the methods outlined in this chapter. Through them you will become more confident, alert, responsive, and aware in circumstances where you previously felt uncomfortable and insecure. When you have learned how to focus your concentration, and have discovered the things that join you to your fellow human beings, nervousness and self-consciousness will dissipate, replaced by the strength of your involvement with life.

14

FOR LAWYERS:
Courtroom
Communication
and Comportment

by Sybil Conrad

The nonverbal world of the courtroom is the perfect illustration of the power of body language. To watch a seasoned trial lawyer in action is like watching a symphony conductor: Every movement is well-planned and executed yet looks so natural that the members of his figurative audience—the jury and witnesses—respond in the desired way without knowing why.

When I was a student of the theatre, long before I became a communications consultant, I learned that the various ways I moved my body helped me develop the character I was portraying. For example, soft, round gestures revealed happy, positive feelings, while sharp, jagged movements expressed anger, frustration, and annoyance. Today, lay people and professionals alike have become students of body language in their attempts to improve the way they communicate. But the universal language conveyed by the *un*spoken word is probably still best understood by the good trial attorney because so much of his daily dealings with other people hinges on his instantaneous ability to interpret the reactions and emotions of the jury and the witnesses under questioning.

The successful trial lawyer is also a man in control of his own body language. It's been said that our body language never lies, while the words we speak may be used to disguise our real thoughts and emotions. Since the circle of courtroom communication begins with you, the trial attorney, I suggest you begin your study of effective trial behavior by becoming aware of your own reactions to various situations. Do you know what you look like when you are relaxed and comfortable in a situation? What happens to your face and posture? Do your gestures change, become more fluid and open, perhaps? What about the opposite extreme—your negative reactions to a situation? What happens to your facial expression and body then?

If you can't answer these questions, I suggest you do what student actors do: spend some time studying your own facial and bodily reactions in a mirror. After all, a good trial lawyer is a performer. You must accept this statement as fact before you can expect to become successful in a courtroom. Moreover, when you understand your own motivations and body impulses better, you'll be more adept at interpreting the nonverbal world of the courtroom, with all its pathos and humor, its compassion and intransigence.

BODY LANGUAGE DOS AND DON'TS

All law schools offer courses in litigation and, as part of those courses, most instructors outline some elementary rules of body language. John Bartels is one of them. In his Pace University School of Law course in trial advocacy, Bartels introduces his students to the concept of nonverbal communication, covering such topics as how to approach a jury or hostile witness and how to address a jury when opening or closing a case. He applies the same acting gestures I learned as a neophyte actress. Here are some rules common to both the courtroom and theatre:

• Don't wave your hands about excessively. It will probably be interpreted as a sign of nervousness.

• Be especially careful to keep your hands away from the "fig leaf" area of your body. Clutching your hands down there is a sure sign of fear, insecurity, or both.

• Eye contact is your strongest form of communication. But don't abuse it by staring too long at one person, particularly a juror.

- Smile when appropriate. The smile is the most universal form of communication, but it may be regarded as insincere if it's perpetual.
- Bartels's most amusing rule could lead to disaster if ignored: Don't lean over the jury railing after a big lunch, particularly after you've imbibed a glass of beer or a hamburger with onions.

Henry Miller, a governor of the New York State Trial Lawyers Association and adjunct professor at St. John's Law School, has further advice for the inexperienced litigator:

- Don't do anything to make the jury uncomfortable. That includes hamming it up—being overdramatic in your use of your voice, facial expressions, or gestures. Miller says novice trial lawyers, remembering that some professor once told them to look directly at the jury, often overdo it and "stare them to death."

Miller feels, however, that many jurors will forgive a lawyer his excesses, if it's clear to them that the lawyer is simply acting out of his passionate belief in his client's case.

- Be definitive yet subtle in your use of gestures. Miller admits that his courtroom body language has become more restrained, more subtle, over the twenty-five years he's been litigating. He adheres to the advice he once got from a successful veteran lawyer: "You can make the same points even stronger with smaller gestures."
- Summing up, Miller says, "Don't do anything or wear anything that will distract the jury. It's hard enough to win a case on its merits."

APPROPRIATE COURTROOM ATTIRE

Throughout history, the public has distrusted lawyers. Over five centuries ago, Shakespeare portrayed them as villains. In the nineteenth century, Charles Dickens did the same.

Clearly, it's in your best interests as an attorney to try to dispel other people's cynicism about your character and motives. One step in that direction is to use your appearance and your wardrobe to maintain a low profile. All the practicing lawyers—both men and women—I interviewed in researching this chapter concurred: the understated Brooks Brothers-type suit is the safest bet. It's low key and doesn't call attention to itself.

Harvey Weitz, president of the New York State Trial Lawyers Association and editor in chief of *Trial Lawyers Quarterly,* points out that a lawyer, in choosing appropriate attire, should take into consideration both the ideological climate of the area and his client's demeanor. He says that in New York City courts, for example, you can show some individuality in dress, but not in areas further upstate. In Westchester

County, where the juries are predominantly upper-middle class, he maintains that it's better not to "stand out, or be too flashy." In fact, the farther upstate you go, the more conservative your appearance and entire demeanor should become.

"Certainly, don't look too affluent," Weitz advises. "In fact, you'd do well to fade into the woodwork in terms of your dress unless you want to distract the jury from an unprepossessing client. Then you may want to dress flashier."

FOCUS ON FEEDBACK

There are three dynamic factors at play in a trial: the people in the courtroom at any given time; the evidence in the case; and the law and legal precedents relating to the case. In this chapter, I'll concentrate on the first factor—people.

There are no fixed rules on how to communicate because people and situations are fluid, unique, and can't be predetermined. Thus, the key to effective communication in any situation is the ability to correctly receive and react to feedback from others.

The sensitive and *successful* trial lawyer has strong powers of concentration. Even while he is pleading a case and recalling all the appropriate facts and legal angles, he must remain alert to the nonverbal signals coming from the people in the courtroom.

HOW TO USE AND ASSESS BODY LANGUAGE DURING JURY SELECTION

Cases are often won during the jury-selection process. Knowing how to interact with potential jurors and to evaluate their nonverbal "remarks" is crucial for the ambitious lawyer determined to win his case.

In selecting a jury, Harvey Weitz recommends maintaining a low-key style. He uses eye contact to draw out jurors and emphasize that he is interested in their every word. He adopts an informal, nonthreatening manner and keeps the volume of his voice relatively low, to underscore that he and the juror are engaged in a one-on-one communication. If jurors clam up or have any difficulty in responding spontaneously—or if Weitz senses any hostility in their demeanor or the way they phrase their answers—he excuses them immediately.

Based on his experience, Weitz prefers jurors "who haven't been through the paces before, jurors who have not sat on cases tried by lawyers who may have antagonized them, consequently making them jaded or disenchanted by the whole justice system." In short, he feels first-time jurors are less likely to answer in clichés, indicating their open-mindedness and lack of fear.

THE TRIAL BEGINS

Your opening statement should be straightforward, outlining the facts. This is not the time for histrionics. Let the facts speak for themselves.

Henry Miller recalls a malpractice suit in which he deliberately described his client's injuries in the most understated manner possible. But the injuries were so horrible that his contrasting understated manner in describing them actually emphasized the horror. As he recited the list of injuries, he watched the jury for nonverbal signals. Sure enough, juror number four was growing whiter and whiter. At the point when Miller told how the surgeon-defendant had tried, unsuccessfully, to save his client's right eye, the juror nearly fainted and the judge had to declare a recess. This is an excellent illustration of how the facts—or, if you will, gory details—speak for themselves. No excessive body language or rhetoric was needed to heighten the drama.

Harvey Weitz stresses the importance of "scoring points" with the jury throughout the trial, and always maintaining an image that is simultaneously authoritative and respectful. Since most juries are predisposed to distrust lawyers, this image is doubly important. Weitz suggests smiling at specific jurors occasionally during a recess or making any other subtle gesture that will gain their acknowledgment in a positive way.

Once the case is under way, your ability to convey confidence, humility, courage, and sincerity—the quintessential traits of a good lawyer, according to Henry Miller—will have a great influence on the verdict. These traits can be expressed best by your grasp and use of nonverbal communication. Keep close watch over your performance: Are you using your voice to its most telling effect? Are your gestures helping or hindering you in making your points and drawing out witnesses? Are you moving about in the courtroom to keep the jury intrigued, alert, and involved?

If the presiding judge is not too formal, you may want to sit on the edge of the counselor's table occasionally in a relaxed pose. Like any change in the courtroom rhythm, it will help keep the participants awake. You can continue to "score points," even if it means raising your voice or pounding the table. *But always watch the jury for negative feedback.* The slightest grimace, expression of boredom, or aversion of eyes indicates jurors are reacting negatively, so you must change your

tack. Harvey Weitz recommends that you "Rouse them . . . with a positive approach."

First-rate trial lawyers can question witnesses and still sense how the
jury is reacting; a real expert adds the judge's reaction to the equation
as well. If he feels either the jury or the judge are annoyed with his
tactics, he backs off. He does everything in his power to keep both the
judge and jury on his side, since jurors often take their cues from the
judge—who also literally advises them on points of law.

Harvey Weitz likes to concentrate on the jury foreman—or whoever
he feels is most likely to influence the jury. He admits, however, that
there have been times when he's misread the foreman's reactions. With
a wry smile, he recalls a case he thought was going against him because
the foreman didn't like him or anything he said or did. To his utter
amazement, he won the case. Later, the foreman told him, "I voted for
your client in spite of you!"

QUESTIONING WITNESSES

There are conflicting opinions on this vital matter. Every good lawyer
has a slightly different courtroom style, just as good business executives have distinct management styles. Here are a few general guidelines
you can keep in mind as you develop your own unique style.

John Bartels instructs his Pace University law students to stand as far
away as possible from their own witnesses (friendly witnesses), so as to
give those witnesses the opportunity to project their voices and views
unhampered. In contrast, stand close to hostile witnesses to
intimidate—with your presence as well as your pointed questions.

On the other hand, Harvey Weitz says he makes it a rule *not* to
impose himself on witnesses, friendly or otherwise. If, under severe
cross-examination, it becomes obvious to him—and hopefully to the
jury—that the witness is lying, he dismisses that witness immediately.
There have been too many cases in the annals of American law where a
cross-examining lawyer didn't quit while he was ahead with a witness.
The witness then proceeded to lose the case for the attorney.

Most lawyers agree that when they are doing a good job questioning a
witness, they can tell by the reaction of the jury. The jurors seem to act
in unison. Their heads turn simultaneously, first toward the lawyer to
take in his question, and then back to the witness to listen to his or her
answer.

When questioning witnesses—even your own—give due consideration to Murphy's Law. In courtrooms, the unexpected can and often

does happen. If a witness gives a surprise answer, pretend it never happened. Never let your voice betray you. Your facial expression and body language must not reflect your surprise or annoyance. Even if you know you're not making headway with a witness, under no circumstances let the jury know that you know. If ever your own body language could work against you, it's now. Since body language never lies, this is the moment when a clever trial lawyer uses his thespian talents to the limit.

THE SUMMATION

In their summation to a jury, experienced lawyers realize how much body language comes into play. As a rule, they lean over the jury box to become part of the jury. However, this can be a bold move and not every juror likes it. If you lean forward and find the jurors moving back in their swivel seats, you know you might be in trouble.

There is a story of a well-known lawyer who, in his excitement, got so close to the jury he almost brushed against a juror. "I'll keep this trial going until December," the lawyer shouted.

The irate juror responded, "You won't keep me here that long, mister!"

Weitz remembers one of his own summations. Dramatic though it may have been, it had not prevented a juror from falling asleep and even snoring. The other jurors tried to awaken him, but Weitz reassured them with his usual confidence. "Don't wake him up. When the time comes, I'm sure he'll vote the right way." When the juror awoke, embarrassed, Weitz put him at ease. "It's okay, Mr. Phillips. We all know it's very hot in here."

As Weitz puts it, "Every lawyer is a salesman."

If you know you have done your job well, you can afford this casual banter with a jury. But if, by the end of the trial, you have not done your homework and not performed well, no end of humor can save you.

IMPRESSING JUDGES—A GREATER CHALLENGE

In courts where there are trials *without* juries, your effectiveness in communicating with the judge is basic. In fact, you must communicate so well with the bench that everything you say and do must indicate you are well prepared and in full command of your case. Judges are impressed by plain speaking and a down-to-earth delivery. If any outward trappings help with judges, it's a lawyer's observance of courtroom decorum and a touch of gray at the temples, a manifestation of an attorney's veteran status before the bar.

The atmosphere in juryless courtrooms is generally quiet and dignified. When you are only playing to one person—the judge—your performance should also be quieter and more dignified. When pleading your case before a "hot bench" (the slang term for the one-judge bench in the lower courts) be very careful of your body language. Never let exaggerated gestures and overblown rhetoric come between you and the facts. Judges want facts, not dramatics.

In the appellate courts, where several judges preside, you will have even less time to make lengthy, dramatic speeches. In the twenty minutes you will probably be allotted to argue your case, you have to marshal the facts and compress your powers of persuasion. You must also know how to deal with the barrage of questions that may come at you from the bench. In such situations, keep in mind the following communications techniques:

• When machine-gun-fire questions are coming at you from the bench, your success lies in your ability to listen and respond with deliberation. Not only listen, but give every indication that you're listening. Stand alert. You might bring your head slightly forward to signal your rapt attention. While a body that's too relaxed won't win you any plaudits from the judges, neither will a body so tense that you look like a West Point cadet.

• Enthusiasm for your case and your ready knowledge of the facts should show in your stance, your voice, and your assured manner.

• As soon as you move up to the podium, place your feet squarely on the floor, a sure sign that you are balanced and in complete control.

• Keep your body still and avoid the sway common in attorneys who have had little or no training in public speaking. To get out of the habit of shifting your weight continuously from one foot to the other, you might place your hand on either side of the lectern to steady yourself. But don't keep it there when you should be gesturing in order to emphasize an important point.

• There is nothing so distracting as a wavering voice to make your listener believe you are nervous or insecure. If your voice has a tendency to waver, try deep-breathing exercises. Concentrate on speaking in phrases. If you want to accentuate certain words, practice inflection—pausing before the word or raising or lowering your pitch to emphasize it.

Jack K. Colman, a respected New York City-based lawyer with the requisite touch of gray, recalls an experience he had in the Appellate

Division of the New York State Supreme Court. Given the situation, he felt he had to resort to the ultimate form of body language—physically leaving the courtroom—in order to make his point.

After being bombarded with questions followed by laughter from the judges, Colman began to feel that his case was not receiving the sober attention it deserved. He acted impulsively, almost instinctively, based on his many years as a trial lawyer.

"If it please the court," he interjected, "I believe there is one duty the court owes the respondent—to consider the respondent's brief and deliberate seriously before rendering a decision."

There was immediate silence. The minute all eyes were upon him, Colman dropped the brief on the table in a sweeping gesture—as dramatic as it was noisy—turned on his heels, and left the courtroom.

Fortunately, Colman's unorthodox behavior worked in his favor. Three weeks later, the Appellate Division decided in favor of Colman's client. This is certainly a good example of the dramatic gesture involving emphatic body language. However, I do not advocate similar behavior until a lawyer has had enough experience in the courtroom to develop a "sixth sense" about what will impress a judge or jury.

Colman used body language to his advantage another time during a conference in a judge's chambers. Colman was representing parents adopting a child. The natural parents were also present to sign the adoption papers.

In an apparent good mood, the judge offered, "It's a hot day. Take off your jackets."

Facing the judge stood the natural father, the natural mother, and beside her, Colman.

The judge looked directly at the young woman, who was only nineteen.

"Do you know that you're surrendering your child to adoption?"

She nodded.

"Do you realize that when you sign these papers, your baby will no longer be yours?"

Visibly shaken, the girl nodded again.

Raising his voice and looking even sterner, the judge continued his questions, each one more penetrating. Colman could feel the quivering body beside him. A glance at her ashen face warned him that in another second, she might change her mind or faint. And his clients might lose their claim to the baby they had loved and cared for during the past nine months, the required time before a couple can file a petition for adoption. Colman's only hope was to somehow distract this young girl from her absorption.

Instantaneously and deliberately, Colman jabbed her with his right elbow. "I'm so sorry," he said. "Did I hurt you?"

The mood had been broken. The girl came out of her stupor and made no response.

"Sign the papers," the judge said. And the adoption was complete.

Surely, another excellent example of body language working for a quick-thinking attorney.

15

DOCTOR–PATIENT RELATIONS: Self-Evaluation Checklists for the Concerned Physician

by Elaine Posta

All available statistics from the country's medical schools and medical associations indicate there will be a glut of doctors in this country in the near future. This trend is already manifesting itself in doctors' diminishing patient loads. The American Medical Association reports that its members had 112 patient visits per week in 1980, down from 122.7 in 1979 and 120.6 in 1978. However, the same survey shows that despite the drop, doctors' work loads have stayed about the same. Doctors spent 44.5 hours weekly on patient care in 1980, little change from the 44.9 hours in 1979.

More time spent with each patient is just one of the ways doctors in private practice are beginning to respond to the increased competition in the medical services marketplace. And the competition is sure to get more intense before it shows any signs of abating—possibly at the end of this century when the first members of the "baby boom" generation start flooding into the geriatric wards. Until then, the ambitious doctor would be wise to evaluate himself and his practice in depth to discover ways he can improve his relations with current patients as well as market his services better to prospective patients.

THE CHANGING DOCTOR-PATIENT RELATIONSHIP

Physicians are seeing a different patient from the one who came for treatment ten years ago. Today's patient is better educated about medical matters and his or her own body. The media continue to barrage the public with information about the latest medical treatments and procedures; nutrition; preventive medicine; holistic and orthomolecular health programs. The public also has ready access to more detailed data concerning the undesirable and long-term effects of various proprietary drugs. A curious layman can consult the *Physician's Desk Reference* or simply read the newly required "patient package inserts" that accompany pharmaceutical products.

These more knowledgeable and sophisticated patients frequently arrive in their doctors' office with concerns and fears that are difficult for the doctor to assuage. With much of the mystery taken out of medicine, doctors are no longer imbued with godlike characteristics. Instead, they may find themselves on the defensive with overly skeptical or even hostile patients who demand a full explanation of the treatment chosen to allay their ailment.

Contributing further to this role confusion between doctors and their patients are the warped and idealized portraits of doctors on television soap operas and prime-time serials. Dr. Kildare, Ben Casey, Marcus Welby, and Trapper John, M.D. are idealized miracle-workers. Their TV-world triumphs lead the public to *expect* superhuman prowess from their doctors, both during diagnosis and in operating rooms. Thus, the public is conditioned to believe that any time a "cure" is not effected or a symptom is not relieved, then the doctor must have goofed and should pay for it.

Superimposed on an already-tense doctor-patient relationship are other disturbing trends. There's a growing medical-consumer movement whose platform calls for "patients' rights." As a consequence, we have the doctrine of informed consent, and patients' use of the Freedom of Information Act to gain access to their medical records. Finally, there's the explosive rise in malpractice litigation.

As a consequence of these developments, many doctors are responding by practicing so-called "defensive medicine." They order expensive and often unnecessary tests and paint an alarmingly gloomy picture of possible adverse effects of therapy, or dire outcomes of surgery, simply as a method of self-protection. This exacerbates the situation even more.

Against this backdrop, it is the rare doctor today who remains unaffected by these changes. Indeed, many doctors are taking positive steps to adjust to the new medical environment. They are enrolling in courses to learn how they can adapt their practices to keep pace with contemporary societal attitudes. They are beginning to practice preventive medicine and encourage their patients to take responsibility for maintaining good health. They are hiring management consultants to find out how to run their offices better—streamlining administrative procedures and decreasing patients' waiting time while simultaneously increasing their comfort level. Some doctors are even taking courses to learn how to market their own services more effectively—and even advertise their services if necessary.

THE IMAGE FACTOR

In the past, doctors thought of themselves strictly as men of science. The notion that they, like other professionals, possessed a marketable "image" was not within their purview. Increased competition for patients has brought many doctors around on this issue as well. Today, the savvy doctor realizes that there are ways he can alter his image—the way lay persons perceive him—to make himself, his office decor, and staff more pleasing to current and potential patients.

Image consultants, myself included, approach an assignment for a doctor in the same manner as an assignment for any other type of professional or small-business person. We start with the doctor himself. We analyze him from the inside out: What is this man's self-image in his role as doctor? How would he like to be perceived by his patients? What's the reality—in short, how *is* he perceived? Finally, what changes can we make in this doctor's persona—his overall appearance, dress, body language, voice, and mode of communication—to bring his self-image in line with reality? Next, what changes can we make in those doctor-patient adjuncts—office staff and decor—so that they, too, are consistent with the image the doctor wants to project?

YOUR IMAGE: HOW DO PATIENTS PERCEIVE YOU?

Doctors are attracted to medicine for a variety of reasons. Doctors' attitudes, motivations, talents, and other attributes differ. As a consequence, individual doctors exhibit markedly different styles in the way they practice medicine. And very often, it is the physician's style rather than his ability that determines whether he is appealing to patients.

Many doctors are unaware of their own particular styles, which may be the same they had from the time they left medical school, or may be styles that have evolved over the years. Either way, it's important to know what style—or image—you project in order to decide: (1) whether you like that image, whether it fits the way you feel; and (2) whether all the ancillary aspects of your image—waiting room and inner-office decor, staff deportment, fees—are consistent.

The highly respected, personable, and enthusiastic patient-care advocate, Dr. Paul Rosch, is a leader of the movement to improve private doctors' relations with patients. As well as being the president of two professional societies (American Institute of Stress and New York State Society of Internal Medicine), he is a clinical professor of medicine at the New York Medical College and an editorial consultant for *Colloquy*, the journal of physician/patient communications. The magazine is recommended for doctors who wish to improve their patient rapport. (It can be ordered free from CPC Communications, P.O. Box 4010, Greenwich, CT 06830.)

Dr. Rosch has also sketched, in caricaturized fashion, the ten most common types of doctors. His descriptions are based on W. A. Steiger's article, "The Process of Primary Holistic Care," in the *Journal of Holistic Medicine* (vol. 2: pp. 137ff., 1980). Being as honest with yourself as possible, check off which type(s) you are, based on feedback you've gotten from others over the years concerning your practice style. Then go back and check the type you would ideally like to be:

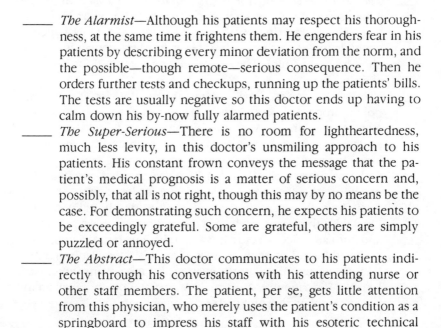

_____ *The Alarmist*—Although his patients may respect his thoroughness, at the same time it frightens them. He engenders fear in his patients by describing every minor deviation from the norm, and the possible—though remote—serious consequence. Then he orders further tests and checkups, running up the patients' bills. The tests are usually negative so this doctor ends up having to calm down his by-now fully alarmed patients.

_____ *The Super-Serious*—There is no room for lightheartedness, much less levity, in this doctor's unsmiling approach to his patients. His constant frown conveys the message that the patient's medical prognosis is a matter of serious concern and, possibly, that all is not right, though this may by no means be the case. For demonstrating such concern, he expects his patients to be exceedingly grateful. Some are grateful, others are simply puzzled or annoyed.

_____ *The Abstract*—This doctor communicates to his patients indirectly through his conversations with his attending nurse or other staff members. The patient, per se, gets little attention from this physician, who merely uses the patient's condition as a springboard to impress his staff with his esoteric technical knowledge. He's usually well versed in the latest medical procedures and sounds like a professor of medicine as he describes patients' physiology and biochemical makeup in the dense jargon of his profession. His diagnosis is, literally and figuratively, delivered over his patients' heads. But his staff admires him greatly. Does the unenlightened patient? Another name for this type: The Show-Off.

_____ *The Jolly*—This doctor is also out to impress—his patients, in this case. He's a man on top of the world. Each patient receives a booming verbal greeting, a hearty handshake, perhaps a slap on the back. The doctor's plush office trappings and his expensive, possibly custom-made clothes further attest to his success and importance. His patients are duly impressed. While warmth and congeniality on the part of a doctor are welcome, this type of physician may overdo it.

_____ *The Dour*—The exact opposite of the Jolly, this rumpled figure always gives the impression that he just lost his last friend. Complaining constantly, this doctor convinces his patients, nevertheless, that he will somehow manage to persevere and actually make a diagnosis and prescribe a treatment. He often appears extremely disorganized.

_____ *The Loving*—This doctor is on a first-name basis with all his patients and gives the impression that he's always at their service. His phone rings constantly. He thrives on his patients' dependence even though he's beset by their demands. Hypochondriacs love him. They're exceedingly grateful for his availability.

_____ *The Formal*—As the label implies, this doctor's style is formal, polite, proper, and standoffish. He addresses most patients formally as Mr., Mrs., or Miss. He may be constitutionally incapable of changing, for when he tries to loosen up and be one of the boys, his jokes—out of character and often off color—merely embarrass everyone. He's considered a moralist, although his patients and colleagues do respect him for his dignity.

_____ *The High Fee*—Nattily dressed in a superbly tailored suit pinched at the waist, he charges fees in line with his wardrobe—and with an office decor that was surely done by a decorator. He invites the kind of clientele who share his appreciation for the finer things in life. His time, energy, and money are showcased lavishly. His patients expect such demonstrations and may reciprocate by showering him with extravagant gifts for his services—

in addition to paying his high fees. This type could also be called the High Society Doctor.

_____ *The Crusader*—This intense physician is always advocating some cause, which may only be a passing fad. He waged a successful campaign against his patients' high-protein eating habits and now he's turned to recommending five-mile jogs as the answer to their—perhaps society's—ills.

_____ *The Mechanic*—This doctor probably missed his calling as an army sergeant. He's a busy nuts-and-bolts specialist who hasn't got time to "fool around." He instructs his patients to state their problem succinctly and cuts them short if they ramble on. His crisp examination is proof that medicine is a mechanical science, not a human art. Patients had better be prepared to accept his exacting medical instructions without questions or deviation. He's an authority figure and won't be brooked.

While Dr. Rosch acknowledges that these are extreme types, his stereotypes still describe certain doctors we all know. At the same time, many doctors are a combination of several of these general types. That's fine. Just know, in depth and detail, what kind of physician you want to be. Once you know this, you can assess whether your office staff and decor fulfill your image goals.

PATIENTS: WHAT TYPE(S) WOULD YOU LIKE TO ATTRACT?

A doctor may well want to factor into his image equation the type or types of patient he would ideally like to attract. Dr. Rosch gives a few examples of various types of patients.

One is the hypochondriacal patient, often female, who broods about every symptom and can never receive enough reassurance. There is also the aggressive, demanding person who knows it all and virtually practices medicine without a license; in this individual's view, it's your role simply to write out the prescription for the drug or treatment he or she has already decided is needed. Then there's the captain of industry, whose very presence intimidates everyone in the waiting room—including your staff. He immediately begins ordering your assistants around and takes possession of several telephone lines. He walks into the treatment room before being summoned and proceeds to tell you, the doctor, how busy he is so "let's get on with it." Of course, he'll be too busy to undergo any treatment right then, but since you're just another employee to be ordered about anyway, he informs you he'll let you know when he's ready.

The experienced doctor will have encountered these and many other types in his practice. However, a preponderance of one type of patient to the exclusion of others indicates that the doctor may be doing something to attract such patients. Analyze your clientele to discover if this is true in your case. If so, analyze why and decide what you could do to attract a more balanced, or even radically different, clientele.

STRIVING FOR THE IDEAL DOCTOR-PATIENT RAPPORT

Given all the potential and actual combinations of doctor and patient, let's examine the essential ingredients that go toward forging the ideal doctor-patient relationship.

How well you communicate with your patients has a lot to do with certain philosophical notions you hold. It's probable you've never articulated them to anyone, maybe not even yourself. For example, do you believe a physician's attitude and demeanor should be the same for all patients? Or should you alter your style to suit the patient sitting before you? If so, how flexible should you be? Where do you draw the line?

The bigger question, though, is whether there are common denominators that should universally apply, regardless of the nature of the patient's problem or the personalities of the participants.

All of the doctors I interviewed for this chapter believe that the ideal doctor-patient relationship is a partnership based upon mutual trust, understanding, and respect.

Are Your Relations with Patients Based on Mutual Trust?

"Obviously, the patient must trust the physician," says Dr. Rosch, "since the patient has placed his well-being, perhaps his life, in the doctor's hands. The patient must have confidence that the physician is competent and is continually acting with the patient's best interest as his first priority."

Unfortunately, it's difficult for patients to judge a physician's competence because they have neither the expertise nor have they done the comparative shopping among doctors that would allow them to make such an evaluation. Fortunately, a doctor can *earn* his patients' trust if he, in turn, trusts rather than patronizes them. Ask yourself:

_____ Do I listen to my patients' symptoms with an open mind regardless of who the patient is?

_____ Do I let my patients give a full account of their problem without cutting their explanation short?

_____ Do I treat my patients based on what they've told me—as well as based on what I think they've left out of their description? Do I probe what I think is missing?

_____ Do I take ample time with all patients so they don't feel like they're being rushed through an assembly-line operation?

Do My Patients and I Understand Each Other's Points of View?

"Effective two-way communication is the key to both solving the patient's problem and building an enduring doctor-patient bridge," Dr. Rosch believes. "A good doctor remains alert to feedback, verbal and nonverbal, from his patients. He motivates, rather than orders, his patients to follow his prescribed course of therapy by whatever means necessary. Each patient is unique. Some patients require cajoling; others must be commanded because orders from an authority figure reduce their responsibility for the outcome; still others want to be given good, solid reasons for choosing one course of treatment over another."

Ask yourself:

_____ Do I factor in a patient's age, social status, prior experience with doctors, education level, and emotional state in deciding the best way to approach him or her to elicit cooperation?

_____ Do I give my patients a full explanation of their problem in language they can understand?

_____ Do I offer concerned patients a full explanation of alternate courses of therapy and discuss the risk-benefit ratio, again, in language they can understand?

_____ Do I keep an open mind about forms of treatment a patient may believe in and want to discuss?

Do My Patients and I Respect Each Other?

Dr. George Hogben feels that his patients often have the answers to their problems and, with guidance from a doctor, can do much to heal themselves. In fact, the word "doctor" comes from the French root word "docere" meaning "to teach."

Dr. Hogben, founder/director of the National Foundation for Wholistic Medicine and assistant clinical professor of psychiatry at Mount Sinai Medical Center in New York, feels that many doctors have a tendency to get too serious with patients about their illnesses. He sees his mission as one of helping his patients develop a sense of joy about life. Along with Norman Cousins, author of *Anatomy of an Illness,* he encourages patients to laugh. He wants his patients to develop a lifestyle of awareness so they can interpret what their body is saying and use those signals to reestablish physiological harmony.

"Illnesses often strike people who have lost the meaning of life or people who are experiencing inordinate stress," says Dr. Hogben. "For example, many people see themselves as failures. That's their self-image. Should they suddenly experience a great success, this creates stress—disharmony in the system—because it contradicts their self-image. In such a case, healing becomes a matter of helping that patient rediscover who he is, his own inner person. Healing should be a joyful event."

Though there is certainly no pat formula that will engender a feeling of mutual respect between doctor and patient, there are certain attitudes that facilitate such a robust, productive relationship. Ask yourself:

_____ Do I present a professional yet approachable image?

_____ Do I believe lay persons are capable of holding informed opinions about their own bodies and the treatment of their ailments?

_____ Am I a role model for what I preach? (For example, do I refrain from smoking in front of patients while advising them to abstain? Am I an overweight doctor advising patients to lose weight?)

_____ Do I keep up with developments in my field as well as related fields and apply them in my day-to-day practice of medicine?

_____ Do I try to educate patients to take responsibility for their own health, offering them guidelines on preventive medicine?

YOUR OFFICE STAFF: ARE THEY YOUR GOODWILL AMBASSADORS?

Because patients encounter a doctor's staff members before they meet him, they're apt to enter the consultation room with preconceived notions about that doctor's capabilities. A doctor should make sure those preconceived notions are favorable.

Your receptionist, nurse, or technician is responsible for creating that important first impression with patients. Indeed, the initial impression is made when a patient calls to make an appointment. As in any business, a receptionist's telephone etiquette is the crucial public-relations link with the outside world. Does your receptionist answer the phone with a smile in her voice? She should be warm and friendly while maintaining a businesslike posture.

Your receptionist or secretary should be equally cordial when a patient calls to talk to you. You should establish a policy about such calls so your receptionist knows precisely what you expect. Orthopedic surgeon Dr. Bernard Jacobs tries to take calls from patients— particularly follow-up calls from patients who have just left the hospital after surgery—immediately. If he can't, he gets back to them quickly. He has instructed his secretary to place his telephone messages in a pile in order of urgency, the most urgent on top. Should a patient call to ask a question Dr. Jacobs has already answered more than twice before, he points this out to the patient and instructs his secretary to field future calls of the same nature.

When patients come to your office in an anxious or frightened state, your staff can do a great deal to ease their discomfort. Your receptionist and/or nurse should greet all patients warmly, *by name,* and make them feel special. Some small question such as, "How's your leg today?" shows concern and interest. On the other hand, your staff should stay in control of any interchange with clients. If a patient gets too chatty, interfering with a staff member's work, the staff member should politely excuse herself: "Mrs. Jones, I'd love to chat with you longer, but I've got to finish this for the doctor. Would you excuse me, please?" Having made a polite excuse, the staff member should break eye contact with the patient and resume work at her desk or pick up the telephone. If the patient definitely has another question, however, he or she should not be ignored. The staff member should indicate she'll get back to the patient in a minute.

Smiling, cheerful staff members brighten the atmosphere of the whole office. A receptionist should greet patients as they enter the office with a smile, and smile at any patient sitting in the waiting room whose eye she might catch from time to time.

Like yourself, your staff members should dress professionally, avoiding overly casual attire such as jeans or mix-and-match slacks and tops. If you do not require your staff members to dress in all-white uniforms, you should still insist they meet your dress standards. Dresses, skirts, or well-coordinated pants ensembles (I prefer dresses and skirts) are the most appropriate attire for medical receptionists. Doctors look the most professional *and approachable* in either a well-tailored and fitted white coat over a good pair of slacks; or wearing a blazer or handsome, subdued sports coat. Some doctors look good in a formal three-piece, pinstripe suit while others look too intimidating and businesslike to the average patient. The worst clothing offense is the doctor who showcases his mod wardrobe professionally. Such attire confuses patients because such a doctor doesn't look serious enough.

Needless to say, grooming is just as important as dress. Make sure the overall impression both you and your staff create is that of tidiness, conservatism, and cleanliness.

Dr. Robert Giller, a New York City-based doctor who specializes in nutrition and preventive medicine, has trained his nurse to act as his eyes and ears in taking down patients' complete medical histories *before* they meet him. It is also her job to make patients feel welcome by engaging in small talk.

If your nurse or receptionist is charged with this task, make sure he or she knows *exactly* what to ask, look for, and listen for during the patient interview. Conduct several dry-run interviews with him/her if necessary. Any staff member with this crucial assignment is an appendage of yourself. Make sure he or she knows what you expect, both in the way of information and demeanor. Also, make sure you take the time to read what your staff member has written down so you don't re-interview the patient—leaving the patient annoyed, and convinced of your office's general inefficiency.

WAITING TO SEE THE DOCTOR

In researching this chapter, I surveyed a number of friends and acquaintances to elicit their opinions of doctors—which ones they liked and disliked and why. Precious time "wasted" waiting for the doctor ranked at or near the top of their list of genuine complaints. Patients are no longer as *patient* about long hours spent in waiting rooms. *Their* time is valuable too, they feel; and they resent having it wasted, particularly if it happens consistently. If this is the case, the people I surveyed will frequently change doctors, or just give up needed treatment in a show of disgust because they cannot afford the time, aggravation, or tedium they experience in the reception room of some "disorganized" or "inconsiderate" doctor.

It's easy to see why a patient who is left to bide an hour's time in a crowded waiting room may label a doctor—or, by extension, his staff—disorganized or even greedy, especially should the patient discover that four other people sitting in that room also have five o'clock appointments. This is neither considerate nor efficient scheduling.

Dr. Jack Kern, a Manhattan dentist, has a practice that operates like clockwork because he and his staff make it a priority. His receptionist calls to confirm your appointment a day or so before, making you feel she and the doctor are looking forward to seeing you. If he has an emergency and gets thrown off schedule, the receptionist also calls and gives you the option of still coming and possibly waiting or rescheduling your appointment for another day. Should you, the patient, arrive considerably late for your appointment *without* calling first to see if appointments can be switched, you may be told firmly but politely that the doctor will have to see you on another day. Once I was a half-hour late for my appointment and Dr. Kern's receptionist gave me another appointment because my tardiness would disrupt his schedule and inconvenience other patients. Rather than being annoyed, I admired Dr. Kern for his solicitude toward his other clients. I was never late again.

If you are a surgeon or other specialist who frequently finds himself unavoidably detained, your staff becomes even more pivotal in your ability to placate disgruntled patients. If your receptionist has not been able to reach clients to warn them of a delay, then she must apologize for the delay upon patients' arrival, and keep them appraised of the situation continually. When patients understand the reason for the delay, they are apt to be more sympathetic than angry.

OFFICE DECOR: IS IT CONSISTENT WITH YOUR PERSONAL STYLE?

Dr. George Hogben is an example of a physician whose personal image and office environment are in perfect harmony. Both Dr. Hogben and his office are unpretentious, relaxed, comfortable, open, and completely natural. He dresses neatly but gives the impression that clothes aren't that important to him. You might call it that homey, college-professor look. He is non-judgmental, has a good sense of humor, and is easy to talk to. Patients tend to think of him as "my friend."

Dr. Hogben's inner office is equally functional and comfortable. In his office he has a small sofa, several wooden-armed upholstered chairs, an area rug, a well-stocked bookshelf, prints on the wall, and no draperies—the last in order to let in the maximum amount of light. It's uncluttered and pleasant.

In contrast, Dr. Robert Giller projects the opposite effect in both his personal appearance and office decor. Dr. Giller tends to look younger than his years, a trait that was not necessarily an asset when he first began to practice medicine. Thus, at that time, he sported a beard to attentuate this feature. Today, he maintains his professional image by taking the advice of his friend Halston, the famous clothing designer. In the office, he always wears a crisp white shirt with a blue tie and pants and a Halston-designed white coat. It is immaculately tailored and fits him perfectly.

His office is decorated in grays and whites and there is a feeling of spaciousness about it. The furniture has simple, clean lines and the lighting is recessed. The waiting room has a calming, almost antiseptic effect on patients. Dr. Giller's treatment rooms are equally attractive and sparse. Each has one small mirror, white walls, two plain chairs, and an all-white table in the middle of the room covered with peach-colored sheets. Here, too, the lighting is recessed, soft, and indirect. Just lying on the table waiting for the doctor could put you to sleep. The artwork throughout his offices contributes to the soothing environment. Dr. Giller designed his offices himself. They've been featured in *The New York Times* architectural section.

Although I think Dr. Giller has, in many respects, the perfect in age and office decor for a doctor, it is not recommended for all physicians. Consistency is the key here. Ask yourself, Does my office decor carry out the feeling I would like to engender in patients? Does it suit my personal style?

Here is a checklist of the minimal requirements every waiting room should meet. Beyond this, how much you decorate your office is a matter of personal style and taste:

_____ Is there enough furniture to accommodate the maximum number of patients I have waiting at any one time?

_____ Is the furniture comfortable and arranged in a way that insures a modicum of privacy?

_____ Are there enough magazines—current rather than two years old—and other diversions for waiting patients?

_____ Is the light adequate so patients can read?

_____ Is there an adequate supply of free brochures and pamphlets on general health, nutrition, exercise, or other medical subjects?

_____ Are the artwork, window, and wall treatments neutral rather than jarring?

_____ Does the rug on the floor muffle the sound of footsteps?

_____ If my practice includes children, do I have a separate section with games and puzzles to amuse them?

_____ Can the ambience of my waiting room be characterized as clean and relaxed, yet professional in all respects?

YOUR FEES: ARE THEY APPROPRIATE AND STANDARDIZED?

Many doctors try to avoid discussing fees with their patients. Dr. Rosch, for one, believes this is a mistake.

"The doctor-patient contract involves a financial transaction which may significantly influence the treatment program," Dr. Rosch points out. "Unfortunately, many doctors refuse to discuss the subject with inquiring patients. Instead, doctors refer patients to their office staff, who may treat the subject in a cold, impersonal fashion, rather than exhibit genuine concern about the patients' ability to pay or other financial contingencies."

In my own survey of my friends, this delicate issue of doctors' fees also came up. Some people said they resent it when a doctor recommends a long-term treatment program for them, but then refuses to estimate its costs, as if the expense were no object where health was concerned. To some patients, it is a vital matter, central to their decision whether to proceed with the doctors' program. Many people also told me that they're afraid to broach the subject of fees with their doctors, since they get the subliminal message that it's off limits, a topic that's embarrassing to the doctor—somehow beneath his dignity.

A more forthright attitude about your fees could make your patients feel much more comfortable about discussing alternative treatment programs with you. Similarly, office fee-collection practices should be clearly outlined to new patients, by either the doctor or his staff, to avoid any later misunderstandings or surprises when expected bills arrive in the mail. To ignore the fact that money has a profound effect on a patient's attitude toward you and your services is an equally profound mistake.

YOUR GOAL: BETTER PATIENT RAPPORT

Fortunately, there are, as I've outlined, many positive things a doctor can do to maintain or restore a good working relationship between himself and his clientele. In Dr. Rosch's words, "Any doctor who remembers to treat the whole patient, not just his or her illness, is a doctor whom patients will revere. Many times it is more important to know what kind of patient has the disease than to know what kind of disease the patient has. In the final analysis, the secret to being a respected doctor is in truly *caring* for your patients—and *showing* it."

PART IV

SPEAKING UP: PUBLIC-SPEAKING TECHNIQUES FOR ALL OCCASIONS

16

MAKING MEETINGS
WORK FOR YOU

by Jack McAlinden

Meetings are a fact of business life. This chapter will show you how to turn meetings to your advantage.

Whether you're chairing a meeting or attending someone else's, you should view any meeting as an opportunity to speak up confidently. Meetings are highly visible situations. You can make meetings work for you by putting on a star performance or you can come away from them embarrassed because of your poor performance—or worse yet, no performance at all because you failed to open your mouth once the entire time. The choice is yours.

Whether the meeting is large, bringing together your fellow department heads to discuss next year's budget, or small—you and your secretary reviewing the day's mail—a meeting always involves more than its ostensible subject. A meeting is a showcase for your management skills: your problem-solving skills, your planning and organizing skills, your time-management skills,your people-sensitivity skills, your delegation skills, and, of course, your communication skills. A meeting gives others the opportunity to see how you deal with your colleagues (i.e., your management style) and how well you transform ideas into action (i.e., your implementation ability). In other words, meetings give others the opportunity to evaluate your professionalism. This is true whether you lead the meeting or your contribution lasts thirty seconds.

The guidelines below suggest ways to improve your performance in each stage of a meeting, from initial planning through follow-up:

STEP 1: PREPARE FOR EVERY MEETING

This holds true whether you or a colleague convenes the meeting. You can't do your best at a meeting unless you know ahead of time why the meeting was called and who is going to attend.

Establish Goals

Whether you are the meeting leader or a participant, decide your business and personal goals for that meeting. Suppose you called a meeting of your peers and superiors to present your plan for marketing a new product. Your *business goal* is to get approval for your marketing proposal. Your *personal goal,* on the other hand, is to demonstrate your capabilities to your superiors, people who are in a position to influence the course of your career within the company.

Another example: Your boss has called a meeting to discuss ways to make his staff more productive. Your *business goal* is to offer several good suggestions, perhaps in written form, ready to be handed out at the meeting. Your *personal goal* may be to gain more responsibility and power within your department.

Making both your business and personal goals explicit to yourself will help you participate enthusiastically and remain attentive even in relatively dull meetings.

Analyze the Other Participants

To sell others on your ideas, analyze who those others are. Ask yourself:

• Whom should I invite to this meeting? Or who has already been invited?

• Who is the key decision-maker at the meeting, officially or otherwise? What are that person's preferences as to meeting time, place, and format?

• How important is the subject to the other participants? Who will be pro and con my ideas, and why? Who might feel threatened by them? Who may gain if my recommendations are approved?

• How can I present my ideas so that the maximum number of participants agree with me? What evidence will the participants find convincing?

Realign Your Goals in Accordance with Other Participants' Goals

Now that you've fully considered the preferences and prejudices of the other attendees, take another look at your business and personal goals for the meeting. Are they realistic and achievable given the participants and the time frame? If not, adjust your goals.

Consider whether other formats, in addition to or in lieu of one large meeting, might be more effective for achieving your goals. Could one-on-one discussions prior to a large meeting save time or build more support? Would a series of smaller group get-togethers be more productive? Also, consider whether these other formats and approaches would actually enable you to exceed your modest goals and achieve *more* than you originally intended. Again, adjust your goals accordingly.

Determine the Probable Outcome of the Meeting

In general, there are three possible courses a meeting can take: the desired outcome (from your point of view, that is), a neutral outcome, and an unfavorable outcome. Acquainting yourself with these three possible scenarios ahead of time will minimize the "surprise ending" factor. Because you have anticipated the range of outcomes, you can cope more authoritatively with whatever occurs.

STEP 2: DEVISE A MEETING PLAN

If you are chairing the meeting—or delivering a segment of it—you must formulate a meeting plan. A meeting plan has a beginning (the down-to-business opening), a middle (the agenda of points to be discussed), and an end (a decisive close).

Down-to-Business Opening

This type opening is straightforward and positions the meeting in the direction you want it to go.

John, for example, has called a meeting to recommend a new computer system to the company's data processing committee (his business goal). This committee moves slowly and cautiously and demands proof to support all assertions. John's boss—and his boss' boss, who designed the current system eight years ago—are on the committee, together with the heads of all departments that are dependent on the computer.

John has done a lot of research on the subject and wants to display it, at the same time building credibility for his recommendations (his personal goals). Below are two ways he might open the meeting:

Option One   "Good morning. I'm glad to see all of you here and complimented that you could take the time to join our discussion of the new computer system. Have we had a time with the Z140! As you know, it never worked. But I'm happy to announce that I've evaluated a lot of systems and found a great replacement. . . . "

Option Two   "We're here to decide on a computer system that best supports our growth plans for the 1980s. I'll review the changes in our computer needs, and then we can discuss how a revised Z140, and the new Z150 and A210, stack up. . . . "

Option One might be termed the "unplanned opening." John said whatever came into his head and, unfortunately, he wasn't particularly diplomatic about it. Option Two is a good example of a "down-to-business opening." It eliminates the chitchat and tells all assembled *why they're there.* You should never assume that everyone knows why the meeting was called. This opening also states *what they will get out of the meeting.* It incorporates John's analysis of the situation and avoids antagonizing one very important participant—John's boss' boss, the man who designed Z140 in the first place.

Agenda

The second part of a meeting plan covers the substance of the meeting. It is a detailed agenda—for your use only—listing all the points you want to make during the course of the meeting. The agenda lists the main points—or recommendations—and subpoints of your argument, presented in logical sequence; the desired outcome for each alternate recommendation; and the steps that would be required to implement each recommendation. Bear in mind that it's difficult, if not impossible, for any group of people to absorb more than four main points in one sitting.

John's meeting, in outline form, might look like this. (The roman type denotes the agenda that participants would receive; material in italic type would be on John's agenda only.)

OPENING

Purpose: to choose a computer system for the future.

Value of Meeting to Participants: enable them to review their computer needs and decide how the present system can be revised or replaced to meet those needs.

AGENDA

1) Brief overview of Z140's operating history.
   * the applications it was designed to fulfill.
   * the applications it does fulfill.
   * discrepancy between above two points.

2) Discuss present unfulfilled computer needs and future needs. Be prepared to talk about your specific needs. *As each department head speaks, write down his/her requirements.*

3) Discuss how Z140 might be revised to fulfill needs. Estimate cost and time required for revision. *List on a chart.*

4) Description of how the new computer system Z150 would meet the needs. Estimate cost and time required to install the new system. *(Visual aid: chart showing Z150's applications.) Ask for comments.*

5) Description of how A210 would meet the needs. Estimate cost and time required for installation. *(Visual aid: chart showing A210's applications.) Ask for comments.*

6) Agree on next steps.

Note that John chose to create consensus on the subject. He asked all the important users of the company's computer system to comment so that: 1) they would feel they were contributing to a joint decision, and 2) the designer of Z140 would realize the opposition to Z140, in its existing form, was universal. Instead of inviting others to speak, John could have made a formal presentation, outlining Z140's faults and extolling other systems' virtues but, having analyzed his listeners, he ruled out this approach.

When deciding how to present your agenda, ask yourself such questions as:

* What are the major points I want participants to remember after the meeting is over?

- What is the best way to support these major points—with visuals, statistics, open discussion, historical examples, quotes from experts, some other means?
- Where am I using too much documentation? Will it confuse participants, put them to sleep, turn them off? Where do I need more?

John distributed his agenda to department heads before the meeting for a specific reason: He wanted each department head to come to the meeting prepared to outline his computer needs.

Whether you distribute your agenda ahead of time depends on the topic, company practice, and how much input you expect from the participants. If the topic is complex, requiring some background before the average person understands it, you might circulate a short reading list or background report, asking participants to do some homework prior to the meeting. Conversely, if the topic is familiar and noncontroversial, you may not need an agenda beforehand.

If you *receive* an agenda for someone else's meeting, look it over thoroughly. If, in your opinion, the agenda distorts the facts or contains glaring omissions, you may want to bring that to the meeting leader's attention before you agree to attend. For example, suppose your boss has already agreed to create a more responsible job for you. In the new job, you will have a larger staff and do minimal traveling yourself. You thought your boss had already agreed to these conditions—until you receive an agenda for a meeting he is calling with you. The agenda includes discussion of a trip you will take to the Far East next spring and nothing at all about increasing your responsibility or staff size. This is a clear signal to iron out the misunderstanding with your boss *before* agreeing to such a meeting.

Decisive Close

End the meeting by restating the meeting's purpose and what the participants gained by attending. Finally, ask for action: state what you want the participants to do as an immediate follow-up to the meeting.

For example, prior to the meeting, John reasoned that no decision on the computer system would probably be reached after just one meeting. His desired outcome would be for the group to endorse system A210. That seemed unlikely. An unfavorable outcome—to revise Z140—seemed equally unlikely. The meeting actually resolved itself as John expected—somewhere between his desired result and a neutral outcome. After two hours, the group agreed that a new system was needed and that two of the three choices would not meet their needs. However, the remaining choice needed further investigation before it was adopted.

John was ready with an appropriate, decisive close:

> We met today to decide on a new system. We've reviewed our needs and determined that neither the revised Z140 nor the new Z150 system would work. The A210 should be evaluated further. I'll get the answers to your questions on A210 in time for our meeting next week. In the meantime, please let me know if you think of any additional questions for me to research concerning A210.

If John had not anticipated the probable outcome of the meeting, he might have been caught off-guard and delivered this off-the-cuff close:

> Well, I'm sorry you couldn't come to a decision today. I think the A210 is a super system and that we should have it. Let me know if you change your minds.

Compare the two closes. The first is strong, the latter is weak, making John look as if he failed in his mission to sell the A210 to the group. By anticipating a range of outcomes, John closed the meeting in control. He appeared authoritative even though he did not achieve his desired outcome 100 percent.

STEP 3: OPEN THE MEETING FORCEFULLY

The hour of the meeting arrives. If you called the meeting, deliver your down-to-business opening confidently. Avoid embroidering the two brief sentences that succinctly state the meeting's purpose and what the participants will gain from their attendance. Deliver your opening using appropriate gestures and physical skills. You may well feel a little nervous as you begin to speak; channel that nervous energy into your eye contact, gestures, and voice. Even an informal meeting is a public-speaking forum. Approach it that way.

Stance   This is one of the most important physical delivery skills. Whether you are conducting the meeting or participating, sit straight in your chair. When you speak, sit forward with your feet on the floor. Keep your arms free to gesture; don't let them rest limply on the table or chair arms. This is an alert position. It commands attention, makes you appear more enthusiastic and full of energy, and adds color (inflection) to your voice. When you're *not* talking, lean back in your chair, a gesture that signals others to participate. To regain control, sit forward again.

Eye Contact   Speak to each person as an individual. Use eye contact to make your points, by letting your eyes rest briefly on everyone in the room, even those sitting to each side of you. When there is one key decision-maker in the room, still include the others. After all, they may be key to the implementation of your proposal. Avoid staring at the tabletop, floor, ceiling, or your notes.

STEP 4: LISTEN INTENTLY TO OTHERS

Listening is a skill. It's a crucial skill in business because it enables you to evaluate feedback from others accurately. During a meeting, active listening will tell you how others are reacting to your ideas (and to your meeting plan) and give you the ability to respond appropriately, whether the overall reaction is positive or negative.

Most of us think we are listening any time we're not talking. This isn't necessarily the case. Although listening may begin when we stop talking, listening is an active skill that demands more than mere silence on our part. It demands self-discipline, complete concentration, and an ability to interpret what we're hearing.

Richard, a product manager, is an example of a person who didn't know how to listen. He was invited to a meeting, chaired by the company's director of marketing, and asked to present next year's marketing plan for his product. The director of marketing opened the meeting by reviewing the sales figures from the current year's campaigns. During the whole time the director spoke, Richard was staring at the ceiling, drumming his fingers on the table, and sighing deeply as he mentally repeated to himself his own opening remarks. In his justifiable concern with his own message, Richard not only lost sight of his personal goal for the meeting—to impress the other participants with his competence and professionalism—but also lost the support of the director of marketing before he even uttered a word. The director of marketing, alert to cues from others during his own presentation, noticed Richard's inattention and resented it.

Give Your Full Attention to the Speaker

Listen with your body as well as your ears. Look at the speaker, not the ceiling, the floor, the speaker's scuffed shoes, the pencil about to roll off the edge of the table. Looking at the speaker forces you to hear what he or she is saying.

Often people use note taking as an excuse for looking away from the speaker. Take notes if you must, but you shouldn't need to take notes continuously. Jot down a line or two, then put your pen down and resume watching the speaker.

Assess Other People's Mode of Communication

The most "persuasive" listening is based on awareness of other people's thinking and speaking habits. For instance, some people will probably agree with you if you let them interrupt your presentation and restate your argument in their own words. However, if you overreact to their intrusion—which might even be a rude outburst—you may defeat your own purpose, which is to get them to agree with you.

An example: Peter was presenting his reasons why the company should underwrite the costs of a new super-elegant package design for a premium perfume. Mary, Peter's boss, interrupted.

"Peter," she said, "all this looks great on paper but I'm really concerned about the cost. That gold foil paper would be the most expensive we've ever used and I'm not sure we can justify it."

If Peter weren't accustomed to Mary's style, he might have gotten defensive and said, "But I've shown how the upscale positioning of this product, using the new package design, will allow us to hike the price and actually increase our profit margin. What more could you want?"

Mary's retort: "I want something more than your pretty pictures and vague cost estimates before I agree to such a radical plan."

Ideally, Peter should have provided Mary with some breathing space. When Mary interrupted, he should have said, "Yes, this would be a major new step for us." (long pause) Mary's response: "On the other hand, I agree the change would result in higher profit margins if we position the product right..." (She pauses, thinking). "It's all very interesting. Keep talking."

By acknowledging Mary's concern and pausing several seconds, Peter could have forestalled her immediate negative reaction.

Absorb the Thrust of the Speaker's Argument, Not Just Assorted Facts

Look beyond the speaker's charts and statistics. What is he really proposing? What are its ramifications?

If you are confused, or if you think the speaker could express himself better, take advantage of a pause and rephrase to confirm your understanding of what he's saying. After all, if *you* are confused, other people in the room may also be confused. Clarifying the speaker's ideas will advance the discussion and save time in the long run.

Scott, the new director of customer relations, switched off the overhead projector and turned to the group: "To become more responsive to our customers," he said, "I'm proposing that we shift service responsibility from the branch offices to regional centers. This would ensure consistency in our response to service calls. In addition, I recommend we computerize and have each regional center record the source and nature of every service call, the time it takes to complete the job, and the personnel required."

James thought for a moment and said, "If I understand this right, what you're proposing is really a complete restructuring of our service organization with much greater control by the head office."

That's precisely what Scott was proposing. All James did was tie together in one sentence the series of steps Scott outlined in his presentation. That one sentence helped everyone else to see just how radical a change Scott was proposing.

Determine the Implications of the Speaker's Message

Once you understand the crux of the speaker's proposal, you are in a position to lead a discussion of its merits. Ask yourself, "What then?" to determine the issues raised by this proposal. Whom will it benefit and whom will it harm? What are the long-term pros and cons?

Let's return to Scott's proposal for the regional service centers. James might continue, "Scott, while I agree that consistency and control are important elements of good customer relations, won't this centralization plan of yours be bad for the morale of our branch office personnel? They're the people who actually call on our customers and embody the company's good image. We have a hard enough time attracting capable people and I think your plan may make it even harder."

James led the discussion by first finding an area of agreement, then going beyond the proposal's obvious benefits and exposing some potential disadvantages. To get himself thinking along these lines, he said to himself, "Suppose we adopt Scott's plan. Then what?"

STEP 5: STAY IN CONTROL OF THE MEETING

If you called the meeting—or during the segment you present—it is your job to assume the leadership role. Your body language—standing up or sitting forward in your chair to signal that you want to speak; sitting down or sitting back in your chair to turn the floor over to someone else—is one way you assert your leadership. Another way is by summarizing to confirm your understanding of what a speaker is saying, as James did in the above example. This technique can also be used to condense both sides of an argument before taking a vote, or to confirm that everyone agrees before moving on to the next point. To confirm that the group has reached a consensus, you might give your summary and then pause, making eye contact with the person who is most likely to agree. Feeling the weight of your gaze, that person will probably speak up and reinforce what you just said.

Finally, make handouts work for rather than against you. It is seldom advisable to distribute handouts or samples before you talk about them. Every person in the room will see the item in a different context and shoot a barrage of questions at you. One way to combat this is by displaying the handout, discussing it, and then making it available at the close of the meeting. Or you may turn relevant points or diagrams into visuals and project them. There are times, however, when these procedures may not be appropriate. If the meeting was called to discuss the draft of a written document, everyone may need a copy.

STEP 6: BRING THE MEETING TO A DECISIVE CLOSE

As you did when you opened the meeting, deliver a formal, *planned* closing statement—not "I guess that just about wraps it up." Make it short. Restate your down-to-business opening in the past tense. Remind the group why you assembled them for the meeting and remind them what they got out of the meeting. Your last words should be a one-sentence statement embodying the action you want them to take. Keep this action step brief and specific.

STEP 7: EVALUATE EVERY MEETING

Learn from every meeting you attend. The best way to improve your performance in meetings is to spend a few minutes evaluating how well you achieved both your business and personal goals in a given meeting. Then briefly rerun your performance during each phase of the meeting process: the preparation phase, the planning phase, the opening phase, the listening phase, the controlling phase, and the closing, action phase. Determine what went well so you can do it again. Consider what you might do differently next time.

STEP 8: FOLLOW UP

Keep in mind that the efforts you make *after* a meeting also build your reputation as a doer. When appropriate, distribute written summaries of agreed-upon actions to stimulate implementation of your proposal. Then follow up later to see what has actually been accomplished.

CONCLUSION

I've outlined eight steps in taking advantage of meetings. Like any other skills, they require practice. Start with the plan. (Even when you're called to an impromptu meeting, think quickly through your goals, the participants, and alternate outcomes. Develop a down-to-business opening for your segment of the meeting.) Work on the subsequent steps, observing what happens when you and others use these skills, and when you do not. Finally, look for increased professionalism in how you treat people and move ideas to action through shorter, more productive meetings.

Copyright 1982 by McAlinden Associates, Inc.

17

HOLDING YOUR OWN IN PRESSURE-CONFRONTATION SITUATIONS

by Dr. Ray L. Steele

"I blew it," my client confessed. "I knew it the minute the reporter walked out the door. But what could I do about it then?"

Luckily, the television cameraman also blew it—the tape did not record—so my client got a reprieve. Instead of running on the six o'clock news on Friday, the interview was rescheduled for Monday morning and my client gained a whole weekend to prepare for it.

Don't count on this kind of luck to get you through your next media interview—or tough-confrontation situation. Strokes of luck like that happen once in a lifetime. Heed the words of Samuel Johnson: "A man of genius has been seldom ruined but by himself." If, at any point in your career, you may have to face a TV camera or a hostile audience as a spokesman for your company, start preparing for the experience now by absorbing the suggestions in this chapter. The half-hour it takes you to read the next few pages may save you countless hours of embarrassment when some hard-nosed job interviewer or journalist catches you off guard and unprepared to deal with his tough questions.

CONFLICT—YOU MIGHT AS WELL ACCEPT IT

Thomas Schelling, in his book *The Strategy of Conflict,* divides up the universe of conflict theorists into two camps. There are those who view conflict as a "pathological state and seek its causes and treatment," and those who "take conflict for granted and study the behavior associated with it."

I fall into the latter camp because, unfortunately, I believe conflict is here to stay. It's a normal, even acceptable, element of communication —*provided* at least one party to the conflict understands how to control it. In any adversary situation, make sure you are the party who not only understands what's happening but takes steps to keep the minor conflict from erupting into a full-scale war.

Setting yourself up for a success in conflict situations begins when you adopt the right attitude. The following suggestions lead to the development of a constructive attitude. Adopting these attitudes will help you do two things: gain the upper hand when you're in danger of losing it; and keep the upper hand once you've achieved it.

Constructive Attitude: View adversaries as fellow human beings.

Good communication takes place on a human-to-human level. Granted, you should show respect, possibly even deference, to people in positions superior to yours—your boss, for example; the president of your company; a prospective employer; a U.S. senator. However, in most cases it is at the human level and not at the status/role level that barriers to effective communication are broken down and persuasion or breakthroughs occur. And this generalization holds true whether your adversary is one individual or a hundred individuals comprising a hostile audience.

If you hide behind your official role as company spokesman to deliver a harsh defense of a controversial corporate issue, you're inviting the other side to deal with you in an equally harsh manner. But if you place your audience in a position where they must deal with you on a human level—an individual level—you make it more difficult for your audience to maintain a hostile stance. Why? Because their hostility, in this person-to-person context, begins to border on socially unacceptable behavior. Such human-to-human positioning places your opponent under intense pressure to deal with you in a civil manner or risk being criticized for behaving boorishly as a person. This type of pressure is not only hard for opponents to ignore but a type of pressure which you have the power to control.

As you face your critics, keep in mind that neither you nor they were born lawyers, corporate vice-presidents, consumers, or talk show hosts. These are simply roles all of you assumed in adult life, roles that have nothing to do with anyone's value as a human being.

The next time an angry mother accuses you of defending a company that is polluting her children's drinking water, you might point out that you have children too and you feel the same way she does about preserving the environment for future generations.

Constructive Attitude: Recognize that you must meet some of your audience's needs, not just your own, to be credible.

The natural tendency of most people is to become defensive when they are being attacked. How refreshing it is when someone occasionally admits he—or his company—might be partially or even largely responsible for something that went wrong. Often he, or his company, is not just a little responsible, but a lot responsible and everyone witnessing the confrontation knows it. Much better to utter a quick *mea culpa* and get on with more positive topics—like how you or the company intends to solve the problem—than to spend the whole time trying to shore up an untenable position.

The corporate attorneys reading that paragraph are probably cringing. No, I am not suggesting corporate spokespeople should admit negligence. Far from it. Rather, I'm suggesting that spokespeople grant that the public has needs too, needs which, perhaps, the company is not meeting. Let me offer an example drawn from my experience preparing corporate officials to square off against their critics in public forums.

Ten years ago, I counseled the spokespersons for a public utility that was under fire due to a lengthy cold-weather power disruption. The state public utilities commission responded to the outcry by scheduling public hearings in various locations served by the company.

Now if you believe such forums are anything more than an opportunity for the public to vent its collective spleen, for the utility to suffer a verbal beating, and for the public utility commission to appear responsible and concerned, perhaps I could interest you in the purchase of a small bridge in Brooklyn! Indeed, such meetings, where public emotions are running high, are almost ritualistic. For a company to profit— or at best hold its own—in such a situation requires careful planning, role playing, rehearsals, and a detailed "audience-needs analysis."

The last item may be the most crucial for the company forced to make the most of such questionable PR "opportunities." I say this because effective communication between adversaries is always need-based. That is, it hinges on reaching a compromise between your needs and the other party's needs. If you fail to acknowledge any of the other party's needs, you simply enlarge the conflict when your objective should be to contain it.

Unfortunately, my client refused to acknowledge any of the public's needs in the first few hearings and stuck to the official line: Bad weather is an act of God. In the process, the company exacerbated its problem, akin to pouring gasoline on a smoldering fire. The result: flaming emotions engulfed everyone while the public utility commissioners, who would eventually be ruling on future company rate increases, looked on.

After one or two disastrous hearings, company officials became more amenable to suggestions. An audience-needs analysis revealed that, due to the power outage, many consumers had suffered some real discomfort. Whether it was more psychological than financial did not matter. These consumers needed the company to acknowledge their problems up front. This was not so hard for company officials to do since many of them lived in the same areas and had also been inconvenienced. The breakthrough in communication came when company spokespeople finally admitted, from the podium, that they understood and had also suffered due to the lack of service. A few even described their experiences in detail. The power disruption was thus transformed into a shared *human* problem with which all assembled could identify. While absolutely no legal responsibility or negligence was admitted, spokespeople did concede partial responsibility for failing to foresee the magnitude of the storm. The audience responded to this expression of regret. The heckling stopped and feelings of goodwill between company officials and the consuming public gradually reemerged. The tenor of subsequent meetings became more positive as company officials promised to institute programs that would minimize the impact of future storms on the utility's operations. The ultimate irony was that the public utility commission later granted the company a rate increase, using the rationale that the company needed the money to improve maintenance in anticipation of natural disasters. The company has maintained a permanent team of trained speakers ever since this incident.

Constructive Attitude: Keep an open mind.

There is always more than one way to solve a problem or implement a new program or avert a potential crisis. Sure, there's your way, which took you several weeks to formulate. But there are also several other ways that probably never even occurred to you.

Keep an open mind when alternative suggestions are thrown at you during the course of a meeting or a talk show discussion. The more willing you are to be flexible and consider other ideas, the less likely you'll become embroiled in a verbal brouhaha. Develop the ability to shift ground and "think on your feet." It will make you appear more in control to the audience. Recognizing that other people have good ideas, too, is *not* a sign of weakness on your part. Indeed, the fact that you can adapt to feedback from your foes is a sign of strength.

Constructive Attitude: Explain exactly what you mean.

When dealing in pressured circumstances, you should be aware of some basic human truths about language and misunderstandings. The most important is: *Words do not have absolute meanings. Words have as many meanings as there are people sitting out there listening to you.*

We all rely upon our past experiences as a filter through which we view language. In confrontation situations, people are especially prone to rely on their own peculiar definition of a word or term rather than the more commonly accepted dictionary definition—or, for that matter, *your* definition of the term, which you yourself have given. My advice to you is to take that extra five or ten seconds and explain what you mean by the term "sales conference." Do you mean a quick get-together to discuss quarterly results and short-term strategy? Or a leisurely quasi-holiday at some remote resort to engage in some in-depth, long-term product planning? If you don't explain *your* meaning, you risk your audience's missing the point, or worse yet, attaching a meaning to your words quite the opposite of what you intended. Therein lie the makings of a conflict.

Define terms that are critical to your message by using such handy verbal devices as, "as you probably know" or "as you may know." Then give your definition. Such lead-ins will help you explain what you mean without appearing to be talking down to your audience.

Much innocent conflict is caused by the careless use of language inappropriate to a particular audience. Know the background of your listeners and their level of familiarity with the topic well enough to select language they'll understand. Be particularly careful when using buzzwords of your profession, whether engineeringese, legalese, or undefined acronyms. Will every one of your listeners understand that by GSA you mean General Services Administration? Or do you mean Girls Scouts of America? In general, keep your language simple and direct. Use colorful terms, slang, or graphic terminology only after you've considered its usefulness in getting your message across to that particular audience. The more you are able to select language that is common to the experience of the audience, language that is direct and straightforward, the greater chance you have to be understood—and to avoid raising any unnecessary red flags.

Constructive Attitude: Be goal oriented.

Before you engage in any potential confrontation situation—whether it's a job interview or question/answer session—you must decide what you hope to gain from the encounter and then keep that goal firmly in mind at all times.

In preparing clients for such encounters, I'm often struck by their absence of purpose. They haven't the faintest idea why they're submitting to this potentially unpleasant experience except that "it's part of my job," or someone "asked me to do it." This lack of purpose was highlighted by a consulting assignment I undertook for a huge industrial conglomerate. I was retained by the CEO to prepare each of the division presidents and a few corporate officers to give a short presentation at an important stock analysts meeting. I worked with each company officer individually. I opened each session by asking the man to describe (1) the overall purpose of the meeting, and (2) the purpose of his presentation within the context of the larger meeting. Of the twelve officers, two understood the purpose of the meeting in the same way as the CEO, but only one saw his individual presentation in the same light as the CEO. I can assure you that before I allowed any of them to open their mouths at that stock analysts meeting, to a man they shared the CEO's conception of what was about to take place.

Why is a goal so important? Because it helps keep you on course when the trick questions come flying at you. If you have clearly and carefully determined your purpose for being there in the first place, you can use it as a beacon, avoiding the shoal waters when the seas get choppy. A clear goal also helps you prepare for the encounter and formulate an agenda—the list of crucial points you are hell-bent on covering before the meeting comes to an end.

Constructive Attitude: Be realistic.

Don't agree to participate in a potential conflict situation unless you've done a personal cost-benefit analysis and know, realistically, what you stand to gain or lose by the encounter. To increase your chances of gaining, heed advice like that contained in this book. (If the encounter is really critical, hire a professional speech consultant to act out the situation with you ahead of time.) Leave nothing to chance. Thorough preparation is still the best way to counter opposition and hostility.

In most cases, I find that well-prepared clients benefit from engaging in these pressure situations. For, among other things, each time they go through one, they become better prepared to deal with the next.

HOLDING YOUR OWN IN QUESTION/ANSWER SESSIONS

Now let's examine how some people manage to snatch defeat from the jaws of victory in very specific pressure-confrontation situations such as the Q/A session.

I have witnessed the demise of many a good public speaker who was unable to respond appropriately when the questions came at him from the floor. I have also seen average speakers come to life during the Q/A period and rescue what would have been remembered as a very dull evening.

To shine at Q/A sessions, you must put into practice all of the constructive attitudes I have just outlined, with particular emphasis on preparation and anticipating problems.

Prepare for the session with the same intensity you devote to your formal speech, perhaps more. If you have a limited background in the subject and inadequate time to prepare for the Q/A session, do a quick cost-benefit analysis as I suggested earlier. A good Q/A period provides the audience with a forum for probing the depth and breadth of your knowledge, which is only partially apparent in a formal speech. Such a session also allows the audience to get a better perspective on your true commitment and interest in the subject. If you don't really know much about it, couldn't care less, and really are pressed for time, consider avoiding the Q/A conclusion to your presentation. There are several ways to do this while minimizing the damage to your reputation as a so-called expert or spokesman. You can talk beyond the time allotted for the formal part of your presentation, leaving no time for questions. You could pull the old politician's trick of suffering a last-minute schedule change that permits you time for only two questions. Or, even better, anticipate any tough questions in the body of your speech.

You should have a clear purpose in agreeing to a Q/A session, just as you need a purpose for engaging in any type of confrontation situation. Make the session serve that purpose.

An example underlines this point. Before he announced his 1980 candidacy for the presidency, John Connally, the former Texas governor, visited Pittsburgh to speak to an influential corporate and university audience as part of the American Experience program. He was invited as an opinion leader and former government official who had dealt with world trade and economic issues. He was not invited as a candidate for the presidency of the United States.

John Connally is known as extremely intelligent and articulate. But that night his performance was not up to par—at first. Although he covered the topics he was assigned, his twenty-minute speech seemed to be a paste-up job, a haphazard collation of five old speeches assembled during his flight to Pittsburgh. It was not vintage Connally, the forceful speaker, and the audience was clearly disappointed. The applause was halfhearted.

What happened next was a revelation to me. I ask you to decide whether this soon-to-be-announced presidential candidate, speaking before an audience of important people, knew what his purpose was that evening? Did he accomplish his purpose by the way he handled the Q/A session?

When Connally called for questions, he announced that he would deal with topics not just on the matters covered in his speech, but in any area. Only one hand went up. Mr. Connally recognized the questioner by name, listened to his very broad query on the current state of America's domestic affairs, and then delivered a surprisingly dynamic statement on how domestic affairs *should* be handled by government. After a couple of very brief answers to follow-up questions, he got another broad question which enabled him to make a compelling statement on the handling of foreign affairs by the president. Shortly thereafter, he got an opportunity to do the same by means of a question on the nation's economy. Three key topics for any presidential candidate had been introduced and Connally had met the challenge.

Quite unlike the nervous, polite applause he'd received earlier, the enthusiastic roar of approval he received this time lasted three minutes. In subsequent conversations with audience members, I heard not one comment about the "lousy speech." Instead I heard ringing praise of Connally's forthright position on domestic affairs, of his keen insight into economic matters, and of his sensitivity in matters of diplomacy.

Obviously, Connally had not been pleased with his assigned speech topic. But rather than confuse and alienate his audience, which had come to hear him talk on that subject, he prepared some remarks that saw him through the twenty minutes until the main event—the Q/A period. The period lasted thirty minutes and presented Connally with an appropriate forum for achieving his goal: to position himself as presidential material. He may have planted those three key questions to make sure they were asked—or he may just have been lucky.

Anticipate probable questions, whether negative or positive. Place yourself in your audiences' shoes and make up a list of likely questions. Prepare answers for those questions. If you've come up with a good list, you'll find that most of the actual questions are at least related to the answers you've prepared. A transitional phrase or two will allow you to segue to your preplanned answer.

Some speakers prefer to include mention of controversial issues within the formal speech, thereby placing such issues in a favorable context for later discussion during the Q/A session. Or a speaker might bring up the issue himself while being questioned, thus diffusing the issue before his opponents can seize on it.

A client of mine used the former technique—addressing the subject himself during his formal presentation—to very telling effect during a potentially nasty stockholders meeting. This man was the chairman of a multinational company. He and several of his executive team had been accused of reaping personal profits from some of their corporate activities. The story made front-page news. (Of course, the story that later exonerated them appeared on page 26 of the business section.)

The company's stockholder relations staff knew that certain corporate gadflies would bring up the matter at the annual meeting and that their goal would be to embarrass the chairman. The company's speechwriters decided that the best defense was an offense and placed the topic as item six in the speech the chairman would deliver. It would immediately follow some upbeat corporate financial news and a few routine topics.

Little was left to chance. The chairman rehearsed the speech before a large group, and it was videotaped. Then the chairman, the chief speechwriter, and I reviewed the videotape. The feedback was unanimous: the juxtaposition of the bad news concerning the vital matter of the chairman's character and morality following the almost ritualistic good news about corporate profits was incongruous. Trust in the chairman's leadership was the real issue and it had to be met head on.

The speech was restructured on the spot. After some brief welcoming remarks and before any other business was mentioned, the chairman explained he was departing from his formal report for a moment to cover a matter of concern to many. Then he laid the matter to rest with five minutes of "impromptu" remarks about the controversy. In the process, he reaped a harvest of praise for his forthrightness and courage, and diffused the issue so well that it never even came up during the Q/A session.

When you anticipate an angry questioning session, one method of verbal control is to limit the time for each question. Explain the ground rules on time up front so it doesn't look as if you're ducking the issue later when you abruptly end the session.

In lieu of a standard question period, you may also allow the audience to interrupt your formal presentation with questions. Again, establish the ground rules up front. Then make it clear by your vocal inflection and gestures that questions are welcome. If the interruption occurs at a bad moment, be polite—"Just let me finish this one point and I'll get back to you."

Graciousness, in fact, is an important attribute of effective speakers. Always treat your audience with courtesy, patience, and kindness, even when they don't reciprocate. Be understanding and help your audience or attacker in the biblical spirit of turning the other cheek. For example, if you get an awful or stupid or uninformed question, don't attach a negative label to it. Instead, restate the question so it makes more sense and credit the questioner with asking an interesting question. Suddenly you'll find the audience is on your side for saving a fellow human being from embarrassment.

Always take your time in answering a question. In fact, in instances when a questioner is extremely hostile, it is often wiser to let him ramble on for a while and vent his anger before you interrupt him to point out that he hasn't asked a question yet. He may still come up with a statement that affords you the opportunity to formulate a question for him—one that leads right in to one of your prepared answers.

Remember, people ask questions for all kinds of reasons—to get attention, to get something they already believe confirmed, to air a grievance, to show resentment of your position. Before you answer, determine why a question was asked, then begin the process of deciding if or how you will handle it. Do not feel pressured to respond immediately to every question.

Ask for a restatement of the question if you're puzzled by it or don't understand why it was asked or just want to buy some time before you answer. You'll find that very few questioners will ever repeat their question using exactly the same words. You'll be amused to discover that some people can't even remember the question once they get it out of their mouths. Dan Rather, the CBS anchorman, tells a story about the time President Lyndon Johnson used this technique on a reporter who had asked a question as hostile as it was convoluted. LBJ paused, smiled and said, "Well, first of all, I don't think you can even repeat that question." He was right. The guy couldn't. And the resulting laughter got LBJ off the hook.

Another useful technique is to restate a negative question in your own words. This does two things: It gives you the chance to place the question in a more favorable light and it buys you time to think about your answer. It also makes you look like a thoughtful speaker who is simply making certain everyone in the room heard the question.

There are also some nonverbal techniques you can deploy in your battle to stay in control of your audience. One is to direct attention away from an angry group in the audience, give the questioner among them direct eye contact when he or she is asking the question, then break eye contact and deliver your answer to another part of the audience. When you're finished, take a question from that part of the audience and avoid looking in the direction of the troublesome group for the rest of the session.

Also, keep in mind that the audience has eyes as well as ears and gets as much from seeing *how* you answer a question—by your body language—as they do from listening to the *content* of your answer. Every time you get a tough question, it will be your nonverbal reaction that the audience will pick up on first. Learn how to use your nonverbal reaction to your advantage.

If you get a difficult question, don't be afraid to smile and let the audience see that you know it's difficult but are not distressed by it. That facial gesture will make you appear in control and discourage other pot shots.

When you get an impossible question, you might want to come out from behind the lectern and stand in front of the audience, microphones notwithstanding, to demonstrate your willingness to speak candidly. Dan Rather, in his book *The Camera Never Blinks,* recalled how two of Nixon's aides, Robert Haldeman and Ron Ziegler, tried to make their boss appear more forthright in the first months of his presidency. They removed the lectern and teleprompter used by his predecessor, LBJ, and had Nixon conduct press conferences using only a standing microphone. Rather described the effect as positive. The use of one lone microphone was driving home the point that the President was engaging his audience "live, direct, naked, except for his own intellect and courage."

One cautionary note in this discussion of verbal and nonverbal candor: To advise anyone to lie to an audience would be the height of folly, let alone an ethical breach. The long-term odds are against any speaker pulling off a public deceit. The immediate benefits accrued by intentionally misleading people are far overshadowed by the consequences when you are finally exposed.

Having said that, let's discuss those instances when you may not wish to give a complete answer. From time to time in dealing with complex issues, you may find yourself facing an unfriendly, completely biased and perhaps largely uninformed audience. In such a situation, your attempt to answer a hostile or extremely difficult question could backfire and substantially erode any progress you may have already made in winning the audience over.

Under such conditions, it is crucial that you listen carefully to both the content of the question and the tone of the questioner. If, on quick reflection, you determine it to be a trap or leading question, there is no reason to fall into the trap. You may say the question demands an answer far too complex for the time allotted, suggest that the audience would be bored with all the details, and promise to answer the question privately afterwards. Then immediately take another question before the questioner can make a retort. Momentum is as important here as in professional football games. You could also say you don't have enough information to give a good or complete answer and promise to get back to the questioner later. Use humor and quip that if you had the answer to that one, you'd be rich, the president, whatever; then MOVE ON TO THE NEXT QUESTION. As speaker, you are in charge of the pacing and as long as you maintain the momentum, you keep control.

Remember your purpose in making the presentation and don't let a single hostile or competitive audience member ruin your opportunity. You will, of course, sustain some loss of audience confidence for ducking the question, but the alternative may spell disaster for your whole presentation. To answer that one trick question that might confuse the whole point of your speech with the audience listening at a 25 percent level of efficiency (which is average) is foolish.

Finally, when cornered, admit what most successful people figured out long ago: No one has all the answers. Be willing to say occasionally, "I don't know," or "I made a mistake." President Kennedy knew admitting a failure could be turned to advantage. He did so after the abortive Bay of Pigs invasion. As the saying goes, "It's a big person who can admit his failures."

TAKING THE TERROR OUT OF TELEVISION INTERVIEWS

While all the techniques covered previously have some relevance in mastering the television interview, the pressure of making contact with such a vast audience strikes terror in the minds of most first-time TV guests, no matter how experienced they are as public speakers. Otherwise articulate spokesmen suddenly freeze or choke up when confronted with that little red tally-light on the top of the TV camera. This needn't happen if you are well versed in the subject matter and apply the previous techniques and those I'm about to give you.

These techniques have been tested and proved successful by scores of my clients who have faced the challenge of a potentially hostile television interviewer. Before accepting them as your own, let me interject one cautionary note; it could be credited to any number of TV reporters and consultants, but was actually articulated by Dan Rather. He said, "My theory is, if you are on television often and long enough, there is no place to hide. You are going to come across for what you are ... Eloquence alone, the power of speech, will not sustain a bankrupt politician [or businessman]. An honest man doesn't always come across well on television. But his honesty usually does."

The following techniques will help you come across better, but they're no substitute for solid information and honesty.

Always watch the program in advance, if humanly possible.

This will give you familiarity with its operation, style, format, and the kind of audience it attracts. Pay particular attention to the interviewer's public persona. Many a businessman has been stunned to find that Mr. or Ms. Friendly TV Personality off camera becomes a fire-breathing demon when the cameras go on. If you take the time to watch the host in action, you know what to expect. On-camera surprises should be reduced to a minimum. This is one surprise you should eliminate entirely.

You need a goal.

Know why you have accepted this TV opportunity and what you want to accomplish. Once again, prepare a list of probable questions, anticipating the worst as well as the best, and prepare suitable responses. In most cases, you'll find there are one or two key ideas that you must get across right off if the audience is going to understand your position. Those are your "communications objectives," and no matter where the interviewer may try to lead you with his or her questions, make those points early.

Position yourself—or organization—correctly.

Positioning is nothing more than selecting the most positive, least damaging approach as the basis for your response. Even the most negative topic has a bright side. Go for it. Seize every opportunity to make yourself—or your organization—look good.

Every issue has several facets. Enlightened self-interest, which is why you're reading this book in the first place, dictates that you select an approach that showcases you or your organization as responsible—doing what you or it should be doing. That is positioning.

Suppose you are the spokesman for a large bank. The reporter notes that the law may soon be changed to make nationwide banking legal. He asks your opinion: Won't such a law be detrimental in its long-term effects because it will enable greedy large banks to gobble up the nation's small banks? He has now positioned you as a "greedy large bank"—unless you say something to counter that positioning. If you're smart, you'll reposition your bank as a responsible member of the corporate community. You might say, "If the legislature decides to change the law as you suggest, obviously it would be because our lawmakers see some benefit to the country by such a move. In any case, this is a capitalist society and the laws of the marketplace are such that no large bank, greedy or otherwise, could keep expanding for long if it remained insensitive to the needs of local citizens. . . . "

However, if your circumstances are so ethically questionable that you cannot reposition yourself (and that is rarely the case with my clients) then my advice to you is to fix the problem before the interview rather than try to position your way out of it. No glib talk will substitute for having a viable position from the start.

Express yourself succinctly.

Television is a headline medium. If you can think in terms of "speaking in headlines," you'll stand the best chance of getting your message across to that huge, amorphorous TV audience out there. Remember, you're competing with the refrigerator, the dog, screaming children, and quarrelsome spouses for the viewer's attention. Make it easy for distracted viewers to get your point. AND DO IT UP FRONT. Don't say, "I'd like to answer that question with an anecdote, something that happened to me on the way here," and then deliver the punch line of the story two minutes later. If the program is live, the host will probably interrupt you before you get to the punch line to deliver a commercial. If the program is taped, your whole long, rambling answer will probably end up on the cutting room floor.

State the punch line up front. If you have a good example to support your statement, present it briefly. Give the highlights. The little details are fodder for print journalists, *not* TV reporters. If your example is good but can't be condensed to less than one minute, ask the interviewer if he or she would like you to give an example. If the answer is yes, go ahead. Then the length of the story becomes their problem. Be warned, however, that they may still interrupt you or encourage you to hurry it up.

Keep in mind that television is an information and entertainment medium. A good interview—and guest—is entertaining, effervescing with good quotes and compelling visuals. Use gestures. You'll find they'll add color and inflection to your voice. Use simple, direct language the whole world can understand. Speak in headline sentences, use brief anecdotes—and humor when possible to brighten your commentary. Be personable and deal at the human-to-human level with even the most hostile interviewer. Use the interviewer's first name to put the interview on a friendly, informal basis. And never be afraid to chuckle at yourself. It creates a powerful image of self-confidence.

I'll never forget how the triumphant Ronald Reagan began his speech as he accepted the 1980 Republican nomination. He said that for the first time in a long time he'd seen himself in a movie on prime-time television that night, referring to the brief biographical film introducing his speech. He said it was one of the joys of the evening for him, a reference to the fact that his old, grade-B movies usually air at three o'clock in the morning. That ability to use humor—especially pointed in this case since the opposition liked to characterize him as a lousy-actor-turned-lousy-politician—helped him to appear both personable and likeable. Those are two traits that are invaluable on television.

TELEVISION INTERVIEW DON'TS

Having just covered what to do to look your best on TV, I'd like to list those things that tend to backfire on the television screen.

• Don't look directly in the camera. Talk to the host. Typically, the host or interviewer will be sitting right next to you. Look at him or her, not at the camera, when you talk, unless you wish to direct a comment very specifically to the viewing audience.

• Don't read from notes on camera unless it's absolutely necessary. Television is a very personal and intimate medium. As a viewer, I don't want you sitting in my living room reading your key points to me like a schoolteacher. That's the image you create if you insist on reading to me.

• Don't let the machine-gun interviewer get away with bombarding you with a string of questions. Either pick one of the questions and answer it or ask the interviewer which of his questions he'd like you to answer first.

• Don't fall for the paraphraser who puts words in your mouth—"In other words, Mr. X., what you are saying is . . ."—and then totally distorts what you just said. Correct the interviewer immediately by saying, "No, Mr. Interviewer, that is *not* what I said. I said . . ."

• Don't tolerate the interrupter who won't let you finish a sentence. Let him finish interrupting you—at least you can be polite—and go back and finish your original thought. When you're through, ask him if he has another question, or deal with his interruption.

• No matter what the interviewer does or says, *never* lose your cool, turn hostile toward the interviewer or try to mimic his/her style. Rarely will you beat interviewers at their game and, in the attempt, you may lose the audience's confidence. After all, it's the host's show and the audience has some loyalty to that host. You're a one-shot guest. They couldn't care less about you. Your job is to be a courteous guest and keep your sights fixed on the main chance—to cover your communications objectives.

• Don't arrive at the studio two minutes before air time and expect to look composed. Arrive well ahead of time and look around. This will increase your comfort level and give you time to relax and review your notes.

• Once the red light is on, don't be distracted by the camera crew or wild gestures from the show personnel. Keep your eyes fixed on the host and let him or her worry about making the show work.

• Finally, don't accept any TV invitation unless you're prepared to make your host look good. By that I mean *provide your host with an interesting show* that will keep viewers tuned in and coming back for more next time. The only way to ingratiate yourself with a TV reporter or talk show host is to put on a good performance. You are performing when you are on television whether you care to see it that way or not. The host certainly knows it's a performance. Take your cues from the host. Note his or her high energy level, gestures, sense of showmanship, and the underlying message being put out that "I'm glad I'm here. There's no place I'd rather be."

JOUSTING WITH JOB INTERVIEWERS

During employment interviews—or in testimony before governmental bodies—you should concentrate on two areas: recognition of the opportunities embodied in the other person's questions, and active use of listening skills throughout.

The kinds of questions asked in interviews or at hearings are generally either open-ended or closed questions. A closed question is one requiring a direct or limited answer, often a simple "yes" or "no." Job interviewers and legislators normally lead with such questions in an effort to control the direction of the dialogue or to obtain specific information. My advice is to respond directly and briefly to such questions, unless to give too little information will mislead those present. In that case, explain why you can't give a simple answer to the query.

Open-ended questions are broad and wide-ranging: "How would you describe yourself?"; or "What mistakes have you made during your career and what have you learned from them?" If you're prepared for the interview, you'll relish these questions because they afford you the opportunity to bridge into your prepared answers. If the question is outrageous in its breadth, however, by all means ask a question back to narrow the focus. You might say, for example, "Do you want me to describe myself as a professional or as a father and husband?" Or "I assume you mean mistakes on the job. . . ."

Use your eyes as well as your ears to judge how involved the other party is in the interview. Active listening skills will help you evaluate both verbal and nonverbal cues.

For example, use affirmative head nods, facial expressions and an intermittant "uh huh," "yes," or "I understand" to indicate you are actively and—in the case of a government hearing—respectfully paying attention. Take notes only when appropriate and never avoid direct eye contact with the interviewer.

Don't allow your mind to wander, even in excruciatingly boring hearings. Keep checking your body language to make sure you're not signaling the interviewer that you're suffering from MEGO, the acronym used in personnel circles for the "mine-eyes-glaze-over" syndrome. Slouching and other physical positions that look too relaxed give this impression. Furthermore, if you're slumped down in your chair and suddenly you sit up straighter when you're hit with a particularly difficult question, the effect is as good as saying, "You got me."

PRACTICE FOLLOWS KNOWLEDGE

Having read this chapter, you now know what to do the next time someone starts backing you into a corner. Theoretically, that is. Practice these techniques in quasi-pressure situations so you'll be prepared when an all-out attack is launched against you. I've never yet worked with a client who, if willing to practice these techniques, didn't find his performance demonstrably improved in rugged pressure-confrontation situations. It's a high-risk area, but the person who can keep his head when his colleagues are falling apart is the person whose image as a leader will continue to grow, and whose career will continue to prosper.

18

SPEECH DELIVERY: How to Keep an Audience Listening

by Elayne Snyder

All public speaking is a performance. And good delivery is part of that performance. Make no mistake about it, your audience considers your voice, tone, manner, style, gestures, and dress as much a part of your performance as your message.

Good delivery of a speech helps listeners concentrate on what is being said. *It does not attract attention to itself.* Rather, your delivery should be perfectly suited to: your audience; the time; the place; and the occasion of your speech. Let's take these points in order:

The Audience

Let's say you've been asked to give a speech on the general topic of group dynamics before a convention of mental-health professionals. You are told that 300 people—about half men and half women—will be present. You know they are not dewy-eyed youths with a narrow frame of reference, but mature, professional people who are looking for new ways to deal with the problems they encounter daily. In short, you will be addressing your peers, who will want to *use* what you have to say. With this information, you know your speech should be pragmatic.

Time of Day

This is important to your delivery because it affects you and your audience. How will it affect you? If you are scheduled to speak at 9:00 A.M. and you happen to be a night person, you will have to psych yourself up to be alert and alive that early. In addition, you must be especially arresting in your opening to get all the other night people in the audience to pay attention. On the other hand, if you're the last person on the agenda at 8:00 P.M., you will have to be particularly lively to compensate for audience fatigue.

The Place

If you are addressing a large group assembled in an auditorium or hotel ballroom, you must keep your delivery more formal. Your talk will need to be well planned because there will be fewer opportunities for impromptu digressions from the topic or questions from the audience.

On the other hand, if you are speaking to a smaller group, of thirty or less, in a classroom or conference room, you should employ a more casual, conversational style. In such surroundings, interruptions for spontaneous questions, short digressions, and off-the-cuff banter are in order. Audience involvement should be encouraged.

If you are speaking at a luncheon or dinner meeting, you will be in competition with waiters scurrying about and banging plates, not to mention informal table talk among members of the audience. In such situations, you must be prepared to just stand quietly at the lectern until the bustling stops and you capture your audience's attention.

The Occasion

Before you write your speech—let alone deliver it—the most important thing to know is *why* you are giving it. What's the occasion? In our hypothetical example, you know you will be speaking at a group dynamics conference sponsored by a national business association, and you will therefore tailor the length and the approach accordingly.

CHOOSING A SUBJECT

Your delivery should also be tailored to your topic—which you generally choose yourself. Of course you want to select a subject your audience will respond to. Because you know the kind of people who will attend this conference, you can make an educated guess about their social, educational, and economic status. These factors will, of course, affect the content of your talk and the language you use to deliver it. They will also determine how you dress. The outfit you choose should make you feel comfortable and in synch with your audience.

If you decide to give a formal speech, it should be carefully prepared, well rehearsed, and delivered with the aid of notes or an outline, but *not* read word for word. (A talk that is not read is known as an "extemporaneous speech.") Nothing is more deadly than a talk that is read rather than spoken.

THE DELIVERY OF YOUR SPEECH

The moment of truth arrives. You are on stage waiting to be introduced. As the host moves to the microphone to introduce you, be aware that your delivery has already begun. *The moment you are in view of the audience, your body language and appearance are sending them messages.* Be sure your body is speaking well of you. Ideally, you should look and feel comfortable, poised, and energetic.

You should listen attentively to what is being said, but you shouldn't overreact. On the other hand, don't act so casual that you ignore what is being said, either. Nor should you fiddle with your notes or examine the ceiling.

At this point, the audience should be looking you over. Be glad they are. After all, you didn't come there to be ignored. Look back at them if you feel like it—it's your chance to begin eye contact, the most powerful form of communication there is. When the introduction is over, rise easily from your chair (if you are seated) and approach the lectern.

Acknowledge your introduction with a nod to your host, and take a few seconds to orient yourself at the lectern. Look at your audience from time to time as you arrange your notes on the lectern and adjust the microphone. Finally, step back about six inches from the lectern, take a couple of relaxing breaths and begin.

All this takes about fifteen seconds, but it is an important time. It gives your audience a chance to adjust to you so that when you do begin, they'll be ready to listen to what you say instead of eyeing your clothes, your hair or whatever.

Once you begin to speak, you have about thirty seconds to capture their attention. If your audience is not favorably impressed with your opening remarks, they'll start thinking their own thoughts instead of listening to yours, and you'll have an uphill battle trying to recapture their interest. So it's important to work hard on your opening remarks—and not just on *what* you say but on *how* you say it.

Even if you have an audience of a thousand people, you should speak in a conversational, informal manner. The reason is simple: every person in that vast crowd is responding to you as an individual. So talk to them as though each person has your undivided attention.

How do you do this? Through proper eye contact. Eye contact is, perhaps, the most important technique of delivery. It rivets your audience's attention and reveals your emotions to them. In turn, your audiences' eyes reveal their reaction to you.

However simple eye contact may seem, it will probably take a conscious effort on your part. This is because few of us are used to being the center of focus for hundreds of eyes. We tend to look away from so much attention. Resist the impulse. *Look at your audience, not at your notes, or the floor, or the ceiling.*

Eye Contact Techniques

If you are talking to a small audience of twenty or thirty people, be sure that at some point during your talk, you look directly into the eyes of each person there. Don't miss anyone. They'll feel it, even if you don't.

If you are talking to a large audience of one thousand or more, you can still give the impression of talking to each person in the audience. You do this by looking in various directions and actually stopping to focus on one person briefly. Pause for about ten seconds maximum, then move on. Proceed slowly in a different direction and look again at one person. Eventually your eyes will have swept the entire audience so that everyone will feel you have acknowledged their existence. Those you have looked at directly will have that special warm feeling, the feeling that comes from direct contact.

One way to establish eye contact during the first thirty seconds of your speech is to ask a question. You don't need notes for that. You can also cite an anecdote or quotation you know by heart.

HOW TO PUNCTUATE YOUR SPEECH

Pauses, gestures, and tone of voice are the "punctuation" of oral communication, and they are every bit as important to your speech as the words you use. Together with eye contact, the pause, the gesture, and voice tone send messages to your audience that you'll never get across with mere words. Thus, you should rehearse them just as thoroughly as you rehearse the words of your speech. Think of pauses as periods, gestures as exclamation marks, and voice quality (pitch and pacing) as italics, question marks, and dots and dashes.

Let's discuss these elements individually.

Pauses and Gestures

To get an idea of the power of the pause, I suggest you watch the "Tonight Show" and observe the master of the pregnant pause at work—Johnny Carson. Notice Carson's deadpan, slightly wicked stare directly into the camera after one of his guests has committed some gaucherie. His silence sometimes lasts three or four seconds, an eternity in television. But his eyes and facial expression tell you all you need to know. That look and the pause that accompanies it are eloquent beyond words.

When it comes to gestures, Hamlet's instruction to the players in Shakespeare's tragedy is still the best advice for any performer. He said, "Suit the action to the word and the word to the action." By that he means be sure word and gesture match. Never wave your arms about just because you feel static standing there. Sometimes just standing there is the best body language.

Newscasters and commentators are worth watching and imitating for the economy of their gestures. Also note their facial expressions, which sometimes say more than words ever could.

Pacing

Pace your speech carefully. Don't try to set any speed records. Remember, there is no such thing as a "speed listener." Most professional speakers, actors, and other performers speak at a rate of about 125 words per minute. They speak slowly at places they want to emphasize, and quickly on those points that are easily understood. *They do not go along at an even rate, like a metronome.* That bores people to the point where they are soon not listening at all.

Pitch

Vary your pitch as well. Your voice is a flexible instrument. Use your high and low tones to color your delivery; otherwise even the most startling statements will sound monotonous.

Record your voice on an audio cassette and listen to it to get some idea of how you sound to others. But don't be supercritical of the quality of your voice. Instead, concentrate on what you can do to enhance what you have.

Take comfort from the example of Louis Armstrong. He had the ultimate in raspy voices, yet he was one of the great song stylists of this century. Why? Because he put color and feeling into that rasp of his. His phrasing was elegant and his energy level incredible. You can be sure he wasted no time wishing he sounded like Bing Crosby or Frank Sinatra. Armstrong created his own style. That should be your goal, too.

PUBLIC SPEAKING AS CONVERSATION

Think of public speaking as good conversation with a friend. In this way, you will automatically begin to incorporate the foregoing techniques into any speech before an audience.

For example, if you were trying to tell a friend that two people you both knew had developed a close rapport, you might hold up your hand, cross your index and third fingers and say, "They're just like that." The gesture enhances your statement, and your friend immediately gets the picture. So would an audience.

Very often the words without the gesture are not completely clear. For example, suppose you describe someone as a big man. It could mean that he's fat, or tall, or it could have to do with his character rather than his physical attributes. But if, when you tell me he's a big man, you puff out your cheeks and make a great circle with your arms, I know he's fat, and you've given me a description of just how much fatter he is than you are. If you mean he's tall, I'll get the message if you extend an arm above your head so I know how much taller he is than you are. If you mean he is a man of character and you nod your head and give the word "big" a special intonation indicating admiration, I'll get your meaning immediately. In all these cases, the gesture is needed to explain the words.

DELIVERING THE IMPROMPTU SPEECH

Most of the techniques of delivery used in the more formal extemporaneous (i.e., unwritten) speech described earlier also apply to impromptu speaking. There are some differences, however.

Strictly speaking, the impromptu speech is one made on the spur of the moment, without notes or props of any kind. Despite that definition, you probably will have a little time to organize your thoughts before you speak. Use that time wisely.

For example, if you are going to a meeting of the local school board, you probably have some idea what is going to be discussed and you probably have an opinion about it. So if someone asks you to support a resolution granting teachers a raise, you are not totally unprepared. After the subject is broached—and *before* you raise your hand to speak—figure out how you want to make your point. When you do get the floor, rise and speak up loudly and clearly; make your point succinctly; and sit down. Rambling on and on destroys the impact of your delivery.

As Ruth Gordon wrote in her play *Over Twenty-One,* "The best impromptu remarks are well prepared in advance." You should remember this maxim, particularly if a question-answer period will follow your speech. If you've spoken on a subject before, you probably know what questions will be asked so you can prepare yourself beforehand. Some speakers get a reputation for being quick-witted during the question-answer period because it is assumed they have never heard the questions before and, therefore, the witty answers are off the cuff. Their secret is knowing their subject so thoroughly that nothing takes them by surprise. They are well prepared with their "impromptu" answers.

19

THE ART OF EXTEMPORANEOUS SPEAKING

by Robert L. Montgomery

Over the years, I've been a participant in about fifty speech contests. I've been a judge of another seventy-five. And I have never won a contest—or seen anyone else win a contest—when the speech was thoroughly memorized or delivered from notes.

Why don't either of these speech-delivery techniques win awards for speakers? Memorizing a talk word for word is the worst way to present a speech because it is totally unnatural. Even a child can recognize a memorized, or "canned," speech in less than a minute by the faraway look in the speaker's eyes and that faraway ring to his or her voice. Memorizing eliminates spontaneity. Furthermore, it's possibly the most arduous, frustrating, and undependable method of mastering a speech.

Then what's wrong with referring to notes? For the average speaker, nothing, provided you don't have your head buried in them, losing eye contact with your audience in the process. Most speech trainers, in fact, recommend using a *written outline*. But it must *be* an outline, not a mass of unwieldy notes. After all, the definition of the word "extemporaneous" is ". . . previously planned but delivered with the help of few or no notes."

There are various types of outlines. For instance, the dean of professional speakers in the United States, Dr. Kenneth McFarland, uses an outline consisting of key sentences. Other speakers use key words rather than sentences to highlight their talks. But the method I recommend doesn't rely on words at all. It calls for pictures!

A PICTURE IS WORTH A THOUSAND WORDS

The best way to recall the main points of a speech is to form a mental picture of each of the key ideas in your speech. I've used this method for many years. Mark Twain—celebrated as a public speaker as well as a writer—was also an exponent of this method. His speeches were always long and filled with human interest anecdotes. To him is ascribed the apt quote: "It usually takes more than three weeks to prepare a good impromptu speech."

Mark Twain always spoke without notes. He used a system of mental pictures summing up his key points. To fix those pictures in his head, he would walk through a park, for instance, in the town he was visiting, shortly before it was time for his appearance. He would look around and try to relate what he saw to key ideas in his speech.

For example, he might take his first main point—in the form of a sentence or phrase—and picture it lying on a park bench. He might picture his next idea hanging from a tree, and the third idea sprouting up from a flower bed. His fourth point might be floating in the water fountain while his fifth was perched on the bandstand.

Thus, when Twain got on the platform to give his speech, all he had to do was picture himself once again walking through that park, and each of his key ideas would pop into his mind in logical order. As he strolled by the prominent park landmarks, the key ideas associated sequentially with the bench, tree, flower bed, water fountain, and bandstand would flow out fluently, naturally, and spontaneously.

Twain was using a virtually flawless method of mental association: key ideas in picture or object form, linked to real objects in the park. What could be easier?

SPEECH NOTES IN THE FORM OF PICTURES

While Mark Twain may have used no notes at all—which is the ideal method—you may want to use them yourself in order to feel more secure. But I recommend that your notes—like Twain's—be in picture rather than sentence form. I find this method allows for a more natural, spontaneous, polished delivery, giving the impression that you are speaking completely off the cuff.

Here's a personal example of how a speech might be converted into picture form. Even though the speech was given at least ten years ago, I can still recall it clearly. Why? Because to conjure up the speech in my mind, all I have to remember are my notes—which were in the form of mental images.

The talk was entitled "Tools of Leadership," and the subject was human relations—how to get along with other people. Here's what I used as cues in my mental outline:

- a coffee can with $100 bills overflowing from it
- a copy of *Reader's Digest,* opened to page 70, with a question mark on the page
- the word CASH, as an acronym for four human-relations principles
- a bank giving away money

These images were all I needed to give a talk that I could polish off in three minutes or expand to fill an hour. Here's how I did it:

The can of coffee with the money spilling out of it reminded me of the image I wanted to conjure up in the audience's mind to open the talk: "The ability to deal with people," I said, "is as purchasable a commodity as sugar or coffee. And I, personally, would pay more for that ability than any quality on earth."

Then I said: "Those words were spoken by John D. Rockefeller, Sr., the richest man who ever lived. What he was talking about is something we call 'human relations.' He used to give speeches on the subject. After his talks, he'd give out new dimes to his listeners, one dime for every person in the audience. And that was done in the days when a dime was still worth ten cents!"

Then, by way of transition, I asked my audience a rhetorical question: "What does it really cost to practice good human relations?"

My next mental picture was that copy of the *Reader's Digest* open to page 70, with a question mark on the page. This reminded me of my next point, the answer to the question I've posed:

"*Reader's Digest* took a poll of major corporations, asking them this question: 'Of the last twenty-five employees discharged from your company, what were the reasons?' The *Digest* reported that 70% of the employees were fired for the same reason—their inability to get along with their fellow workers."

Now I was ready to swing into the heart of my talk—those four human-relations principles that spell out CASH. So I said next:

"Here is evidence that our jobs, our income, and even our friendships depend on our ability in human relations. So I propose a four-point program for better relations with the people you work with or socialize with."

The "C" of my acronym CASH popped into my head next and reminded me that the first principle I wanted to discuss is, *Don't Criticize, Condemn or Complain.* (In truth, I pictured more than just the opening letter of the word CASH. I pictured a big sign reading "CCC" for the three C's—criticize, condemn, and complain.) I followed with a story about Abe Lincoln on human relations, and two personal anecdotes. All three examples reinforced the rule, *Don't criticize, condemn, or complain.*

The "A" of CASH—and the mental picture of a dozen roses—reminded me of principle number two: *Give honest sincere Appreciation.* I followed that up with a quote by Mark Twain and a story about a friend of mine. The word "*A*ppreciation" and the flowers reminded me of both stories.

Next came the letter "S," which stood for the principle: *Become Sincerely interested in other people.* I quoted Bernard Baruch, told a second story drawn from Abraham Lincoln's life, and finished with two personal experiences. (I also pictured a pair of cauliflower ears; these signified listening and reminded me of my supporting evidence.)

My fourth and last principle, signified by the "H" in the acronym and a visualization of a coach motivating a football team with a pep talk, was: *Have a Hearty enthusiasm.* The "H" emphasized the word "hearty" since just ordinary enthusiasm is not enough. Then I quoted Longfellow, Norman Vincent Peale, and others on enthusiasm. I also threw in my own observations and experiences to support the principle.

I then pointed out to the audience how the principles I had just recited to them spelled out the word CASH.

Then, I conjured up my last mental image of a bank giving away money. I closed by saying: "I have for each of you a copper plaque of Abraham Lincoln. You get 100 of these for a dollar at any bank." And I had aides distribute a brand-new shiny penny to each member of the audience.

My final words were, "I can't afford to give out new dimes as John D. Rockefeller did, but put this penny in your pocket or purse and it will be a reminder to practice the CASH principles for better human relations."

And that's it! All I need to remind me of the entire talk even ten years later is a handful of mental images.

I prefer to keep my images in my head when I give a speech. But until you get used to this method, you may want to draw yourself some pictures on 8 x 10 or 4 x 5 index cards. (Avoid using paper; it rattles in microphones and is generally difficult to handle.) To prevent your index cards from getting out of order, you may want to punch a hole in the corner of each, run a string through it and tie a knot.

MEMORY SKILLS APPLICABLE TO EXTEMPORANEOUS SPEAKING

Another easy memory system to use for speaking extemporaneously is the *stack-and-link method*. Stacking and linking key ideas is a remarkably simple and yet almost foolproof system for speakers. (It will also help you to remember lists of any kind.)

The objective is to put abstract ideas into concrete form and link the ideas together. The more outrageous the mental picture the easier it is to remember. Here's an example of how the system works: Let's say you're going to give a speech on early American history and you want to talk about the formation of the original thirteen colonies. Here's how you concretize the ideas and *stack and link* them together:

Picture a *deli*cate china plate, *deli*cate china *ware*, on the floor in front of you. Jammed into the chinaware is a huge fountain *pen;* on the pen is a *Jersey calf*, a *new* calf; on the calf is *King George;* on King George's face is a *cut. Connecting* the ends of the *cut* is a Band-Aid. On his head is a *mass* of ice. Seated on ice is a movie starlet named *Marilyn.* In Marilyn's lap is an ocean *liner,* pointed *south.* On the liner is a single smokestack and jammed into it is a ham, a *new ham.* The ham is wrapped in a song sheet that reads: "Carry Me Back to Old *Virginny.*" On top of the ham, pushing it down the smokestack, is the *Empire State Building.* There's a weathervane on the building at the top in the form of an ocean *liner* pointing *north;* the wind is blowing north. On the deck of the ocean liner is a hen, a *Rhode Island* Red *hen,* cackling.

There you have, stacked and linked, for easy recall, the thirteen objects that tell you instantly the thirteen original colonies in the order they joined the Union. The italicized words give the clues.

Did you immediately identify the correct order of the states?

Delaware
Pennsylvania
New Jersey

Georgia
Connecticut
Massachusetts
Maryland
South Carolina
New Hampshire
Virginia
New York
North Carolina
Rhode Island

And, in case you're asked, if you have the hen lay a bottle of Vermont Maid Syrup, you'll recall the fourteenth state, Vermont.

You can transform any abstract ideas into concrete object form. Love is easily symbolized by a heart, patriotism by a flag, inflation by using a dollar sign with wings on it. The Ten Commandments, or any concepts, rules, or regulations can be visualized in object form.

Most professional speakers and teachers use the stack-and-link method of association or the system of mental pictures associated with familiar items or objects. With a little practice you can master these methods and use the one that works best for you. But, remember, practice is the best instructor. It takes hard work to make any system your own.

OTHER FORMATS FOR WRITTEN OUTLINES

Although I prefer the visualization method, there are other ways of outlining a talk. Here are two.

• The first is the *key word* outline. A speaker I know gave a five-minute talk on "Safety in Hunting" with this kind of outline. His opening was, "Four out of five hunters who were killed in the United States last year were killed by someone in their own hunting party." On his outline, the first line read: "Four out of five hunters . . ."

The remainder of his talk was summed up in just a few key words. These words referred to safety reminders. Here is his outline as it appeared on an 8 x 10 card in large red letters:

1. Plugged barrels
2. Trespassing
3. Ricochet
4. Booze and guns
5. Lost

The entire talk was based on those key words. Our speaker closed his talk with the same startling, sobering statistic he used to open the speech. I could give the essence of the talk from memory now that I know the key words and the one statistic. And I've never been hunting!

First, I would make the point that you should always clean the barrel of your gun before you go out to pursue your prey. A plugged barrel could easily backfire and kill the hunter. Second, I would caution against trespassing on private property, whether "Keep Out" signs are posted or not. Under the new laws, signs are not necessary. Furthermore, the owner of the property could mistake you for an intruder or even a robber and shoot you. That happened recently in Wisconsin. Next, I'd say that bullets ricocheting off trees or rocks are often the reason for accidental shootings. I'd then talk about the hazards of drinking while hunting. And I'd wrap up my speech with a warning about how hunters should stay together in a group, to keep any individual or individuals from getting lost.

If this kind of outline appeals to you, you could put together an equally brief outline to help you recall the details of your own presentation. On the other hand, to recall these points from memory, *without any notes,* all you have to do is form a mental picture for the opening statistic and each of the five key ideas discussed above.

• Example number two is what I call a *key phrase* outline. It is also simple and easy to use.

The speaker who gave the following talk used an 8 x 10 card with the key words in large one-inch-high lettering. (Incidentally, you should always *print or type* your outline. Remember, you are *not* going to read an outline. You are only going to glance at it to jog your memory.)

To illustrate his talk, this speaker used four slides of a group on a backpacking expedition. I've never been backpacking, but by using his outline—and doing a little background reading—I could give the main ideas of his speech.

Here is the exact outline:

SLIDE #1: (picture of a group hiking in the woods).
           What is it?
           Who can do it?
           Where to go?
           When?
           How?
SLIDE #2: (picture of a hiker with a closeup of the backpack).
           Equipment:
           Pack.

Bag.
Tent.
Food.
Cookware.
Water.
Boots-lightweight. Why?
SLIDE #3: (picture of a group camping in the hills).
Easy.
Exercise.
Fresh air.
Carefree.
Low cost.
Nature (bears).
SLIDE #4: (picture of hikers sitting around a campfire).
FUN!

Even without the slides, the words and phrases above in outline form are all that are needed to relate the story to others.

OPENINGS AND CLOSINGS

Although, as I've said, you should *never* memorize a talk word for word, you *should* memorize the opening and closing of your speech. There's a saying, "By their entrances and exits you shall know speakers—whether they are amateur or professional." So make sure you know the opening and closing of your talk by heart. After all, these are the two most vulnerable areas of a speech—and the parts people tend to remember most.

Even speakers who insist on reading their speech should know the opening and closing by heart, so they can look at their listeners at these critical points. While you're practicing the opening of your speech, keep this important point in mind: *You never get a second chance at a first impression.*

PART V

CAREER ADVANCEMENT VIA SELF-PROMOTION

20

LIFE PLANNING:
How It Can
Benefit You

by Helga Long

Successful careers—indeed, successful lives—don't just happen. They are the product of a continuing program of long-range day*dreaming.*

Dreaming?

Yes, *dreaming*. We all have a dream, a vision, a purpose, a goal we want to achieve before we die, but too many people don't know, on a conscious level, what that goal is. They've never forced themselves to verbalize their secret ambition and, thus, go through life fulfilling other people's expectations and other people's dreams.

Life planning is the never-ending process of stating and attempting to achieve your dreams. Your short-term career goals will change from year to year, but your one true ambition in life never changes. It is the purpose to which your whole life is dedicated.

Do you know what yours is?

THE BENEFITS OF LIFE PLANNING

At this point, you're probably saying to yourself: "I neither know nor care. How is some idealistic goal in life going to help me get a promotion or put my son through college? The daily grind of making a living long ago stripped me of my youthful dreams."

The fact is that the absence of a dream, a "design for living," may just be the reason why you get so few promotions and aren't making more money. When author Gail Sheehy asked 60,000 people from all walks of life to fill out an extensive "Life History Questionnaire" for her book *Pathfinders,* she discovered that the people who are the most successful and satisfied with their lives have at least two things in common: they tend to have more close friends than others and they are more devoted to a cause beyond themselves. These "pathfinders," according to Sheehy, find more meaning in life and enjoy it more than those with no lifelong goals to propel them forward.

Perhaps Theodore Roosevelt said it best, though a mite harshly: "If a man does not have an ideal, then he becomes a mean, base and sordid creature...." He could have added "...a creature whose thinking is muddled and whose approach to life is generally passive." Instead of exerting control over his life, such a man tends to let life—or the fates, destiny, whatever you want to call it—do the controlling. It's an unfortunate truism that a man who does not know where he wants to go usually ends up going nowhere.

The antidote for this malaise is life planning. It is a process I teach to executives, particularly people who have just lost their jobs and feel a momentary lack of direction. By and large, my "students" are involved, high-powered, motivated individuals who commit themselves easily to the life-planning mode of self-discovery because they immediately grasp its benefits.

One form of life planning is management-by-objectives, which helps people identify goals and gives them standards by which to measure their performance. However, with life planning, the arena is the wide expanse of a person's life. Management-by-objectives, in contrast, applies only to the circumscribed world of the corporation and employees' performance there. Life planning helps people develop a sense of priorities in all aspects of their life, from their personal life to their careers. It allows them to see the forest instead of getting lost in the trees.

DEVISING A LIFE PLAN

A life plan is a timetable for reaching not only your life's goal but the myriad of smaller goals that preoccupy you on a daily basis. The reason for a life plan is to focus your thinking so that you can make the most efficient use of your mental and physical energy over a specified period of time—one lifetime. Your objective is to channel your energy into a manageable number of interim goals, realizing that the more focused you are, the more concentrated your energy will be.

Step One

Your first task is to discover, if you don't already know, your primary goal in life, your *raison d'être*, the fixed purpose around which everything else in your life revolves. For some people, this task takes them on a joyride of self-discovery. For others, the process is far more arduous, requiring them to travel backwards in their own psyches to a time in their youth when dreams still seemed capable of becoming reality.

There are a number of questions you might ask yourself in order to bring your primary goal into focus:

• Who am I? And what do I want to accomplish in life?

• On my deathbed, looking back over my life, what would give me the most satisfaction?

• What types of successes in my everyday life give me the greatest sense of accomplishment?

It's possible that you will come to know your life's goal after just one sitting. However, most people must repeat these and similar questions to themselves on a number of different occasions before they get close to the truth. Each time you ponder such questions, take notes— randomly. They may not make much sense at first, but when you compare your jottings from several introspective sessions, you will begin to see patterns emerging.

One of my clients—an executive in the steel industry—took over a month to discover tht his major ambition in life was *not* just to be president of his company. After filling several notepads with lists, he finally admitted to himself that he derived an even greater pleasure from his role as father than he did from his role as power-wielding executive. Those rambling lists led him to this realization even though they were filled with such secondary goals as "I want to hold a local political office...live in a restored English Tudor house in the suburbs...drive a Mercedes...put my five children through college ...travel around the world some day." But buried within those lists were several continuing themes. Many of his goals involved his children and the kind of upbringing he was giving them.

Another constellation of this man's goals concerned his desire to help solve the country's important problems, such as environmental pollution and unemployment. Rereading those notes, it suddenly hit him:

His mission in life was to nurture children who, as adults, would be committed to working for the public good. When he repeated that life goal to me, it rang true. He reminded me of Joseph P. Kennedy, a man who certainly made an impact during his own lifetime, but continues to do so even today through his sons and daughters' dedication to public service and charity work. This steel executive was in the same mold.

A happy man is generally a man whose occupation and lifestyle are congruent with his lifelong goal. For example, a man with a strong sense of organization, a flair for words, and desire to educate would probably gain the most satisfaction as a textbook editor or a writer of educationally oriented material. A man with a scientific bent and a profound need to help others on a one-to-one basis would make an excellent doctor. From the time I was quite young, I knew I wanted to have an impact on the quality of people's lives some day, and I feel I am doing that as the head of an executive search firm and through my executive-career-counseling work.

Step Two

Once you have stated your life's goal in one sentence, you are ready to begin implementing that goal. A career, defined as a "succession of jobs that form a coherent pattern," is one tool for helping you achieve your ultimate goal. Thus it is important that you plan your career as a general might plan a battle, or a football coach might map out the plays for the big game.

First, ask yourself, "Is my profession or occupation helping me to complete my life's work?" If your answer is no, go one step further and ask yourself, "Is there a way I can make my profession or vocation congruent with my fundamental goal?" Often, there is. For example, a young lawyer who is a rising star in his firm, but feels unfulfilled nevertheless, might look to see where he can make a contribution— such as taking on a few *pro bono publico* clients. An auditor employed by a large public accounting firm might take advantage of one of the firm's minority outreach programs and become a visiting professor of accounting at a predominantly black college for two years. A manufacturing executive working in a "smokestack" industry such as steel or oil refining might become a member of the Sierra Club and work toward the conservation and preservation of wilderness areas of the country. It's been my experience that most executives can make satisfactory mid-career transitions *without* totally changing occupations, engaging in extensive retraining, or moving into a new industry.

Ideally, the life/career planning process should begin as soon as you graduate from school. With his long-term objectives clearly in focus, a young man can make sure that jobs or promotions he accepts make an integrated contribution to his overall life and career goals. Furthermore, he can avoid two of the worst career pitfalls: task orientation and job orientation.

To avoid task orientation, never allow yourself to lose sight of your job's true objective. A personnel director is supposed to interpret management's policies to employees, as well as to reflect back to management any important unmet employee needs. Any personnel director who views himself primarily as a record keeper misses the point. He is task obsessed to his own detriment.

A job-oriented person also overlooks the big picture. To avoid this pitfall, recognize that the jobs you hold, and the order in which you hold them, are extremely important. So before you accept any job, ask yourself, "Where could this job lead?"

Remember, it's never too late to begin the life/career planning process. Now is an excellent time to start whether you are 25 and just embarking on your career or 45 and stalled in a job you dislike and in a lifestyle that makes you uncomfortable.

Step Three

Once you have figured out how your profession or occupation complements your larger goal in life, you are ready to begin the nuts-and-bolts process of life/career planning.

A *Personal Career Plan* codifies your short-term goals, those interim steps that move you toward the eventual fulfillment of your overall ambition. A Personal Career Plan is mapped out in five-year increments. It should answer the following questions:

1. What career and/or personal goals would I like to accomplish in five years? Ten years?
2. What would I like to be earning in five years? Ten years?
3. What kind of lifestyle would I like to have in five years? Ten years?

The answers to such questions will provide you with a list of short-term goals. In formulating these goals, don't rely purely on logic. This type of decision making should be creative and bring your emotions, values, and beliefs into play. You may also want to consider the emotions, values, and beliefs of your wife, since she will become a partner in any important decision affecting your personal life.

Step Four

Next, you must focus on implementation—how you plan to achieve your short-range goals. Suppose, for example, that you are a middle manager working for a large bank as an economist—a staff job. One of your goals is to move into a line position as a corporate loan officer. You would ask yourself:

1. What special training will I need to qualify as a corporate loan officer?
2. What books could I read on the subject?
3. What internal political roadblocks may be thrown up to prevent such a lateral career move?
4. Will my boss be a help or a hindrance? Is there some other influential bank officer who might help me achieve my goal?
5. What is the probability of eventually becoming a corporate loan officer at my present company? Are my chances any better at another bank, perhaps a smaller one?
6. What is the educational and experience level—and age—of the average person who becomes a corporate loan officer?

When you have discovered everything there is to know about how to become a corporate loan officer, you must formulate a short-term game plan that outlines the progress you expect to make toward your goal over the next year, perhaps over the next several years.

The physical format and the exact timetable of your Personal Career Plan are up to you. Some men are extremely methodical about their plan, laying it out precisely on a chart, or in some other schematic format, in, say, six-month increments. Other men keep their goals and implementation plans in their heads or make rather disorganized-looking entries on the subject in a small notebook. I make no recommendations concerning format or scheduling. Whatever works for you is the structure you should adopt.

Step Five

This is the hardest step of all, because it requires that you stop dreaming and start *doing*. This is the stage at which some men discover that the reason why they aren't moving ahead is not external—such as a boss who won't credit a subordinate for his ideas, or an employer who does not promote from within. Instead, the reason is internal, psychological in nature. A man may have a neurotic fear of success that he has never

confronted, indeed, never realized he had. He erects his own roadblocks and detours to prevent himself from ever achieving his stated
goals.

In implementing any Personal Career Plan, a man should expect to
slam up against many barriers and hurdles. The question to ask yourself
is, "Am I willing to do what is necessary to remove this barrier, even if
the prospect is very uncomfortable?" To remove a barrier, you may
have to sharpen your public speaking skills by enrolling in a Dale
Carnegie course, for instance. Or maybe you're having trouble writing
succinct memos and reports, so that a business writing course would
be in order. On the other hand, your problem may be emotional and/or
psychological, so seeking private or group counseling from a professional might be beneficial. No matter what the barrier, there is a way
through it. It's up to you to decide how to handle it and then do it!

Don't be lazy. Too many people mistakenly believe that wishing for
something is the same as going after it. It isn't. Good intentions are a
beginning but they must be translated into actions. Whenever you find
yourself muttering, "I don't want to do _____," "That's too hard,"
"Give me a break, world," it's time to figuratively give yourself a good,
hard kick in the rear. Whatever your goal, you must go after it with all
the energy you can muster.

In addition to laziness, there are several other pitfalls that can trap
people attempting to implement their life/career plans. One involves
mistakes.

Expect to make mistakes no matter how well you've worked out your
personal game plan. In fact, do more than expect mistakes; in the words
of Buckminster Fuller, "Embrace mistakes." Mistakes serve a useful
purpose because they wake you up and force you to take stock of a
situation. So you got fired. Are you going to sit and brood about it for
the rest of your life? Maybe being fired was the figurative "kick in the
rear" that you needed in order to get moving again along a constructive
pathway.

Never castigate yourself for a mistake or let it stymie you. Instead,
analyze your mistake and transform it into the proverbial blessing in
disguise.

Finally, make sure you meet your self-imposed deadlines and accomplish your short-term goals no matter how small. Why? The reason
concerns your morale. Self-esteem is developed by degrees. A strong
self-image is acquired by (1) setting goals for yourself, minor ones at
first; (2) achieving those goals within the time frame allotted; and (3)
receiving praise from others about those accomplishments. If you

consistently fail to accomplish your interim goals, you set up a pattern of failure that will gradually sap your self-confidence and erode your self-esteem.

Should you fail to accomplish several goals in succession, sound the alarm. It's been my experience that there are generally two reasons why a man fails to accomplish minor goals: either his goals are not realistic to begin with; or he is not motivated enough. If the former is true of you, scale down your goals so that they are realistic and *do-able*. If your problem is one of motivation, consider going to a career counselor or confiding in a friend about your self-doubts and disappointments. Whatever you do, *do something*. Don't accept your shortcomings or other obstacles as "just the way things are."

Step Six

Continually revise and update your life/career plan based on any new information you discover about yourself or others. A life/career plan is not engraved in stone. It exists merely to provide you with a framework for advancement. You are its author and you can alter its content anytime it appears to be leading you astray.

LIFE PLANNING LASTS A LIFETIME

The kind of self-conscious personal planning we've been discussing is not something that ceases with retirement. Hardly. In fact, retirement may be the ideal time for you to rechannel 100 percent of your energy into your life's goal.

I think there is nothing sadder than a person who retires from life when he reaches sixty-five and leaves his job. Such people have planned their own obsolescence, often moving to retirement villages where they spend the rest of their days searching for new hobbies to occupy their waking hours. Their "real life" is over and they figure they'll just coast and enjoy themselves for the remainder of life's ride. The problem is that too many of our senior citizens who have chosen this lifestyle don't enjoy themselves. Secretly, they're miserable because they have withdrawn from involvement with the larger issues confronting humanity.

If you are approaching retirement, don't let it become a goal in itself. If you do, I guarantee you'll experience a tremendous letdown. This is the same letdown you'll feel at any age if you achieve an important goal without having a follow-up goal right behind it. With a new goal to pursue, you avoid that awful feeling of emptiness that results when a personal triumph disintegrates with the passage of time. Whenever you find yourself saying, "Is this all there is?," you know you're momentarily without goals. It's an uncomfortable, rootless feeling. Don't stay in that place for long.

21

PERSONAL PUBLIC RELATIONS: A Do-It-Yourself Program

by Carl Terzian

You're unhappy and angry—and you just can't understand it. It should have been you, not Jack, who's being promoted to senior vice-president. You're already a group vice-president with fourteen years of loyal service to the company. The senior vice-presidency was your next move. But that promotion writeup in the business section of the newspaper is Jack's, not your's.

Or maybe you're a dedicated doctor with a jealous wife on your hands. She and some of the other doctors' wives were playing tennis yesterday, but it was Sheila Johnson who drove home in a new Rolls-Royce, not your Peggy. You know you're as good a doctor as Dick Johnson, so why is his practice growing so much faster than yours? It doesn't make any sense.

If a company is considering three equally qualified candidates for a major senior management promotion, the executive who looks the best, can speak well, is involved in the community, who mixes well socially, and who possesses that special quality called "class," always has the edge over his competitors. A self-employed professional man who can boast these attributes will also find it easier to build his practice or increase his sales.

People prefer doing business with competent business and professional men—better yet, competent *and successful* business and professional men. But who is the successful man? He's the man who is *perceived* to be successful by others. And it's high visibility and good personal publicity that make others perceive a man that way.

PERSONAL PUBLIC RELATIONS—WHAT IS IT?

Good personal public relations means garnering deserved recognition for yourself that will help you advance in your career. It does *not* mean notoriety or personal aggrandizement.

High visibility of the right kind can be financially rewarding as well as satisfying to one's ego. Even many publicity-shy professionals now realize they must take an aggressive marketing stance if they are to survive, let alone succeed, in today's competitive marketplace. That could include advertising their services, a practice heretofore unheard of among doctors, lawyers, and accountants. Today, it's becoming commonplace.

When you hear the words "publicity" or "personal public relations," you probably visualize a story about you in the newspaper, or imagine yourself being interviewed on a television talk show. That's part of it, the most glamorous part. But a well-rounded personal publicity program encompasses much more: hosting receptions, giving speeches, writing articles, receiving awards, meeting people, taking a leadership position in the community, sending gracious letters. These are all aspects of the do-it-yourself personal public relations program I will outline for you in the following pages.

DO-IT-YOURSELF PR

After more than twenty years as a personal public relations counselor to over six hundred clients, I am convinced that a person's *attitude* is the real key to any successful self-marketing effort. A person simply cannot expect to achieve his publicity goals unless his marketing program receives his highest priority.

To be effective, a public relations program has to be long term. It will take a consistent commitment of energy, time—perhaps several years' time—and resources on your part. A few well-placed bylined articles, even several important speaking engagements, by themselves, won't land you your dream job or double your business overnight. But a wholehearted dedication to the all-important and all-encompassing job of selling yourself will.

When I'm retained by a client, I take him or her through a three-phase program. Although phase three yields the tangible results, the preparatory phases one and two are equally crucial. Without a public relations counselor to prod and guide you, it will take self-discipline to work your way through these phases. But do not neglect the fundamental steps or your lack of preparation may create embarrassing moments for you just when you least expect them.

PHASE 1: ANALYZE YOUR GOALS

Why are you embarking on this publicity effort? If your answer is, "To get ahead in my field," think some more. That goal is too vague. What is your specific goal or goals? Make sure you know what they are before you proceed any further.

Once you can state your goal(s) in one sentence, you must challenge each of them. Do you have a full knowledge of any sacrifices that may be required to achieve your goal(s)? Are you willing to make those sacrifices?

Successful business executives often come to me to explore the idea of running for elective office. "I've achieved most of my business goals, yet I feel unfulfilled," they tell me. Before I even accept them as clients, I have to know whether these people understand what they're getting into. Many times they don't. They still believe the idealized version of American politics they were taught in high school civics classes: the best qualified candidate wins; there's no mudslinging; it's just a matter of hard work, getting to know a lot of new people, and soliciting adequate financial resources to wage a high-visibility campaign. Unfortunately, that's *not* the reality of true-life political campaigning.

During my orientation with such a client, I ask him probing questions as: How much do you *really* know about what it's like to be, say, a congressman or senator? Have you ever been to the state capital, or to Washington, to see what that officeholder does? Have you ever worked in a political campaign? Do you know anything about the political organization of the district? How much do you know not only about politics, but about basic civics, how the American system operates both in theory and practice?

Finally, I query the man about his marriage and family: Do your wife and children share your goals? Do they know the pressures and fishbowl scrutiny they will have to endure? Even if they're willing, do they have the emotional and intellectual stamina to make it through a long, hard-fought campaign? And to embark on a new life if you're elected?

PHASE 2: EVALUATE THE PRODUCT—YOU

Put 100 men and women in a room and ask them to define "personal public relations" and you'll get 100 different answers. Some of them will undoubtedly say, however, that PR is an attempt to cover up a person's flaws and place that individual in a favorable light.

This is an erroneous view of personal public relations. True, personal publicity is an attempt to highlight the positive aspects of a person's character and accomplishments while playing down any negatives. But it should never become a vehicle for distorting the truth or outright lying.

I choose my clients very carefully—especially those seeking elective office—just so I won't find myself promoting an individual who doesn't deserve the recognition. A person's ethics, values, and standards are the key to my decision whether or not to accept him or her as a client. While a potential client may be interviewing my firm, at the same time, I'm also interviewing him. We're both probably evaluating the same things: honesty, integrity, track record, reputation.

I make the same suggestion to you: Before you embark on any self-marketing program that will cast you in the spotlight, be sure you belong there. Do you truly possess that special blend of intelligence, skills, and charisma that deserves—no, *demands*—positive exposure and the rewards that accompany such exposure? Do you have the credentials, track record, and substance to radiate that indefinable quality called "class" I mentioned earlier?

Be honest with yourself. Ask yourself: What are my assets? My liabilities? In what areas am I vulnerable to attack? What can I do to convert any negatives into positives *before* I launch my personal public relations campaign?

David Ogilvy, the brilliant advertising executive, always emphasized that the quickest way to kill a mediocre product is to call attention to it. Unfortunately, the slickest ad or publicity campaign in the world can't combat bad word-of-mouth reviews; there's no humiliation worse than a big brash public failure. So take a searching personal and professional inventory before proceeding further.

On the other hand, you may indeed have all the raw materials for success in your field, but suffer from the uncut-diamond syndrome. In short, your assets have never been integrated into a salable commodity. You need packaging. Maybe your dress is inappropriate for the magnitude of the job or your speech lacks refinement. Maybe you don't read the publications or books that will give you an informed opinion. You may need coaching in the art of gracious entertaining. Perhaps your office decor shows little discernment.

The advice contained in this book is designed to help you eliminate these exterior red lights. I advise you to do so *before* moving on to phase three.

PHASE 3: IMPLEMENT YOUR PERSONAL MARKETING PROGRAM

I define personal marketing broadly as everything from advertising, publicity, and public relations to civic participation and general socializing. Which aspects of the following program you want to stress will depend on your career goals and your personal style and interests. Use my suggestions as a springboard for tailoring a public relations campaign to suit your particular needs.

General Publicity Common sense, dignity, honesty, graciousness, and the right attitude—these are the attributes that impress journalists and other members of the media. For your purposes, the ideal media targets are newspapers—in both the community where you live and the city where you work; trade, professional, and civic organizations' publications; alumni journals; company house organs; and local radio and television news and talk shows. It is people in decision-making jobs with these publicity outlets that you want to meet and cultivate.

Pretend, for a moment, that you're an architect with several professionals working for you. Your firm has just been retained to design three exciting new buildings. You'd like the firm to get some publicity focusing on these projects. Your new clients have no objections. Where do you begin?

You would tell the media about your projects in a press release. Quite simply, a press release is a news story. It should be brief, to the point, and state the facts: *who* you are; *what* your firm is about to do; *when* it will do it; *where* it will be doing it; *why* it is doing it; and *how* it will accomplish its goals. If your story has a visual angle—as an architect, yours certainly does—be sure to include with the press release high-quality 8 X 10 black-and-white photographs. In this case, you might include photos of your architectural models. Since your objective is *personal* publicity, make sure you're in the photograph looking at the models. Don't just stand there stiffly staring in the camera, though. Editors like candid shots. These are photographs where the subjects appear to be caught up in what they are doing (for example, explaining the architectural features to the client).

If you've never written a press release before, or seen one so you can copy its format, I suggest calling your local newspaper editor and inviting him out to lunch to ask his advice. Once the editor hears why you've called, the first thing you'll have to do is wait for him to pick himself up off the floor! Editors rarely get asked how they can help.

My experience is that editors—local editors, at any rate—are more than happy to sit down with you and explain what they look for in a story. (I wouldn't try calling up a harried editor for a big-city newspaper like *The Los Angeles Times,* however.) The editor will probably tell you that when you've got something to say about your product or services, the best way is the simplest. Give a straightforward description of your product or service without hyping it; tell how much it costs; where people can get it; and what hours it's available. If an editor gets such a press release and has further questions, he'll call you or send around a reporter.

Also, he'll tell you that a good human-interest photo with a bright, pointed caption can stand by itself as a newsworthy item.

What's newsworthy? This is where your amateur status as a publicist may emerge. Don't mistakenly assume that anything *you* find fascinating necessarily has universal appeal. Here are some hints about the kinds of items journalists find newsworthy: an offbeat job or hobby; opinions you have on a subject in which you are deemed an expert; contests or high awards you've won; important news events that you've either witnessed or participated in; anything you've done that's highly unusual (maybe you were one of the first Occidentals to visit Red China; you hosted an impromptu reception for the president of the United States when he made a surprise visit to your town; you had the governor of your state as a houseguest). In general, anything that is first, best, worst, a breakthrough, highly unusual, amusing, or timely will pique the curiosity of some editor.

But newspaper publicity is only one aspect of a general publicity campaign. Perhaps you're a professional who takes pride in staying on top of current trends in your field, whether those trends concern emergency medicine or tax legislation. If you've got some strong and *informed* opinions on a particular new development, contact the editors of trade publications and offer to write an article. Also exploit all opportunities to publicize any original research you've done in your field. Trade publications and professional journals are looking for just such material.

If you're a poor writer, it may be worth it to hire a professional writer to ghostwrite the article for you. If you work for a large corporation, a member of the company's public relations department may write it for you, gratis. Why? Because it reflects well on a company if it employs experts and industry spokesmen.

Never overlook a trade or professional publication because it has a small circulation. What the trades lack in terms of readership quantity they more than make up for in terms of readership quality. Bylined articles in trade and professional journals not only give you the imprimatur of an authority in your field, but are also an excellent springboard to the consumer press. Always reprint your trade articles to use as handouts the next time someone asks to see your resume or inquires about your credentials. You might also mail such articles on an FYI basis (for your information) to people in your personal contact file. (More about this file a little later.) Further, you might dangle those articles before print or radio-TV assignment editors as credible bait for a general interview with you.

If you've got something to say that could be of interest to those outside your immediate professional sphere, give your local radio program directors a call. Despite recent legislation, both AM and FM stations in this country still have community service requirements to fulfill to keep their Federal Communications Commission licenses. Granted, being on the air at 6:00 A.M. on a Sunday morning on your local, easy-listening station is not exactly a forum equivalent to "Face the Nation" or "Meet the Press." But, on the other hand, the appearance didn't cost you anything either. And some people out there will be listening no matter what the hour of day or night. Besides, any radio exposure is great practice for bigger and more important radio or television appearances later. The experience will teach you how to organize your thoughts quickly and state your opinions succinctly.

Once you've made the initial contact with a few members of the media, don't have an ulterior motive every time you talk with them. If they call you asking for information, give it to them if possible. But request anonymity if being identified as a source of the information might be damaging to your professional reputation. Once you become one of a reporter's regular sources, you are in a position to ask for a few favors of your own. But don't overdo it.

My final advice to you about dealing with the media is: Never, *never* lie to journalists, or give them the impression they're being used. Yes, in recent years some reporters' ethics have been tested and found wanting. But most respect confidences, quote accurately and generously, and are not "out to get you" because you're a member of "the Establishment." The climate between reporters and the business community has warmed considerably in recent years, I'm happy to report, with both sides ridding themselves of unhealthy preconceptions.

Public Speaking   The platform continues to afford a unique opportunity for dynamic speakers to showcase their credibility, increase their visibility, and make contact with people who may one day become clients, mentors, customers, or just new friends. The career, as well as the personal life, of more than one professional has been enriched— even dramatically altered—by his outstanding performance at the podium.

Beyond the exposure, there are a number of more intangible personal qualities public speaking will help you develop. Speaking experience will increase your poise and self-confidence, force you to develop a winning platform persona, and project an aura of authority and honesty. If you're hot tempered and prone to sudden outbursts, public speaking will soon reduce this tendency as well. Public address sharpens your intellect and communications skills, and teaches you to present your arguments logically and without excess of confusing detail. Finally, it will help you develop a useful, almost instinctive sixth sense concerning other people's reactions to what you are saying.

Getting up on that platform to address an audience is the key to developing inside and outside visibility. To gain greater exposure *within* your company or profession, speak up at internal meetings or at professional conferences, ask questions after someone else has given a presentation, or spearhead discussions in informal workshop sessions. To gain greater exposure *outside* your company or profession, get a list of local organizations from your chamber of commerce and offer to address these groups on a catchy topic related to your field. The Kiwanis, Optimists, Rotary, and Lions clubs are always looking for speakers. Approach the group's program chairman with a cover letter offering to speak on your topic; a brief, one-page outline of the speech; a bio and black-and-white photo of yourself; a suggested introduction for the MC; and a news release the group might want to send to the media about your speech.

If you wonder why you're doing work that might appear to be beyond your normal business commitments, remember that the true publicity value of a speaking engagement lies in all the marketing activities you can create and schedule around that thirty-minute address. For example, try to have the organization arrange a news conference before your speech, where you hand out a boiled-down version of your prepared text and answer questions about it. You can also reprint the speech in toto and send it to the media. And you might use portions of the speech later, in a bylined article on a similar subject.

Fraternal organizations are great forums for beginning speakers, but you should eventually move on and address more challenging business and professional audiences. In general, the larger and more influential your audience, the greater the chance your talk will be publicized. As you gain more experience, avoid the temptation to appear only before friendly groups. Admittedly, it's ego-gratifying to educate and inspire your believers; however, when you possess sufficient confidence, it's equally critical to attempt to reach the indifferent—even hostile—audience.

Of course, writing a speech will mean long hours of research, preparation, and practice. Once the speech is written, record it and listen carefully to the playback to eliminate any weak sections. Fine-tune it for the specific audience. I advise you to restrict yourself to subjects you know thoroughly and can talk about enthusiastically. And, above all, resist the urge to make a blatant commercial pitch for your business or services.

By all means, stick around after you've delivered your speech to answer questions, meet new people, and exchange business cards. Then follow up with gracious letters to the program chairman and any influential listeners who gave you their cards. Who knows? Your note may wind up in the organization's newsletter for extra mileage.

Civic Participation   If you live in a smaller city where business and social relationships intertwine, attaining a position of civic leadership will enhance your reputation as well as advance your career. I'm talking about putting in many long hours of hard work on behalf of the United Way, the March of Dimes, the Boy Scouts, or Junior Achievement—true grass-roots community participation. I'm not talking about heading up a committee and then letting someone else do all the work. Rather than enhance your reputation, this type of passing-the-buckmanship will surely help destroy it. The word always gets around.

When you head a committee or hold down an officer's post, you have to be willing to put in the time and effort to make the organization's programs successful. If you join a fraternal organization like the Lions or Elks, actively take part in those programs which will do the general community the most good. Or you might seek a trustee position for a church, school, foundation, hospital, or college.

What's the payoff? First, the satisfaction of knowing you're contributing to society's betterment. But, on a selfish level, you've now got a legitimate platform for speaking out as an acknowledged specialist in a subject you believe in passionately. With your call for action, you can make significant and legitimate news. If you haven't already cultivated media contacts using the expert-in-your-field angle, then this new role gives you another excellent reason to establish such relationships. In your new role, you may also be called upon as an expert witness or as an authority giving testimony to fact-finding federal committees and commissions. All of this will widen, broaden, and deepen your exposure to other influential members of your community. Finally, when push comes to shove, most people with a contract to let or a product to buy are going to deal with the business or professional man they've met informally at their fraternal club's weekly luncheon, or have heard so much about because of his distinguished service on a charity drive.

While personal and business advancement may be an important motivation for your civic involvement, you must also truly enjoy this type of public service. Otherwise, your ulterior motives will become readily apparent and that can only tarnish your good name.

Philanthropy and Sponsorship   If life has been good to you and your firm now employs hundreds of employees, you might simply continue to manifest the same public-spirited generosity you did when the firm was small. However, instead of monetary contributions, you can now let your donations take other forms. For example, you might lend one of your managers to a charity such as the United Way, UNICEF, or the Junior League, while still keeping that employee on your payroll. Or you might let a worthy group use a spare office for its headquarters.

As an individual, you can also think of highly creative and noteworthy ways to contribute to worthy causes. Instead of making an outright monetary gift, how about endowing a guest-musicians' fund at your local church . . . or sponsoring a guest lecture series at your local college . . . or giving seed money to a Junior Achievement corporation in addition to contributing your business acumen to help those teenagers make their project a success?

Your ability to get publicity for such unusual forms of philanthropy is limited only by your imagination and knack for dreaming them up.

Recreational and Social Clubs   I advise my clients to join at least one downtown luncheon club and one recreational or social club. I also advise them to realize we're living in an era of heightened consciousness about women and minorities. Make sure you're not walking into a hornet's nest by joining a club that could be accused of some form of discrimination. This is *not* the type of association that will help build your good name.

Enjoy golf, tennis, or racquetball for the pure sport of the game; but also use your athletic ability as a social, business, or public relations vehicle. Important business deals are still begun or finalized on the links, or over drinks following tennis doubles or a fast-paced round of racquetball. (Incidentally, play to win. That old chestnut about letting the boss or a potential client win is nonsense.)

Clubs should be used as places where you can entertain guests graciously in sumptuous surroundings. But never let your business discussions over lunch or dinner get so involved that either you or your guest start poring over business documents. This type of blatant commercial behavior is frowned on at the toniest old-guard clubs—and at the best clubs for the newer elite as well.

Well-chosen club memberships can catapult you into an entirely new circle of friends. These new friends may be better read or livelier conversationalists than your old group, in which case, I suggest you develop some new interests and social abilities in line with theirs. Practice the social arts—but without overdoing it and becoming a gadfly or, worse yet, an insufferable boor.

Gracious Letters   I know what you're probably thinking: "What can this consultant possibly tell me about letters that I don't already know?"

Well, I believe that gracious letters are an invaluable form of public relations that most people overlook. I'm not referring simply to the required thank-you notes. I'm referring to those unexpected notes to congratulate friends or acquaintances on a promotion or an award they've received. Maybe a long-lost friend was just featured in a magazine you happened to see by chance. Take the opportunity to renew your friendship with a warm letter.

Letters have more psychological import—and impact—when recipients know you're writing because you want to, not because good etiquette demands it. As a professional, you should remain constantly alert to notable events, small though they may be, which affect your associates and provide you with a legitimate reason for sending a brief congratulatory note.

Personal Contact File   The old maxim that you never know who may help boost your career or business is just as true today as it was yesterday. Keep a "personal contact file" on every man or woman you meet who could by the furthest stretch of your imagination play a significant role in your future advancement.

These 3 X 5-card mini-dossiers should contain the person's full name and nickname, address, phone, how and where you met, friends in common, interests, and any other relevant facts. Every time you get a business card worth hanging on to, add it to your file. After many years, my personal contact file now contains about ten thousand names. David Rockefeller's file is reportedly over thirty thousand names long. When he was still CEO of the Chase Manhattan Bank, three secretaries kept meticulous track of all his acquaintances around the world. When he went on a trip abroad, his secretaries would riffle through the cards and prepare a report, so that he could bone up at a glance on his acquaintances in places as far flung as Kuala Lumpur and Tokyo. He could also refresh his memory whether he should use formal address, first names, or nicknames.

Of course, a personal contact file isn't valuable until you actually put it to work. What that file amounts to is an instant mailing list of important people in front of whom you would like to keep your name. When you are promoted, have your company print a formal announcement that you can send to these contacts. Also send them reprints of any speeches you make or notices of any awards you receive.

If you open a new office, move into new quarters, or are now offering a new product or service, you'll be thankful you've compiled this list of business and personal contacts.

Government Involvement If politics holds excitement for you, I suggest channeling your talents and financial resources into the support of a political candidate, cause, or party. Realistically, your chances for high visibility are greater when you play a key role in a lesser political candidate's campaign (say assemblyman, councilman, or supervisor) than a statewide or national campaign (governor, U.S. senator, or congressman). Your $100 donation to a city councilman is far more important to him than to a gubernatorial candidate.

If you are an authority in your field or a spokesperson for your company or organization, consider testifying before administrative and regulatory commissions, government panels, or legislative committees. If you're nonpartisan and can spare the time, consider pursuing a commission appointment yourself. On the plus side, a commission seat will increase your stature and visibility. On the minus side, you could also find yourself embroiled in controversy or be asked to publicly disclose your financial net worth. Less risky are memberships on blue-ribbon advisory committees, or technical and industrial boards.

Get to know local, state, and national elected—or appointed—public officials. Once you've made their acquaintance, visit them occasionally at city hall, the county board of supervisors, the state capital, and Washington, D.C. Get on party finance committees; it's an excellent way to meet VIPs and possibly become one yourself if your candidate should get into office. And don't just attend testimonial dinners— organize one!

Awards and Prizes   This is an important but tricky component of your personal do-it-yourself PR program. Nothing is as potentially repugnant as having others realize you are trying to engineer an award for yourself.

Of course, the primary question is: What have you or your firm done to deserve special tribute, such as a commemorative or congratulatory resolution passed by a legislative body, a *Congressional Record* mention, a Freedoms Foundation or other patriotic award, an honorary degree, or "Man of the Year" designation?

Here is where a third party—a friend or PR consultant—may be required to intercede on your behalf. This third party can instigate the award and then supervise the arrangements for the awards presentation and attendant publicity. The colorful scroll is one thing, but the publicity opportunities that accompany the award are your real motive.

This hopefully well-deserved acclaim should motivate you toward greater heights of achievement, lend prestige to your endeavors and challenge others to emulate your example.

THE SENSITIVE MATTER OF YOUR PUBLIC IMAGE

The program I've just outlined will play a vital role in developing the most precious thing a man has—his reputation. Imaginative, forthright and discerning personal PR is certainly within the grasp of every motivated man and woman. If you really have something special to offer others, why hide it under a bushel? Market your desirable qualities in a way that will build your reputation—along with your business or career.

22

TWENTY QUESTIONS (AND ANSWERS) ABOUT ATTRACTING (AND IMPRESSING) EXECUTIVE RECRUITERS

by Carl W. Menk

Today, executive search is an estimated $1-billion industry with some 1,700 firms operating in over 3,300 locations throughout the United States. Yet despite its size and growing influence in the business community, the industry remains an enigma to most people.

As president of Boyden Associates, one of the older and larger recruiting firms, I'm continually amazed at how little the average man in the street knows about executive search—what it is, and how it operates. These 20 questions are the ones I am asked most often. The answers constitute a short primer on the industry and will offer guidelines for any encounters you may have with recruiters as you progress in your career.

QUESTION 1: HOW DO EXECUTIVE SEARCH FIRMS DIFFER FROM EMPLOYMENT AGENCIES?

An executive search firm, or executive recruiter, is an advocate in behalf of its clients, generally large, well-known companies. The jobs recruiters fill are middle-to-senior-level management positions and their fees are a guaranteed 30 to 33½ percent of the first year's salary plus expenses, regardless of whether the placement is made.

This contractual retainer arrangement is, in fact, the most notable difference between search firms and licensed personnel agencies. It also accounts for their disparate modes of operation. Because employment agencies and even some firms calling themselves executive recruiters work on a contingency basis—no placement, no fee—their recruitment methods are less thorough. Little research goes into the compilation of their candidate lists; resumes are generally collected through newspaper ads or culled from files; and agents typically meet with candidates only once. The candidate's resume is often circulated to several companies indiscriminately.

In contrast, search firms use magnets to find that proverbial needle in the haystack. Recruiters do everything with careful attention to detail—from an in-depth analysis of the position to be filled, which may take days of discussion with the client, to exhaustive interviews and reference checks with a pared-down list of every conceivable person with the right qualifications. Normally, the client is introduced only to the top two or three candidates for the job.

QUESTION 2: AT WHAT SALARY LEVEL DO I BECOME ATTRACTIVE TO RECRUITERS?

Don't expect much interest on the part of recruiters until your salary reaches $35,000 a year. The typical Boyden search falls within the $45,000–$100,000 salary range.

QUESTION 3: DO RECRUITERS EXPECT TO SEE A CORRELATION BETWEEN MY AGE, SALARY, AND LEVEL OF ACHIEVEMENT?

The answer is yes, with qualifications.

Since it is against the equal opportunity laws for either a recruiter or potential employer to ask you your age, you might assume that such correlations are no longer being made. This isn't entirely true. Resumes typically contain the dates candidates worked for each employer; therefore, a little simple arithmetic will give anyone reading a resume an approximate age.

I don't know of any reputable recruiter who would rule out a good candidate solely because his "age–wage ratio" wasn't attractive. However, recruiters may examine such a candidate more thoroughly. Recruiters also recognize that a number of significant variables affect a person's salary: the industry (heavy industry, glamour industries, and nonprofit institutions tend to pay less at the middle-management level); function; line versus staff positions (line positions, such as sales, that directly impact profits always pay more); and location (the South, and smaller cities usually pay less).

With the preceding qualifications, the following age–salary guide will give you a yardstick to measure your own performance:

AGE	SALARY	
	Above-Average Achiever:	*Superstar:*
23–25	$18,000–$25,000	$34,500–$37,500
26–29	$26,000–$29,000	$39,000–$43,500
	(age = salary)	
30–34	compensation starts exceeding age and diverges at an increasing rate	$45,000+

QUESTION 4: IN ADDITION TO SALARY, WHAT OTHER CREDENTIALS WOULD MAKE ME ATTRACTIVE TO A RECRUITER?

Recruiters are impressed by the obvious—good schools, coveted awards, and outstanding employers. Their favorites are such companies as General Electric, IBM, Procter & Gamble, and General Motors—companies that are mature and well-managed, and have established reputations as training grounds for future industry leaders.

When you are planning your career moves, keep three factors in mind. First, in terms of career progression, it's harder to move from a smaller company to a larger one than vice versa. So if your first employer or employers are large corporations with $1 billion or more in sales, you have much more flexibility later on in your career when you want to change jobs with the aid of a recruiter.

Second, you won't look attractive to recruiters if you're changing jobs at a pace that exceeds six moves during your entire business career, good explanations notwithstanding. While the average American worker may hold ten different jobs before retirement, as a recent survey by the National Bureau of Economic Research revealed, this type of job-hopping is *not* acceptable in managerial ranks. The only managers who may be able to change employers more rapidly without negative consequences are those working in the retailing, advertising, publishing, broadcasting, or aerospace industries. Among recruiters, such industries are jokingly known as "revolving doors."

Finally, to make yourself attractive to recruiters, never underestimate the power of personal publicity and good word-of-mouth reviews from your peers. Recruiters aren't, by nature, gamblers. They stay with the sure bets and leave the long shots to the employment agents. So if you maintain high visibility in your field and *appear* to be an expert in your area, some recruiter somewhere is probably tracking your career already and has clippings on you tucked away in his files for future reference.

QUESTION 5: HOW MUCH INFORMATION SHOULD I PUT ON MY RESUME? WHAT ABOUT ITS FORMAT?

A resume will never get you a job. All it's intended to do is get you in the door for the initial interview.

Resumes should get right to the point: Who are you (name, address, phone number)? When and where have you worked? What impact did you have on each company's performance during your tenure there? What is your background (education, marital status)?

I suggest you put the description of the job you are seeking in a cover letter. That way, you can modify the description to appeal to the person receiving the resume. The purpose of the cover letter is to tell the recipient how to interpret the information on the enclosed resume.

I'm often asked if honors, achievements, organizations, sports, and hobbies belong on a resume. The answer depends on the position you are seeking and your region of the country. Here are some general guidelines:

• If you are going after an analytical, technical, or scientific job, a more academic resume is in order. Such resumes should include scholastic honors, grants received, technical papers of note, and memberships in professional societies. Civic projects, sports, and hobbies are secondary.

• In the marketing field, scholastic achievement isn't as important, but who you know and your range of interests are. Thus, I recommend putting your extra-employment activities on such a resume. Organizational affiliations, civic activities, sports, and hobbies may also be helpful on personnel, public relations, and general management resumes.

• Socializing in exclusive circles is often extremely important for entry into law, accounting, and consulting firms whose professional codes, until recently, prohibited advertising or the open solicitation of new business. In these fields, mention of your clubs and civic activities is important as an indication of the level of your contacts.

• Reactions to specific organizations and activities differ depending on the region of the country. In the New York area, employer and recruiter reaction to civic activities ranges from indifferent to negative. Some fast-paced New York City-based companies believe that their executives' energies should be directed almost exclusively to solving company problems.

• Regional variations for the rest of the country are fairly predictable. In much of the Midwest, a traditional solid-citizen lifestyle is still in vogue and membership in the Rotary, Kiwanis, and Lions clubs may score points. Exclusivity is valued in the South and Southwest where the names of country and luncheon clubs often appear on resumes. In New England, however, anyone privy to the old-boy network would be considered pretentious and gauche if he committed his contacts to paper.

• Midwesterners and Southerners often practice a modified version of the old-school-tie syndrome. The employer may not care whether he went to school with a candidate's father, but he does look kindly on a prospect who exhibited enough regional chauvinism to stay home and get his education in good local schools. As for the West, "membership only" luncheon clubs are fashionable in San Francisco and business is often conducted there, while in Los Angeles the situation is more open. Because of the Sun Belt climate, sports and outdoor hobbies appear more frequently on resumes there.

The format of your resume is a matter of individual taste and should reflect your management style. But whatever format you choose, make sure it's easy to read and that information is introduced in order of its importance.

QUESTION 6: HOW IMPORTANT IS MY SO-CALLED "IMAGE" TO A RECRUITER?

It's important that you create a favorable first impression. If you don't, a recruiter may not give you a second chance.

I estimate that 20 percent of my final evaluation of a candidate is based on what happens during the first five minutes of contact. When I meet a candidate for the first time, I consciously try to relax and concentrate on initial impressions—manner of speech, voice, appearance, and poise. These may seem like artificial criteria, but don't discount their importance. While you're sitting there in your scuffed shoes and stained tie, I'm thinking, "Will this person be able to gain the respect of our client? Will he have the polish to handle a lunch with the client?" In short, I put myself in the position of someone with whom the candidate may later be doing business. I note whether the candidate immediately puts me at ease and commands my fullest attention.

QUESTION 7: SHOULD I APPROACH A RECRUITER DIRECTLY WHEN I AM TRYING TO CHANGE JOBS?

You can try writing directly to a recruiter and enclosing a resume, but don't expect immediate results. Executive recruiters are swamped with unsolicited resumes—I estimate Boyden receives over two thousand a week—so you may not even get an acknowledgment unless a recruiter, coincidentally, happens to be working on a search for a manager with your precise background. That's highly unlikely. On any given day, Boyden's U.S. offices are working on about 250 searches. However, the average search takes 90 days to complete and in those 90 days, Boyden will receive some 26,000 unsolicited resumes. The law of averages is *not* in your favor. At best, a recruiter may file your resume for future reference.

QUESTION 8: HOW CAN I INCREASE THE PROBABILITY THAT A RECRUITER WILL CALL ME?

The best introduction to an executive recruiter is an indirect one.

The typical search looks for business talent in all the obvious places: its own files, which are usually elaborately cross-indexed; professional and trade associations' search firms and alumni directories; *Who's Who, Standard & Poor's, Dun & Bradstreet,* and other executive registers; university, trade, and industrial periodicals carrying bylined articles by experts in particular fields; and, occasionally, the local social register. If you want a recruiter to find you, make sure that you're easy to find. See that your name and credentials appear in as many of the above sources as possible.

But the best entrée to a recruiter is still the personal referral. When a recruiter is working on a search, he's wide open for suggestions and often gets leads from previous clients, candidates he's placed in other positions, or from people he's met through quasi-social/business activities such as memberships on corporate or charity boards and civic organizations. A recruiter may even inquire among his country-club peer group or intimate circle of friends, one reason why a large network of influential acquaintances never hurts an ambitious manager.

QUESTION 9: WHAT SHOULD I DO IF A RECRUITER CALLS?

Unless you know the recruiter personally, the first thing you should do is establish the fact that he or she is, indeed, Joe Smith or Jane Jones of the XYZ Executive Search Firm. Without any hesitation, the recruiter should be able to tell you all the specifics about the position he or she has been retained to fill: the exact title and salary range; the level of responsibility the job represents within that company; the company's size, structure, location, and profitability. If the recruiter seems uncertain and prefers to question you in detail about your current job instead, you have reason to be suspicious. Graciously make some excuse, take the person and firm's name and number, and hang up. If you have access to one of the executive-recruiter directories listed at the end of this chapter, look up the firm. Otherwise, find the firm's name and address in the telephone directory. See what classification—"executive search consultants" or "employment agencies"—the firm is listed under in the Yellow Pages. If you still aren't satisfied the recruiter is legitimate, ask a friend or someone knowledgeable about the search industry.

Once you are satisfied, by all means call the recruiter back. An auspicious phone conversation with an unknown executive recruiter has been the key to many a manager's career advancement.

QUESTION 10: DURING THIS INITIAL PHONE CONVERSATION, SHOULD I TAKE EVERYTHING A RECRUITER SAYS AT FACE VALUE?

It depends on the recruiter. Some recruiters are up front about what they want. They have a management position to fill. Would you be interested?

Others aren't as forthright because they feel a period of suspense is necessary to whet a prospect's appetite since they assume he is securely and happily employed where he is. Thus, a recruiter may open the conversation with the let-me-pick-your-brain-for-a-moment gambit. He'll tell you that he wants to describe a job opening to you in some detail in case you happen to know anyone who might be suitable for it.

With this introduction, you will probably assume you have already been dismissed as a possibility. Then the recruiter will develop, logically, all the reasons why this hypothetical friend of yours might want to work for the as-yet-unnamed client company. Don't bother to ask the company's name. The recruiter won't divulge it this early in the game.

The question is: Does or doesn't the recruiter want you, in search parlance, "to reach for the job" yourself? If the job genuinely sounds like one you are well qualified for, he might. If you are interested yourself, say so. However, if this assertion elicits little more than a vague, "I'll make note of your interest," you can assume the recruiter was being honest with you from the beginning. All he wanted to do was pick your brain for the names of possible candidates—and you aren't one of them.

QUESTION 11: IF I BECOME ONE OF SEVERAL CANDIDATES ON A RECRUITER'S LIST, WHAT CAN I EXPECT?

Commentators fond of automotive metaphors have pointed out that getting a job through an employment agency is like taking a sightseeing tour on an overcrowded bus. In comparison, an executive search is more like an exotic adventure into parts unknown while luxuriating in the passenger seat of a sleek, black limousine.

People-assessment is second nature to a recruiter, and the assessment begins the minute you pick up the telephone—long before you've even declared yourself in the running. Once a recruiter is satisfied that you're truly interested in the job and possess the qualifications, he or she will suggest a face-to-face meeting to make sure you look as good as you sound. To remember how you look, many recruiters will take your picture with a Polaroid during the first interview. If the interview goes well, be prepared for one or two more before you are introduced—if ever—to the client.

After the second interview, some recruiters may try to make you feel you're the only person in the country under consideration for the job in an effort to flatter you into cooperating fully. Don't believe it. On a typical search, up to two hundred potential applicants are screened; perhaps thirty are called; and meetings may be arranged with ten or twelve. Only two or three will ever actually have an interview with the client and the front-runner may meet the client some five or six times. All this takes an average of between sixty and ninety days.

QUESTION 12: IF YOU WERE MEETING ME FOR THE FIRST TIME, WHAT WOULD IMPRESS YOU MOST AND MAKE YOU RECOMMEND ME TO A CLIENT?

Screening interviews are designed to probe a candidate's personality and success record, starting with the person's present position and working backwards.

During these interviews, the answers to my *unspoken* questions are the crucial ones. I want to know what's motivated you throughout your career, why you selected certain employers, what prompted you to remain at a job longer than you should have, or how a specific job broadened your experience and knowledge. Any high-powered, self-motivated individual will offer this information before I've asked for it.

I think most recruiters and employers would agree on five traits that are an asset in any candidate no matter what the job: (1) constructive aggressiveness; (2) the willingness to make the necessary sacrifices in order to get ahead; (3) honesty; (4) people-sensitivity and interpersonal skills; and (5) intelligence. The last factor—intelligence—should come through in your record of achievement. Of course, there is a difference between your theoretical intelligence—what I call the "can-do factor"—and how you've demonstrated that intelligence during your career—the "will-do factor." Obviously, any recruiter or employer is going to be more impressed with the latter.

QUESTION 13: DO RECRUITERS SIT IN ON A CANDIDATE'S INTERVIEWS AT THE CLIENT COMPANY?

Many recruiters will sit in on a candidate's initial client interview, often for reasons that have nothing to do with that candidate. For instance, if it's the recruiter's first assignment for a new client, he or she will want to witness how the client deals with candidates, and possibly make suggestions later.

QUESTION 14: HOW SHOULD I HANDLE ANY NEGATIVE FACTORS IN MY BACKGROUND SUCH AS BEING FIRED?

Both recruiters and clients know you're human and expect to hear you demonstrate this. My best advice is to admit your failures but in a way that emphasizes you're a better person today because of them.

I am happy to report that the stigma against the fired executive is abating somewhat, mainly because so many senior managers now fall into that category. One survey in 1977 showed that 23 percent of all top management vacancies resulted from terminations. My personal estimate is that some 25 percent of all personnel placed by executive search firms have been discharged once or were well on the road to it sometime during their career. Should a dynamic executive who has faced an involuntary discharge sometime during his own career interview you at the client company, you can be sure he will have some understanding of your situation and evaluate you accordingly.

If you've been fired, allude to it euphemistically ("I left because of policy differences"; "to pursue other career goals"; "to seek new challenges") but don't think you're fooling anyone. If possible, try to find out what your ex-employer's story will be and structure your explanation accordingly. For example, if you know your ex-employer will say you were fired for incompetence, you might counter, "The job was not challenging and my morale was low, so I unfortunately let my work slip while I was looking for another position elsewhere."

QUESTION 15: WHO WILL CHECK MY REFERENCES—THE RECRUITER OR THE CLIENT?

One of the reasons companies hire recruiters is to take as much of the risk as possible out of the selection process. To do this, most recruiters make extensive reference checks before they introduce a candidate to a client. After meeting a candidate, a client occasionally wants to check a source or two of its own. Of course, the client is free to do so.

QUESTION 16: WILL THE REFERENCE CHECK BE SUPERFICIAL OR IN-DEPTH?

Recruiters' policies on references vary considerably. For lower-paying, middle-management jobs, some recruiters just go through the motions of a reference check. They verify the facts—schools attended, graduation dates, length of service with previous employers—and get one character reference. On the other hand, for a CEO slot at a *Fortune* 500 company, recruiters have been known to retain outside agencies to get a lifelong commentary on the candidate's character and habits.

The norm is somewhere in between these two extremes. At Boyden, we ask the candidate for a list of names and may query him about his choices, particularly if the list is heavy on college professors and light on recent employers. We do not restrict our referencing solely to the candidate's list, however. Our objective is to make sure the candidate and client company fulfill each other's needs. Since most candidates are currently employed, we work closely with them concerning references and exercise considerable sensitivity and discretion.

QUESTION 17: IF I AM THE FRONT-RUNNER FOR THE JOB, SHOULD I PLAY HARD TO GET?

Play it straight rather than hard to get. Encourage the recruiter to sell you on his client. Without question, the recruiter should provide you with an annual report, other salient company handouts, and a full explanation of the job, preferably as it appears on the specifications form. (The "specs" evolve out of brainstorming sessions between the client and recruiter. It's essentially a detailed outline of the position to be filled and the requirements the ideal candidate should possess.)

What the "spec sheet" won't list are the client's real preferences—those unwritten criteria that now constitute discrimination—and the internal political ramifications, if there are any. You've got a right to know these things, so ask. If the recruiter is smart, he'll level with you even at the risk of turning you off, because he certainly doesn't want you to (1) alienate his client on first meeting with a barrage of hostile questions; (2) take the job, then quit six weeks later—since most recruiters would feel obligated to replace you without charging a fee.

If, however, after hearing the recruiter out, you are still uneasy because of rumors you've heard about the company or department from other sources, make the recruiter *prove* his assertions. Ask to speak to key people at the client company or people who have left the company for jobs elsewhere. Your requests should be granted, provided the client is convinced you're the prime prospect and there really is nothing to hide. Companies that are in trouble and having a hard time attracting top talent are often forced to acquiesce to such demands. Desperate companies have even been known to let senior management candidates interview their outside auditors and legal counsel. If that happens, you know you've got the job—if you want it.

QUESTION 18: HOW LARGE A COMPENSATION INCREASE SHOULD I EXPECT?

A 25 to 30 percent compensation increase plus bonus and stock options is average. Moreover, an up-front bonus is frequently added to the package to offset the annual bonus the candidate loses from his current employer.

A company may try to lower the percentage of salary increase by offering various nonmonetary concessions. For example, companies located in a low-cost-of-living region—like the South, where salaries lag behind the national average—often attempt to lure candidates from higher-cost-of-living areas with nonmonetary perquisites that have a positive impact on candidates' lifestyles without the offsetting negative impact on their income tax bracket. The most popular "perks" are the use of a company car, club memberships, 100-percent paid family medical and dental plans, free financial and legal counseling; low-cost and, sometimes, interest-free loans; educational assistance for children; and the purchase of a relocated executive's home to save him the trouble of trying to sell it in a depressed market—and the guarantee of a favorable mortgage rate when he buys a new home.

Remember, a search firm merely advises its client about a candidate's present compensation package. (If you've lied, the truth may have surfaced during the reference checking.) The recruiter recommends the increase he deems appropriate. But the client does the negotiating with the candidate and makes the final offer.

QUESTION 19: SHOULD I INSIST ON AN EMPLOYMENT CONTRACT?

Today, many employers balk at employment contracts, feeling they symbolize a lack of trust on both sides. Good faith aside, they also have a number of other disadvantages from your end. An employment contract could keep you imprisoned in a job you hate or prevent you from working for a competitor. Conversely, it's no insurance policy against your being fired—or having to hire a lawyer to force your employer to live up to the financial terms of the agreement.

In lieu of a contract, ask for a letter confirming your arrangement: salary, bonus, expense account, moving expense reimbursement (if applicable), retirement program provisions, stock options, or, if you're concerned about the new job's stability, a severance arrangement. In the event of a disagreement, a letter of agreement will serve to remind both parties of the terms of the employment arrangement.

QUESTION 20: WHERE CAN I GET A LIST OF RECRUITING FIRMS?

To locate executive recruiting firms which specialize in your field, consult one of the following directories:

Directory of Executive Recruiters (Consultants News, Templeton Road, Fitzwilliam, NH 03447) lists over 2,300 search offices in the United States, Canada, and Mexico; their industries or functional specialties; and minimum salary handled. Price: $12.00 prepaid, $15.00 if billed. The same organization publishes various other lists and executive job information booklets, such as "The Lexicon of Executive Recruiting"; "How to Seek a New and Better Job"; and "Job Marketing," a package of materials covering all aspects of finding and negotiating a new job.

AERC Membership List (Association of Executive Recruiting Consultants, 30 Rockefeller Plaza, New York, NY 10020) is just that. These approximately 60 firms are some of the best in the field and subscribe to the AERC's Code of Ethics. Price: $3.00.

Executive Employment Guide (American Management Associations, Management Information Services, 135 West 50th Street, New York, NY 10020) contains information on some 150 firms, ranging from executive search firms and job counselors down to licensed personnel agencies and job registers. It details each firm's specialty, minimum salary requirement, and willingness to review resumes and grant interviews. A short reading list covers books on job seeking and directories with information on companies. Price: $3.00. Free to AMA members.

ABOUT
THE CONTRIBUTORS

Don Bachman has balanced a many-faceted career in industrial relations, including executive recruiting, training, and labor relations. In 1975 he formed his own management consulting firm, specializing in executive search. With the publication of his book *How to Dress for Success* (1979), Bachman zeroed in on the premise that the image you project can determine whether you continue to climb or stall on the ladder of success. *Firm:* D. E. Bachman & Associates, 48 Oak Avenue, Metuchen, NJ 08840. (201) 548–7242.

Barbara Blaes's background encompasses business management and administration, freelance writing, teaching, and modeling. Most recently, she was director of publications for the Council for American Private Education. Her Southern California-based firm specializes in executive appearance training, with stress on verbal and nonverbal communication (voice projection, goal-setting and interviewing techniques; wardrobe, hairstyle, diet, exercise and body movement). *Firm:* Barbara Blaes & Associates, 13900 Panay Way S214, Marina del Rey, CA 90291. (213) 827–0765.

Sybil Conrad brings twenty years of acting and writing experience to her role as a communications consultant. The author of four novels, she is also the writer/producer of her own radio program, and has acted extensively in TV commercials. She has designed and taught speech courses at Pace University, U.S. Military Academy, University of South

Carolina, and the College of New Rochelle, and is a faculty member at the Human Relations Center and The New School. Her corporate clients include American Cyanamid, IBM, Technicon, and American Express. *Firm:* Conrad Communications, 6 Black Birch Lane, Scarsdale, NY 10583. (914) 725–2360.

Stan Farb is a clothing advisor to some of the most successful men in business, industry, and the professions. Formerly president of his own men's clothing firm, he is much in demand as a counselor on problems of dress and corporate dress codes. For over twenty years he has provided the executive and professional man with rules for proper attire, helping him at the same time to express his own taste and individuality. *Firm:* Stan Farb, Inc., 4643 North 74 Place, Scottsdale, AZ 85251. (602) 946–1567.

Lois Fenton is a well-known speaker, writer, and consultant on executive dress. Since 1960 she has spoken for corporations and conventions nationwide, and aboard cruise ships. She has also been featured in *The New Yorker, The New York Times, Detroit News,* and *Signature.* In 1976, she developed the Executive Wardrobe Engineering seminars to help businessmen project a more professional image; and has since been retained by numerous corporate and institutional clients including Exxon; Sperry Rand; Arthur Young & Co.; and Carnegie-Mellon University. *Firm:* Lois Fenton, Executive Wardrobe Engineering, 721 Shore Acres Drive, Mamaroneck, NY 10543. (914) 698–0721.

Mara Gleckel is a psychotherapist with a private practice in New Jersey and New York City. Her firm specializes in consultation to educational and business organizations, and has been retained by such clients as New York Telephone, ABC–TV, the U.S. Department of Labor, and the U.S. Coast Guard. She is also the originator of the "Ego, Image, and Success" seminars which she has given at Hunter College and Long Island University; and is author of a booklet of the same name. *Firm:* Family Therapy Associates, Inc., 61 East 77th Street, New York, NY 10021. (212) 628–1872.

Phillip Grace, who holds a B.B.A. (management) and an M.B.A. (marketing), is currently a principal in the Georgetown Marketing Institute, a "think tank" of professionals who solve business problems giving special emphasis to marketing and advertising. He has substantial experience in the federal government as a protocol officer; has written *A Silk Purse from a Sow's Ear* (Stelucan Press, 1977), a basic guide for professional and social mobility; and is listed in *Who's Who in the East, Who's Who in Government,* and the *Social Register* of Washington. *Firm:* Georgetown Marketing Institute, 1218 31st Street, NW, Washington, DC 20007. (202) 965-3585.

James G. Gray, Jr., a nationally recognized expert in media and image communication, is author of *The Winning Image* (Amacom, 1981). He serves as adjunct professor in American University's School of Communication, where he created and teaches the course, "How to Project a Professional or Public Image." He specializes in public speaking and television-appearance coaching and seminars. The firm's clients include senators, politicians, diplomats, lawyers, and executives from Xerox, Marriott, NBC, Boeing Aircraft, and the Pentagon. *Firm:* Media Impact, 7510 Old Chester Road, Bethesda, MD 20817. (301) 229-1740.

William Hussey is an advertising, promotion, and public relations executive with over twenty years' experience in sales, marketing, and corporate communications. A specialist in the creation and staging of sales presentations, he coaches salespeople and executives on the delivery of both corporate presentations and formal speeches. His firm also offers a writing course aimed at teaching clear business communication skills to managers. His clients include *Newsweek* magazine; Institutional Investor Systems; American Can Company; The American Board of Trade; Hayden Publishing; and the Bank of America. *Firm:* William Hussey Associates, 96 State Street, Brooklyn, NY 11201. (212) 625-2485.

Helga Long heads her own executive search and human resources consulting firm. The firm is widely known for its innovative approach to search, and for its staff of dedicated professionals. From its original emphasis on recruiting in the consumer goods field, the firm has expanded into a wide range of industries including pharmaceuticals, cable TV, banking, advertising, toys, and industrial hard goods. The firm also offers such other services as industry analysis; minority recruiting; executive compensation; employee benefits planning, labor relations, and plant location studies. *Firm:* H. M. Long & Associates, 820 Second Avenue, Suite 1100, New York, NY 10017. (212) 867-9610.

Jack McAlinden, in more than fifteen years in the field, has helped everyone from young executives to CEOs to discover and build on their strengths to become more natural, persuasive communicators. He founded his firm in 1972 to develop the verbal communications skills of senior and middle management. Since then, the firm has helped companies' R&D departments communicate with their finance departments, helped finance talk to marketing, and even helped the United States get its point across to the European nations, Japan, and Australia—and vice versa. The firm's broad range of multinational clients include Avon, Citibank, International Paper, and McKinsey & Co. *Firm:* McAlinden Associates, Inc., 122 East 42nd Street, New York, NY 10017. (212) 986–4950.

Carl W. Menk is president of Boyden Associates, Inc., an international executive search firm with thirty-five offices throughout the world. Boyden is the oldest major executive recruiting firm in the country, founded in 1946 by Sidney Boyden, a management consultant who felt that executives and companies alike would benefit from a professional approach to filling management vacancies. Boyden is a "generalist" firm, serving a wide range of clients in every industry and job function. *Headquarters office:* Boyden Associates, Inc., 260 Madison Avenue, New York, NY 10016. (212) 949–7600.

Robert L. Montgomery is a thirty-year veteran public speaker and trainer who does frequent commentaries on television. His specialty is coaching in public speaking and memory/listening skills, as well as sales and motivation training. His clients include the American International Group, Corning Glass, Amdahl, and Ingersoll-Rand. He has written numerous books, including *A Master Guide to Public Speaking, Memory Made Easy, Listening Made Easy,* and *How to Sell in the 1980s.* He is also the author of a six-cassette series developed since 1975. *Firm:* R. L. Montgomery & Associates, Inc., 12313 Michelle Circle, Burnsville, MN 55337. (612) 894–1348.

Catherine Gaffigan Nelson is a Broadway *(Whose Life Is It Anyway?)* and film *(Julia)* actress and performer. In 1974, sidelined from show business by back surgery, she established a communications consulting firm to upgrade the speechmaking skills of executives and politicians. She holds a B.A. in English, an M.F.A. in speech and drama, and has trained at the Institute for Rational-Emotive Therapy in New York City. *Firm:* Catherine Gaffigan Nelson, 156 West 76th Street, New York, NY 10023. (212) JU–6–6300/877–4676.

Elaine Posta conceptualized and directed TWA's first flight attendant/employee grooming programs and acted as its PR liaison with the White House. A noted fashion, skin care, and makeup consultant, she has created motivational, career advancement, sales, secretarial, and total-image-projection programs for corporations, government agencies, universities, hotels, department stores, and professional organizations. A partial client list includes Caesar's World and Meridien Hotels; HUD; CETA; Eastern Airlines; NYU; After Six; Erno Laszlo Institute; and Holland-America Cruises. *Firm:* The Image Institute, Inc., 4 East 82nd Street, Suite 5F, New York, NY 10028. (212) 861–2783.

Dr. Shirley E. Potter has specialized in personal communications skills programs for eight years. Through private consultations, seminars, and customized training programs, her clients learn how to build rapport with audiences, develop confidence and ease with themselves and others, increase their skills in "people management," and gain recognition and salary, either where they work now or by changing employers. David Rockefeller, Jr., can attest to her achievements as a trainer, as can other clients from Mobil Oil, Exxon, Harvard Law School, The New York Times Co., Affiliate Artists, and Cornell University. *Firm:* Shirley E. Potter Associates, 146 West 75th Street, New York, NY 10023. (212) 799–5585.

Elayne Snyder offers hands-on help for the speaker who wants to deliver the best. She is a professional speech consultant with a speech degree and broadcasting and lecture experience. She gives her clients knowledgeable and practical help in preparing for any public-speaking challenge. She covers speakers' needs ranging from how to develop an artful introduction and handle an important television interview to delivery of a captivating formal address. Her private clients call Elayne Snyder their "speechmaking secret weapon." *Firm:* Elayne Snyder Speech Consultants, 333 East 49 Street, New York, NY 10017. (212) 759–4943.

Ray L. Steele, Ph.D., assistant provost of the University of Pittsburgh, is also on the faculty of its speech department and Graduate School of Business Management for Executives. He holds degrees in administration, political science, speech/communication/broadcasting, and has studied law. He has worked with Burson-Marsteller in New York City and trained executives from General Motors, Clark Equipment, IBM,

Rockwell International, and Westinghouse. *Firm:* Steele & Associates, R.D. #2, McDonald, PA 15057. (412) 624–4230 day/(412) 926–2474 evening.

Carl R. Terzian is a prominent author, lecturer, and consultant who heads a West Coast-based public relations firm. The firm also offers counseling in governmental affairs, managerial development, and executive speech training and placement. It has served nearly 600 clients since 1969. Each year, Terzian travels nearly 300,000 miles to address conventions, conferences, and sales and management meetings as a motivational speaker. Earlier in his career, he served as a State Department goodwill ambassador in the Eisenhower administration, and handled public-relations affairs for the Lutheran Hospital of Southern California and architect Charles Luckman. *Firm:* Carl Terzian Associates, One Century Plaza, Suite 3190, 2029 Century Park East, Los Angeles, CA 90067. (213) 557–3087.

Jacqueline Thompson is a freelance writer who specializes in business and careers. She is the author of *The Very Rich Book: America's Supermillionaires and Their Money* (William Morrow, 1981), and *Upward Mobility* (Holt, Rinehart & Winston, 1982); as well as being the editor of the women's edition of *Image Impact,* published in 1981 by A&W Publishers. She is also the editor of the biennial *Directory of Personal Image Consultants,* published by the Editorial Services Co., the only directory covering specialists in speech/public appearance, dress and color consulting, personal PR, and motivational career counseling. *Firm:* Editorial Services Co., 1140 Avenue of the Americas, New York, NY 10036. (212) 354–5025.

William Thourlby is an internationally respected clothing consultant. He is the advisor on a continuing yearly basis to companies as diverse as Coca-Cola, Price Waterhouse, and Smith Barney, Harris Upham & Co. Thourlby is author of the bestselling book *You Are What You Wear,* and writes an award-winning, widely syndicated newspaper column with the same title. As a wardrobe consultant, Thourlby draws on his experience as an actor *(The Manchurian Candidate, Will Success Spoil Rock Hunter?),* model (he was the original Marlboro Man and one of the nation's top ten models), motion picture producer, educator (Emory University), and businessman (former owner of two clothing stores). He has also been clothing counselor to two U.S. presidents. *Firm:* William Thourlby, New Line Presentations, Inc., 575 Eighth Avenue, New York, NY 10018. (212) 246–2219.

INDEX